T0361235

ROUTLEDGE LIBRARY EDITIONS: HISTORY OF MONEY, BANKING AND FINANCE

Volume 9

THE MANHATTAN COMPANY

THE MANHATTAN COMPANY

Managing a Multi-Unit Corporation in New York, 1799–1842

GREGORY S. HUNTER

Routledge
Taylor & Francis Group

LONDON AND NEW YORK

First published in 1989 by Garland Publishing, Inc.

This edition first published in 2018
by Routledge
2 Park Square, Milton Park, Abingdon, Oxon OX14 4RN

and by Routledge
711 Third Avenue, New York, NY 10017

Routledge is an imprint of the Taylor & Francis Group, an informa business

British Library Cataloguing in Publication Data
A catalogue record for this book is available from the British Library

ISBN: 978-1-138-70169-4 (Set)
ISBN: 978-1-315-10595-6 (Set) (ebk)
ISBN: 978-1-138-05628-2 (Volume 9) (hbk)
ISBN: 978-1-315-16540-0 (Volume 9) (ebk)

Publisher's Note
The publisher has gone to great lengths to ensure the quality of this reprint but
points out that some imperfections in the original copies may be apparent.

Disclaimer
The publisher has made every effort to trace copyright holders and would welcome
correspondence from those they have been unable to trace.

This picture shows the Manhattan Company's first office (in the building at the right) on Christmas Eve, 1799. Aaron Burr, one of the founders of the company, and his daughter, Theodosia, are the central figures in the panel. To the right is John Stevens, the eminent engineer, who helped the company solve its early problems in supplying water to the city. Standing with him is Daniel Ludlow, first president of the Manhattan Company. *(Courtesy of the Chase Manhattan Archives.)*

The Manhattan Company

Managing a Multi-Unit Corporation
in New York, 1799–1842

Gregory S. Hunter

Garland Publishing, Inc.
New York & London
1989

Library of Congress Cataloging-in-Publication Data

Hunter, Gregory S.
The Manhattan Company : managing a multi-unit corporation in New York,
1799–1842 / Gregory S. Hunter.
p. cm. — (Garland studies in entrepreneurship)
Originally presented as the author's thesis (Ph. D.—New York University, 1988).
Includes bibliographical references.
ISBN 0-8240-4670-6 (alk. paper)
1. Bank of the Manhattan Company—Management—History.
2. Bank management—New York (N. Y.)—History.
 3. Banks and banking—New York—History. I. Title. II. Series.
HG2613.N54C533 1989
332.1'22'097471—dc20   89-48491

Printed on acid-free, 250-year-life paper

Manufactured in the United States of America

TO JOANN

WHO MADE IT ALL POSSIBLE

AND MEANINGFUL

PREFACE

As I look back over the years, Chase Manhattan has been part of my life on a number of occasions. While in college I worked as a Summer Temporary Teller with Chase from 1973 to 1975, spending one summer at the 135th Street Branch in Harlem and two summers at the Dyckman Street Branch in upper Manhattan. Because of this experience, I have a great respect for the many frontline bankers in the trenches of the various branches across the country.

In 1977 I enrolled in the first class of New York University's new training program in archival management. Even before classes began, I was fortunate enough to secure a job in the recently-founded Chase Manhattan Archives under the direction of Linda Edgerly. Over the course of the next year I learned a great deal about what it means to be a professional archivist in addition to learning a great deal about the history of Chase.

After leaving the Chase Archives to establish an archives for the United Negro College Fund, it came time for me to pick a dissertation topic. The Manhattan Company was a natural choice, and I spent the next several years as an intermittent researcher in the Chase Archives. In many cases I was using files which I had processed a few years earlier. My involvement with Chase had come full circle.

There are many people I must thank for the parts they played in the publication of this book. First and foremost are my friends and colleagues at the Chase Archives who provided support over the long term of this project: Linda Edgerly, Anne Van Camp, Sally Brazil, Jean Hrichus, and Ann Gibson. I also am indebted to archivists and manuscript curators at other repositories: Susan Davis and Bob Sink of the New York Public Library, and Tom Dunnings of the New-York Historical Society. In addition, I have been blessed with supportive bosses: Turner Battle and Chris Edley at the United Negro College Fund, and Barry Kalen at ITT Corporation.

A very patient dissertation committee in the History Department of New York University is largely responsible for the successful completion of this project. I can never adequately express my thanks to Tom Bender, Vince Carosso, and Carl Prince for sticking with me over the years.

The other winner of the perseverance award is my wife, JoAnn Heaney Hunter, who defended her own doctoral dissertation just four months before my own. Without her help and support, this project would never have been completed.

This book really was a team effort. My thanks to everyone who was a part of it.

Gregory S. Hunter
New York, New York
October 23, 1989

CONTENTS

INTRODUCTION

> We must leave our example as a
> lesson to posterity to imitate us
> in supporting the cause of
> republicanism which is certainly
> intimately connected with the
> prosperity of our institutions.[1]

> We have in large measure lost sight
> in recent years of the interactive
> and often symbiotic relationship
> between business and society.[2]

The last few decades have been a fertile period for the study
of American business history. Scholars have explored various aspects
of the subject, looking at both individual topics and key industries
and institutions. This volume continues the trend by looking at one
topic (management) within one institution (the Manhattan Company).

Most previous historians, however, have studied the management
of business in a vacuum, separating the internal affairs of
particular companies from the social and political environments in
which corporations existed. Failure to link these two elements has
led to a form of historical myopia. This is illustrated by the

---

[1]DeWitt Clinton to Henry Remsen, March 16, 1808, Folder 3,
Clinton Papers, New York Public Library (hereafter NYPL).

[2]John N. Ingham, review of *American Business*, by James
Oliver Robertson, in the *Journal of American History*, 72, no. 3
(December 1985): 673. Ingham attributes this situation to the power
of the conceptual framework developed by Alfred D. Chandler, Jr.,
which I will discuss below.

1

writings of two key business historians, Alfred D.Chandler, Jr. and Bray Hammond.

Chandler is the dean of modern business history and the person whose terminology and methodology have shaped most discussions of the subject in recent years. Chandler's most influential work was his 1977 book entitled *The Visible Hand*.[3] In this book Chandler studied the growth of modern management, linking its appearance with the emergence of large-scale railroads in the second half of the nineteenth century. According to Chandler, at this time management became the "visible hand" controlling business, replacing the "invisible hand" of market forces. Throughout this book and in his previous studies, Chandler chronicled the relationship between strategy and structure in American businesses. However in doing so, Chandler did not adequately discuss a third factor, political or environmental influences upon managerial decision-makers.[4]

Chandler is not alone in this regard. Fritz Redlich, whose two-volume work in the late 1940s detailed the development of American bank managers, also largely ignored the influence of such external factors as politics and public pressure upon the managers of

---

[3] Alfred D. Chandler, Jr., *The Visible Hand: The Managerial Revolution in American Business* (Cambridge: Belknap Press of Harvard University Press, 1977).

[4] For a review article which makes much the same point I do, see Edward P. Duggan, "Business and the City: A Review Article," *Business History Review* 56, no. 1 (Spring 1982): 76-83.

individual banks.[5]   Both Chandler and Redlich discussed the strategy and structure of American business without providing the much-needed environmental context.

The other side of the coin is illustrated by Bray Hammond. His key work, *Banks and Politics in America*, contained an abundance of context -- political battles, legislative victories, and public outcries. What is missing, however, is a sense of how these matters affected the management of particular banks. Strategy and structure tend to get lost among the political bloodletting.[6]

As with Chandler, Hammond is not alone in his "school" or style of business history. Recently Ronald Seavoy has analyzed the politics involved in the chartering of banks in New York State.[7] According to Seavoy, the trend toward general incorporation and away from individual chartering of corporations was an economic expression of Jacksonian Democracy: the benefits of incorporation were expanded from the elite to the general public. While Seavoy did link economics and politics at the chartering stage, he never explored the

---

[5]Fritz Redlich, *The Molding of American Banking: Men and Ideas*, 2 vols. (New York: Hafner Publishing, 1947, 1951; reprint, New York: Johnson Reprint Company, 1968).

[6]Bray Hammond, *Banks and Politics in America From the Revolution to the Civil War* (Princeton: Princeton University Press, 1957).

[7]Ronald E. Seavoy, *The Origins of American Business Corporations, 1784-1855: Broadening the Concept of Public Service During Industrialization* (Westport: Greenwood Press, 1982).

continuing links *after* incorporation. In Seavoy's book we see numerous corporations born, but never learn about the effects of environmental influences on their growth and development. It is like a story without a conclusion: Snow White without the magical kiss or Cinderella without the glass slipper.

What is needed are studies which relate internal and external aspects of managing individual nineteenth-century business corporations, studies which relate strategy and structure to the local social and political environments. To what extent did particular policy innovations derive from purely internal stimuli? How important were such external factors as competition, public relations, or the threat of political action?

This study takes a step toward answering these questions by looking in detail at the Manhattan Company, one of the earliest multi-unit business corporations in the United States and one of the antecedents of today's Chase Manhattan Bank. My focus will be on how the interaction between management and environment affected the course of the company's development.

The Manhattan Company is of interest because it was one of the major financial institutions in New York in the nineteenth century. The company is interesting as well because its charter and structure were not typical for the first half of the nineteenth century. In an era of restrictive charters and public distrust of corporations, the Manhattan Company received great freedom in structuring its operations and in using its capital. And at a time when banks in the mid-Atlantic region usually did not long stray far from the financial field, a major division of the Manhattan Company supplied New York City with water for almost fifty years. In terms of Chandler's outline of corporate development, the Manhattan Company was a half century ahead of its time.

From 1799 to 1842 the Manhattan Company had three distinct divisions: a water works, a main bank in New York City, and bank branches upstate in Utica and Poughkeepsie. To successfully manage this complicated and somewhat decentralized business, the Manhattan Company's directors and managers had to be particularly sensitive to the social and political environments. As will be seen, few major decisions dealing with any of the Manhattan Company's divisions were made in a vacuum.

In order to understand the significance of the Manhattan Company and its charter, it first is necessary to trace the history of banking and incorporation prior to the founding of the Manhattan Company. This will be followed by a discussion of the nature and significance of the Manhattan Company's charter. Next, separate chapters will explore in detail the management of the Manhattan Company's three divisions: the water works, the main bank in New York City, and the upstate bank branches. Finally, I will turn to the people of the Manhattan Company to test whether or not my conclusions about the company's management are reflected in the career patterns of individual employees. By organizing the study in this way, I hope to show how Chandler's strategy and structure and Hammond's social and political environments were intertwined in the history of one leading nineteenth century American business corporation.

CHAPTER ONE

CORPORATIONS AND BANKING

BEFORE THE MANHATTAN COMPANY

> Today the corporation is known and accepted -- sometimes with varying mixtures of love and hate -- as a legitimate form of private, competitive business enterprise, a form available to Exxon or one's family physician. It was not always thus. Two centuries ago the corporation was much more of a quasi-public, monopolistic privilege, sometimes of a non-business nature, and available only in a restricted manner as a specific grant from parliament or legislature.[1]

> Banking began in the New World [all] of a sudden, under specific governmental sanction, with a pretentious assembly of capital, and in a forensic blaze of controversy. It began with incorporation, and with important exceptions incorporation remained the rule, both in the States and in Canada.[2]

The Manhattan Company built upon a long tradition of corporate development in Britain, the American colonies, and the early nation.

---

[1]Richard Sylla, "Early American Banking: The Significance of the Corporate Form," *Business and Economic History*, 2nd ser. 14 (1985): 105.

[2]Bray Hammond, *Banks and Politics in America From the Revolution to the Civil War* (Princeton: Princeton University Press, 1957), 4.

While people on both continents were familiar with corporations, however, the corporate form was not as prevalent as it is today. The granting of corporate charters remained a carefully-guarded prerogative of the national and local governments, dispensed only to those projects deemed as advancing the public good.

The Manhattan Company and later corporations played an important role in identifying the potential of the corporate form and the desirability of its wider use. At first this involved showing the benefits of pooled capital and limited liability to achieve goals obviously in the public interest -- building turnpikes and bridges, for example. As the nineteenth century progressed, however, the definition of "public service" expanded to include not just internal improvements but almost all areas of business activity. Ultimately, by the middle of the nineteenth century incorporation became something freely available on equal terms to all qualified applicants. In order to appreciate the magnitude of this shift, it first is necessary to trace the tradition of incorporation prior to the Manhattan Company's founding.[3]

---

[3] The corporate form has several advantages over partnerships and other less formal methods of organization: limited rather than full liability; "perpetual" life of the entity even after the death of the founders; and the ability to sue and be sued in court. These advantages go beyond the mere pooling of capital. A convenient statement of these advantages is found in a 1789 petition by the Bank of New York for a state charter even after the bank had been operating for five years. "That standing on the footing of a private company, in which each member is supposed to be personally

The Inheritance From Great Britain

Great Britain, the country which had the greatest influence upon the development of the mid-Atlantic region, did not make extensive use of incorporation for businesses. Parliament passed very few individual charters of incorporation for businesses and no general incorporation laws until well into the nineteenth century. Almost all large business was carried on by unincorporated joint-stock associations, which legally were only expanded partnerships. The United States, rather than Great Britain, was to pioneer the widespread use of the corporate form.[4]

Much of the British aversion to corporations can be traced to a debacle involving stockholders early in the eighteenth century. Speculators inflated the price of stock in the South Sea Company to such an extent that the "bubble" finally burst, causing injury to

---

responsible for all the engagements entered into, it has been found that many persons who would otherwise be desirous of becoming subscribers are deterred by that circumstance from doing so; whereby the increase of the stock of the bank is obstructed and its operations proportionably confined." The petition is found in Henry W. Domett, *A History of the Bank of New York, 1784-1884* (New York: Riverside Press, 1884; reprint, Westport: Greenwood Press, 1969), 32-33.

[4]Ronald E. Seavoy, "The Origins of the American Business Corporation, 1784-1855: New York, the National Model" (Ph.D. diss., University of Michigan, 1969), 52-53. Thomas C. Cochran, "The Business Revolution," *American Historical Review*, 79 (1974): 1454-55.

many shareholders. Public uproar over the matter led to the passage of the so-called "Bubble Act" of 1720, which made the securing of corporate charters for business enterprises almost impossible. The law declared that "acting or presuming to act as a Body Corporate" by any organization not already formed at the passage of the act, should "forever be deemed to be illegal and void."[5]

Incorporated banking in Britain dated from the Tonnage Act of 1694. This bill authorized the incorporation of the Bank of England, which was to become the model for banking in the New World. Alexander Hamilton, one of the key early proponents of banks in America, was greatly influenced by this act.[6]

As a result of the Bubble Act, however, the British banking "system" consisted almost entirely of "private" banks: non-incorporated partnerships and proprietorships. In 1794, the one hundredth anniversary of the founding of the Bank of England, there were only four other chartered banks in the British Isles. In that same year there already were eighteen chartered banks in the United States, only thirteen years after the incorporation of the first American bank.[7]

---

[5]Hammond, *Banks and Politics*, 3.

[6]Ibid., 3

[7]The others banks in Great Britain were: the Bank of Scotland, the Royal Bank of Scotland, the Bank of Ireland, and the British Linen Company (which had banking powers). Ibid., 129, 6.

The British corporate legacy to the American colonies, therefore, was a mixed one. In fact, most of American development was directly opposite the British tradition. Whereas in Britain the development of banks was a gradual process, banking in the New World began suddenly "in a forensic blaze of controversy," to use Bray Hammond's phrase.[8] In addition, most British banks were unincorporated; in the United States just the opposite was the case. The familiarity of Hamilton and other early American bankers with the Bank of England, therefore, was a familiarity with the exception rather than the rule in Great Britain. Finally, banking in Britain developed from a surplus of capital among wealthy individuals looking for investment opportunities, while in the United States banking emerged from a lack of capital among merchants needing additional resources to conduct their daily business. In the United States, the corporate form became the vehicle for *accumulating* capital for worthy projects.[9]

The Colonial Experience

Before the Revolutionary War, charters of incorporation were

---

[8]Ibid., 4

[9]Donald R. Adams, Jr., *Finance and Enterprise in Early America: A Study of Stephen Girard's Bank, 1812-1831* (Philadelphia: University of Pennsylvania Press, 1978). Also Hammond, *Banks and Politics*, 68-9.

granted to American groups both by the English crown and by colonial assemblies. Most of these corporations, however, were for the purpose of establishing either (1) municipalities or (2) religious, educational, or charitable institutions. Very few businesses received charters.[10] Another noteworthy trend was the increase in the number of corporations during the last two or three decades before the Revolution. In fact, all but one or two of the private business corporations in the colonies were chartered after 1760. This foreshadowed the even more rapid growth which was to take place after the war.[11]

More than a dozen corporations chartered in England were active in the colonies before the revolution. About half of these maintained the seat of the corporation in England and remained distinctly English in complexion and control. This was true, for example, of the earliest colonization companies and several famous missionary societies. The rest, however, located their governing bodies in the colonies and quickly became "American" in practice if not in origin.[12]

---

[10]Nelson M. Blake, *Water for the Cities: A History of the Urban Water Supply Problem in the United States* (Syracuse: Syracuse University Press, 1956), 63.

[11]Joseph Stancliffe Davis, *Essays in the Earlier History of American Corporations* (Cambridge: Harvard University Press, 1917), 1:106-7.

[12]Ibid., 1:30, 48.

The colonial legislatures, however, were a more fertile source of corporate charters than the British Parliament. While there was no sharp legal distinction during the colonial period between "public" and "private" corporations, it is convenient to treat the two groups separately. Furthermore, the private corporations may be divided according to the purpose for which they were chartered: religious, educational, charitable, or business.[13]

In terms of public corporations, two main types were chartered in the colonies. The first category involved government entities of various size: municipal corporations and corporate towns. Twenty-four municipal corporations were chartered in the colonies, almost three-quarters of which were located in the mid-Atlantic region. Sixteen of these municipal corporations survived until the Revolution. The second group of public corporations consisted of a relatively small number of administrative boards charged with the oversight of public education and charity on behalf of local units of government. These administrative boards largely were confined to Pennsylvania and Maryland.[14]

Private corporations are distinguished from public corporations chiefly by their large measure of private support and control.

---

[13]This is the distinction which forms the basis of Davis' work. See page 49 of his book.

[14]Ibid., 1:54, 59-60, 74.

However, all private corporations during the colonial period were involved in advancing ends considered to be of broad public value. This is the reason they were granted the benefits of incorporation by the colonial legislatures.

By far the largest group of private corporations in the colonies involved religious worship. The chartering of such religious corporations was clearly seen as being in the public good. As in England, two types of religious corporations were chartered: the "corporate sole," consisting of one person and his or her successors (for example, the parson of a church); and the "corporation aggregate," consisting of several persons and their successors.[15] The distinction in this case was between the person and the institution.

A second major category of private corporations involved those founded for educational purposes, the most important of which were colleges. At the time of the Revolution, there were nine colleges with corporate charters. All of these colleges survive to the present day and are among the leaders of American higher education.[16]

---

[15]Ibid., 1:75.

[16]The nine were: Harvard (founded 1636, chartered 1650); William and Mary (royal charter, 1693); Yale (founded 1701, chartered 1745); Princeton (chartered 1748 as the College of New Jersey); University of Pennsylvania (1753); Columbia (chartered 1754 as King's College); Brown (1764); Rutgers (chartered 1766 as Queen's College);

There also were private corporations chartered for charitable purposes, though the exact number is difficult to determine. In particular, hospitals and mutual benefit societies received charters from colonial legislatures. Some, like New York Hospital which was chartered in 1771, survive to the present day. Others existed for a short period of time to meet a specific need and then closed their doors. The key point is that, as with the other categories of corporations, the advancement of certain charitable causes was seen as being in the public interest.

This concept of "public interest" extended even to business corporations. The colonial, and later the state, legislatures were willing to delegate wide powers to private business corporations because they saw these corporations as advancing the public good. While this justification dates from the time of the Roman Empire, the American innovation was to expand the definition of "public service" to include almost all legitimate business activity. This happened during the nineteenth century with New York as one of the leading states.[17]

During the colonial period, however, relatively few business

---

and Dartmouth (1769). See ibid., 1:84-6.

[17]Cochran, "Business Revolution," 1456. See also Ronald E. Seavoy, *The Origins of the American Business Corporation, 1784-1855: Broadening the Concept of Public Service During Industrialization* (Westport: Greenwood Press, 1982).

corporations were chartered: no more than seven survived from before the Revolution. This was due to a number of factors: the absence of a British tradition of corporate business form, the colonial prejudice against the prominent examples of English business corporations, and the underdevelopment of the colonial economy. The most important reason was the last: because the colonies were dependent on the mother country, the requisite economic, social, and political conditions for widespread corporate development did not exist on this side of the Atlantic. The immature colonial economy did not require the pooling of economic resources to the extent that would be necessary a few decades later. Also colonial legislatures, still sensitive to the debacle of the South Sea Bubble, were leery of issuing corporate charters. This situation began to change near the end of the colonial period. An acceleration in the use of business corporations began which was to continue and expand after independence. Perhaps these nascent business corporations near the end of the colonial period are another indication of the extent to which the mother country and the colonies had drifted apart both economically and socially.[18]

Banks, as we know them today, did not exist during the colonial

---

[18]Davis, *Essays*, 2:328; 1:87-9. Simeon E. Baldwin, "American Business Corporations Before 1789," *American Historical Review* 8 (April 1903): 449-65. Robert A. East, "The Business Entrepreneur in a Changing Colonial Economy, 1763-1795," *Journal of Economic History* 6 (1946): 16-27.

period. There were no commercial banks, or offices of "discount and deposit" as contemporaries would have called them, until after the Revolution.[19] However "land banks" were established in most of the American colonies during the first half of the eighteenth century. With the exception of two relatively short-lived private land banks, all of the banks that actually functioned were created and operated by the governments of the colonies. This is a further indication of the colonial preference for governmental rather than private solutions to public needs.[20]

Unlike "money banks" which focused on mercantile credit, land banks loaned provincial paper money to individuals on the security of real and personal property. Since hard money was so scarce in the colonies, the hope was that paper currency lent by the land banks would facilitate trade and commerce. The land bank system, however, never met this expectation.

The land bank idea first was proposed in 1649 by William Potter of London. The idea soon reached New England, where John Winthrop,

[19]Davis, *Essays*, 2:34. East, "Business Entrepreneurs," 25. Hammond, *Banks and Politics*, 9-10.

[20]As the next chapter will show, this preference continued after the Revolution. When the idea of a water company for New York City was first broached in the 1790s, most people expected a municipal rather than a private company. One of Aaron Burr's more interesting achievements was his convincing of a variety of prominent citizens from different political persuasions that a private company would better meet the needs of the populace.

Jr. and others became its ardent advocates. In 1682 the Reverend John Woodbridge of Newbury, following the lead of Potter and Winthrop, wrote a pamphlet advocating the establishment of a land bank in Massachusetts. The idea then spread to the rest of the colonies.

New York State had a land bank which was a corporate body. By its charter the directors of the bank were given powers to negotiate loans, ascertain the value of securities, receive and hold payments on loans, and sell mortgaged property when forfeited by default. The New York land bank made one issue of currency, in 1737. Despite the date proscribed in the original law for the retirement of the bills, the directors were allowed to postpone retirement for a number of years.[21]

Despite the general familiarity of the colonists with the corporate form and their specific experiences with corporations chartered on both sides of the Atlantic, the colonial era was a relatively quiet time for incorporation. After the Revolution, however, the new states increasingly issued corporate charters of all types. The break with Great Britain was economic and social, as well as political: a new structure had to be developed to meet the needs

---

[21]For additional information on land banks see Theodore Thayer, "The Land Bank System in the American Colonies," *Journal of Economic History* 13 (Spring 1953): 145-59. Also Redlich, *Molding*, 1:5-7, 24, 205.

of the states and nation. The widespread use of the corporate form for business and other purposes became a central part of this new structure.

The Confederation and Early National Periods

The movement toward widespread incorporation began during the revolutionary war. The necessity for large group enterprises to wage the war led Americans to consider all possibilities for collective effort.[22] Though the exigencies of war prevented the immediate establishment of corporations, the foundation was set for rapid growth once peace was secured. This growth was seen first in the chartering of ecclesiastical and other non-business enterprises. Their successes eased the way for other types of corporations, especially those established for business purposes.[23]

A key question involving the first few years after the Revolution is why the corporate form, rather than partnerships, gradually moved to the fore. Before answering that question, however, it would be wrong to imply that corporations completely replaced other forms of collective enterprise. For the next fifty years, each grant of incorporation still required a separate legislative act. Partnerships did not disappear; they continued to

---

[22]East, "Business Entrepreneurs," 26.

[23]Davis, *Essays*, 2:328-9.

exist side-by-side with corporations.

After the Revolution there was a gradual expansion of the corporate form in a nation newly freed from the constraints of an anti-corporate mother country. The interesting thing about this expansion over the next few decades is that there is little evidence of corporations *replacing* partnerships or other forms of organization. Rather, *new* enterprises were given corporate charters. The debate seldom was over whether corporations were usurping the role of partnerships; instead, the debate centered on which new projects should be granted the benefits of incorporation. This, ultimately, may be why corporations expanded after the war: the state legislatures were more willing to consider and authorize new projects.

During the Confederation, however, the actual number of corporations still remained small: the thirteen years of the Confederation resulted in the chartering of but twenty-one business corporations.[24] The explosion was to come between 1789 and 1800. In these years almost 280 business corporations were chartered in the United States. Though this number still may seem small by modern standards, it was a growth unprecedented either in the Mother Country or the colonies.[25]

---

[24]Baldwin, "American Business Corporations," 459.

[25]Davis, *Essays*, 2:8.

Unfettered by Old World ties or constraints, after 1789 Americans embarked upon an experiment in business organization and public policy toward business enterprise. As Ronald Seavoy noted, during the 1790s "franchise corporations" emerged from "benevolent public service corporations."[26] The corporations chartered during this period were seen as delegations of state authority in specific areas. As such, there remained a public expectation that the corporations would serve the commonweal. The fact that the corporations also benefitted their investors apparently was not a great cause for public concern.

The franchise nature of business corporations is obvious in such enterprises as toll bridges, turnpikes, and canals. But even banks were considered to be franchise corporations, agents of public utility. This was because eighteenth and nineteenth century banks issued notes which served as currency for the local community and the nation at large. The existence of a bank in a region made it easier for merchants and others to conduct business. It was the function of note issue, therefore, that the legislatures franchised to different banks. This view that banks existed primarily to advance the common good survived for decades in the new republic, despite, as Fritz Redlich said, "much bitter experience" to the contrary.[27]

---

[26]Seavoy, *Origins*, 104.

[27]Redlich, *Molding*, 1:7-8.

The first commercial bank chartered in the United States was the Bank of North America, which opened in Philadelphia in 1781.[28] This was a successful institution and the model for subsequent commercial banks in all states. In particular, four aspects of the history of the Bank of North America shed light upon the situation in early America and serve as precursors to the experience of the Manhattan Company.

First, the pressure to establish the bank came from a merchant community experiencing a lack of working capital. By pooling their resources, they hoped to formalize what previously had been individual, informal relationships. For some time it had been customary for a merchant with a temporary surplus of funds to make loans to other merchants for short periods of time. The Bank of North America now was to perform this function for the entire merchant community.[29]

Second, opposition to the bank came not only from groups in

---

[28]The best general discussions of the bank are: Janet Wilson, "The Bank of North America and Pennsylvania Politics, 1781-1787," *Pennsylvania Magazine of History and Biography*, 66 (1942): 3-28. F. Cyril James, "The Bank of North America and the Financial History of Philadelphia," ibid., 64 (1940): 56-87. And George David Rappaport, "The Sources and Early Development of the Hostility to Banks in Early American Thought" (Ph.D. diss., New York University, 1970).

[29]Joseph Edward Hedges, *Commercial Banking and the Stock Market Before 1863*, Johns Hopkins University Studies in Historical and Political Science, ser. 66, no. 1 (Baltimore: John Hopkins University Press, 1938), 15. Hammond, *Banks and Politics*, 76.

society with different credit requirements than the merchants, but also from those with different political leanings. In the former category were the agrarians, who had been supporters of Pennsylvania's land bank and who needed longer loans than the forty-five days customary in a merchant bank. In the latter category were the Democrats who made the crusade against the bank a plank in their political platform. Looked at in this way, the fight over the Bank of North America was an episode in the factional struggle between Democrats and Republicans in Pennsylvania.[30]

Third, the nature of the bank's charter was crucial and became a source of some of the factional struggle. The founders of the Bank of North America originally requested a charter with no limit to the bank's capital and no expiration date. While the 1781 charter was perpetual, it limited the bank's capital to $10 million. It also prevented the bank from engaging in trade, a common clause in corporate charters after the South Sea Bubble.[31] The bank lost its charter for a short period of time, regaining a charter in 1787 when Republicans returned to power in Pennsylvania. The new charter, however, was markedly different from the original one. In addition to retaining the prohibition against commerce, it also limited the bank's capital to $2 million and placed a fourteen year duration on

---

[30]Rappaport, "Hostility," 244, 251.

[31]Ibid., 15, 24, 37.

the bank's incorporation.[32]

Fourth, the bank's profitability was a two-edged sword. On the one hand, the profits of the bank helped attract investors and promote the use of the corporate form. In 1782 the Bank of North America paid a dividend of 8 3/4 percent; in 1783 the dividend jumped to 14 1/2 percent.[33] On the other hand, the profitability of the bank helped spur the opposition and rally public support to their position. As George David Rappaport said, "To many Americans, including part of the mercantile community, money was too important to allow individuals to make profits from it, let alone control it." The opposition to the Bank of North America, therefore, became a "crusade" against the spectre of an aristocratic money power endangering the young Republic.[34] Once again, the franchise nature of early banks is clear. The best modern parallel might be public utilities, where the function is considered too important to let private individuals control and profit from it.

In addition to Philadelphia, the other major commercial centers in the new nation soon established banks: Massachusetts chartered a bank in 1784, Maryland in 1790, and New York in 1791. By 1793 there

---

[32]Ibid., 239.

[33]Ibid., 33. This was in line with later banks, whose dividends typically were between eight and ten percent per year. See Davis, *Essays*, 2:103-5.

[34]Rappaport, "Hostility," 70, 245-8.

were twenty chartered banks in the country.[35] The key point in the establishment of these banks was the fact that usually there was no more than one bank in a particular community: the "franchise" of banking was considered to be an exclusive one. There were some exceptions, particularly in cities having branches of the Bank of the United States.[36] But clearly it was not the intention of the early state legislatures to promote competition in banking, especially competition by people of a different political persuasion. The creation of the Manhattan Company was one of the first breaks in the solid wall of monopoly banking on the state level.

Banking had established itself on a sound footing in a surprisingly short period of time. This was a "profoundly radical development," in the words of George David Rappaport.[37] In addition, the success of banking led to a wider acceptance of the corporate form. The next few decades witnessed experiments with the corporate form in other fields. Many of these enterprises also were made possible by the availability of banking resources in the new

---

[35]Davis, *Essays*, 2:59. Blake, *Water for Cities*, 63-4.

[36]In addition to its main office in Philadelphia, the First Bank of the United States established branches in the following cities: Boston, New York, Baltimore, and Charleston (1792); Norfolk (1800); Washington and Savannah (1802); and New Orleans (1805). Hammond, *Banks and Politics*, 127.

[37]Rappaport, "Hostility," 39.

states.[38] Nowhere was this more apparent than in New York State.

Banking in New York Before the Manhattan Company

As I already have discussed, New York State had experience with a land bank during the colonial period. The interest in a land bank continued after the Revolution, becoming one part of a factional struggle which was to dominate the next few decades. In this regard, the New York experience was similar to the Philadelphia situation involving the Bank of North America.

With the departure of the British from New York City in November of 1783, several groups began to think about the establishment of a bank as one means of reviving the shattered commerce of the city. Seven years of British occupation had left New York City devastated. As one newspaper said, "Business is very dead here and money scarce; the British having carried it all away with them."[39]

Thomas Stoughton, a New York City merchant and one of the original directors of the Bank of New York, commented on the

---

[38]Davis, *Essays*, 2:108.

[39]New York *Journal*, May 6, 1784, p. 1. See also Edward Streeter, *Window on America: The Growth of a Nation as Seen by New York's First Bank, 1784-1959* (New York: Bank of New York, 1959), 10-14. Allan Nevins, *History of the Bank of New York and Trust Company, 1784-1934* (New York: Bank of New York, 1934), 2. Forrest McDonald, *We the People: The Economic Origins of the Constitution* (Chicago: University of Chicago Press, 1968), 296.

situation a number of times in his correspondence with other merchants. "Trade was never more Dull in the State of N.Y. than at this period," he wrote to a Spanish mercantile house, "and until the country has forgot she was at war & Industry Spreads her Self, our exports will not be so abundant as we had reason to hope." Stoughton continued that in an attempt to encourage "every branch of active Commerce the most useful establishments are Setting of foot," including a specie bank.[40]

Other merchants also commented on the financial plight of the city. John Delafield, for example, spoke about the problem of inadequate currency. "Money concerns are at Present my chief Study," he wrote to a business contact in Philadelphia. "Continental and State papers, as various and in shapes as Questionable as Hamlets Ghost pass through my office in abundance."[41] Clearly the problems of the city in 1784 went far beyond the resources of individual merchants. In order to have any hope of solving these commercial problems, an institutionalized financial structure was essential.

A second group, however, was inspired more by the promise of a

---

[40]Thomas Stoughton to Farrel Storage Company, Cadiz, March 17, 1784, Lynch & Stoughton Letterbooks, New-York Historical Society [hereafter NYHS], New York, New York. For similar quotes see Stoughton to Messrs. Frederick & Geale, Dublin, April 10, 1784; Stoughton to Frances Bine, April 10, 1784.

[41]John Delafield to Messrs. Deaver and Baker of Philadelphia, April 4, 1784, Delafield Letterbooks, New York Public Library [hereafter NYPL], New York, New York.

good return on their investments than by a sense of helping the community. As has already been shown, early banks were very profitable and therefore attracted the interests of speculators. By serving as an agent for two such speculators, Alexander Hamilton first became involved in the founding of the Bank of New York.

Jeremiah Wadsworth and John B. Church, Hamilton's brother-in-law, were the largest single stockholders in the Bank of North America, holding 104 and 98 shares respectively.[42] Both men, therefore, made handsome profits when the Bank of North America declared its large dividends. Late in 1783 Wadsworth and Church, then in Europe, instructed Hamilton to establish a New York City bank in which they could hold controlling interest. Their developing plans were suddenly interrupted, however, by a newspaper announcement of a proposed New York State land bank.[43]

In February, 1784 two New York City newspapers reported that a plan was afoot to establish a bank with a capital of $750,000. The point which distressed the merchants was that only one-third of each

---

[42]John D.R. Platt, "Jeremiah Wadsworth: Federalist Entrepreneur" (Ph.D. diss., Columbia University, 1955), 135. This represented more than twenty percent of the bank's total of 1,000 shares.

[43]Ibid., 146-9. James, "Bank of North America," 65. John C. Miller, *Alexander Hamilton: Portrait in Paradox* (New York, Harper and Row, 1959). Harold C. Syrett, ed., *The Papers of Alexander Hamilton* (New York: Columbia University Press 1962), 3:514n.

share was to be paid for in cash -- the remainder was to be secured by real estate mortgages.[44] Though the newspapers did not mention Robert R. Livingston by name, Hamilton later reported that he "had reason to suspect the Chancellor was the true father" of the enterprise. Hamilton's suspicions were borne out when Livingston and a number of others petitioned the State Legislature on February 17th for a land bank charter. The proposed charter also contained a clause which would have prohibited the establishment of any other bank in the state.[45]

Thus early in 1784 the sides were drawn for a fight over what type of bank should be established in New York. The division in this matter closely paralleled the divisions on other economic matters, including the arguments over the federal impost[46] and the

---

[44]*The Independent Gazette or the New-York Journal Revived*, February 12, 1784, p. 3. The New York *Packet and American Advertiser*, February 16, 1784, p. 1.

[45]Hamilton to John B. Church, March 10, 1784, *Hamilton Papers*, 3:520-1. Further proof of Livingston's involvement can be found in his papers in the NYHS, especially the following 1784 items: "On the Improvements Made by Corporations," "Thoughts on the Establishment of a Bank," and "Observations of the Proposed Establishment of a Bank." These documents contain a plan almost identical to the one presented in the newspapers cited above.

[46]The five percent impost plan was an attempt to bolster the credit of the Continental Government. Opposition arose "partly from a disinclination to give up power, and partly from the disinclination of the upstate men to do what they felt would favor the city merchants and might increase the land tax." Thomas C. Cochran, *New York in the Confederation: An Economic Study* (Philadelphia: University of Pennsylvania Press, 1932), 159-60.

establishment of a state paper currency.[47]   On one side were the New York City merchants who believed that "Land Banks as such are altogether incapable of answering the purposes of the merchant, as they cannot supply the specie for payment of foreign debts."[48]   In addition, many merchants believed a bank firmly established on specie to be the only way of controlling the postwar inflation and depreciated Continental currency.[49]   This group was concentrated in the downstate, urban region of the state, although some large upstate land proprietors also fell into this camp.   As "federalists" they supported a strong national government for both ideological and economic reasons. The advocacy of a "money bank" based on mercantile transactions was to become an important element of their program.[50]

---

[47]Beginning in 1784 there was agitation for an issue of paper money to replace the specie lost during the last months of the British occupation. The State Assembly passed two paper money bills in 1784 and a third in 1785, but all were defeated in the Senate. Finally, the paper money bill advocated by the upstate interests was passed in 1786. McDonald, *We the People*, 293.   Merrill Jensen, *The New Nation: A History of the United States During the Confederation, 1781-1789* (New York: Alfred A. Knopf, 1950), 320-1.

[48]Extract of a letter from a "Gentleman in Philadelphia" to his friend in New York, dated February 26, 1784, New York *Packet*, March 11, 1784, p. 3.

[49]John Delafield to Messrs. Deaver and Baker of Philadelphia, April 4, 1784, Delafield Letterbooks, NYPL. See also Broadus Mitchell, "Inflation: Revolution and Its Aftermath," *Current History* 24 (May 1953): 258-9.

[50]E. Wilder Spaulding, *New York in the Critical Period, 1783-1789* (New York: Columbia University Press, 1932), 4-10, 101-2.   Jackson Turner Main, *The Antifederalists: Critics of the*

Opposing the merchants and their allies were the followers of George Clinton. In particular, this group was composed of small farmers from upstate, who wanted a bank which advanced their own landed interests. Because of the seasonal nature of their work, the farmers required loans of longer term than those usually given by commercial banks. They also tended to favor states rights and to oppose the formation of a strong federal government. Finally, the farmers did not wish to strengthen the downstate faction (which eventually would oppose them in the struggle over the Federal Constitution).[51]

Both groups realized the benefits a bank could bring. The following contemporary testimony summarized these benefits:

> The great benefits to commerce and society at large, to be derived from well regulated BANKS, especially in republican governments, or where the hand of arbitrary power is restrained by law, is a fact universally acknowledged....A Bank is not only a place of safety for cash, but it renders aid to the merchant and tradesman by discount at common interest. It compels society to punctuality in contracts; -- it enables it to make fresh ones; -- and surprisingly augments the force of doing more business in less time and with greater facility to all parties.[52]

The interesting thing about this statement is that it was not issued

---

Constitution, 1781-1788 (Chapel Hill: University of North Carolina Press, 1961), 48-50, 242. Cochran, *New York in the Confederation*, 17n, 159-81.

[51]Main, *Antifederalists*, 50.

[52]New York *Packet*, February 16, 1784, p. 1. The quote also is found in *The Independent Gazette or the New York Journal Revived*, February 12, 1784, p. 3.

by one of Hamilton's supporters. Rather, it was written to advocate the proposed land bank.

Hamilton took it upon himself to spur the rest of the merchant community to action. He sarcastically commented that the supporters of the land bank believed it to be "the true Philosophers stone that was to turn all their rocks and trees into gold." Hamilton was so successful in his warnings that a second group of merchants began to plan for a "money bank," and called upon him to subscribe. "I was a little embarrassed how to act," Hamilton wrote to Church for whom he supposedly was still trying to establish a separate specie bank, "but upon the whole I concluded it best to fall in with them."[53] It was this union of forces which ultimately became the Bank of New York.

In the ensuing battle, the agricultural and mercantile groups each prevented the other from obtaining a charter.[54] The merchant group, however, decided to open its money bank as an unchartered institution. Their creation, the Bank of New York, opened for business on June 9, 1784. Over the next seven years, the principals of the Bank of New York continued to try for a state charter. Their petitions were rejected by the state legislature in 1785 and again in 1790. This was a reflection of the continuing factional struggle in

---

[53]Hamilton to Church, March 10, 1784, *Hamilton Papers*, 3:521-2. See also Hammond, *Banks and Politics*, 65, and Baldwin, "American Business Corporations," 465.

[54]Hammond, *Banks and Politics*, 65.

New York and the fear that corporations chartered for economic purposes would abuse their privileged position and oppress the community.[55] As Gordon Wood has shown, the revolutionary experience of this first generation of Americans led to a widespread fear of corruption and the consequent establishment of checks and balances on both governmental and private institutions.[56]

Despite the setbacks over its charter, the Bank of New York prospered and grew, paying annual dividends of six percent. This was due in large measure to the sound business practices the bank inaugurated. Among these practices, which were to become standard among banks in New York State, were:

1. Discounts (loans) were made for a short period of time (thirty day maximum).

2. No note or bill would be discounted to pay a former one (no renewal of loans).

3. The rate of discount was set at seven percent per year.

4. Repayments had to be made in bank notes or specie.

5. Money on deposit could be withdrawn anytime "free of expense," but there were no overdraft privileges.[57]

---

[55]Domett, *Bank of New York*, 33-35. McDonald, *We the People*, 390. Nevins, *Bank of New York*, 20.

[56]Gordon Wood, *The Creation of the American Republic, 1776-1787* (Chapel Hill: University of North Carolina Press, 1969).

[57]*New York Directory for 1789*, 114-5.

The Bank of New York's original capital of $51,500 grew to $381,250 by May, 1791. At that time its deposits were $773,700 and its loans and discounts totaled $889,200.[58]

On March 21, 1791 the Bank of New York finally received its state charter. Among the key features of the charter were: the bank's capital was set at $900,000; debts were limited to three times the amount of capital subscribed; property could be held only for purposes related to banking; the bank was prohibited from dealing in trade or buying and selling stock; the directors were required to issue half-yearly dividends on profits; and the charter was to run for a limited time, in this case twenty years.

This charter was to become the model for bank charters in New York until 1825, when the form for acts of incorporation was changed and more stringent restrictions were included.[59] There was, however, one notable exception to this rule: the Manhattan Company. The next chapter will detail the nature and significance of the Manhattan Company's charter and its effect upon the operations of the company. It also will show that factional struggles remained an

---

[58]Louis M. Hacker, *Alexander Hamilton in the American Tradition* (New York: McGraw-Hill, 1957), 80-81.

[59]For the full text of the charter, see Domett, *Bank of New York*, 127-34. For comments on the charter, see ibid., 34-5; Nevins, *Bank of New York*, 20; Sidney I. Pomerantz, *New York, An American City, 1783-1803: A Study of Urban Life* (New York: Columbia University Press, 1958), 184-7.

important element in the course of corporate development.

Conclusion

In the years before the Manhattan Company, the structure of businesses was circumscribed by the social and political environment. One could not freely and easily structure a large business because the corporate form was so closely guarded by the state legislatures. Acts of incorporation were specific and restrictive, rather than general and permissive. This narrow structure clearly influenced the strategies business leaders could follow, a point not sufficiently stressed by Chandler. He attributed the lack of innovative, large scale enterprises to the inadequately developed market. But even if the market had been more mature and the demands of the public more extensive, typical corporate charters would not have permitted businesses to expand into new areas. The political environment in these early years would not support the structure necessary to carry out modern business strategies.

CHAPTER TWO

THE FOUNDING AND CHARTER

OF THE MANHATTAN COMPANY

> In a republican and capitalistic society, government would not be the sole repository of the general public good. In their private activities and enterprises private individuals also secured the public welfare.[1]

While the Manhattan Company built upon a long history of corporate development, in many ways it was more of a leader than a follower. The Manhattan Company became a bridge between old and new concepts of the corporation and its role in American society. The main pillar of this bridge was the distinctly "modern" charter the Manhattan Company obtained from the New York State legislature. This charter gave the company a great deal of freedom in structuring its operations. As a result, the leaders of the Manhattan Company were able to pursue business strategies uncommon for the time, especially diversification.

Despite this freedom, the Manhattan Company remained a nineteenth century corporation, closely bound by public expectations of the common good. Throughout its history, external factors such as public criticism and possible competition led to changes in both the

---

[1]Hendrik Hartog, *Public Property and Private Power: The Corporation of the City of New York in American Law, 1730-1870* (Chapel Hill: University of North Carolina Press, 1983), 146-7.

Chartered 1799

The seal of the Manhattan Company, adopted in 1799. It pictures Oceanus, the Greek god of waters, at the Hilltop, the source of all streams. At his side is an ever-flowing urn, from which flows a symbolic river. The spade in his hand is a symbol of his authority. *(Courtesy of the Chase Manhattan Archives.)*

Manhattan Company's strategies and structure.

The Manhattan Company's charter was modern not because of the state's desire to advance corporate development, but because of a combination of circumstances surrounding the company's founding. The origins of the Manhattan Company can be traced to a mosquito-spread yellow fever epidemic which swept New York City in the summer of 1798.

Americans of the 1790's still were decades away from developing a germ theory of disease. One common theory of the time attributed epidemics to impure drinking water and the decaying wastes found in the streets of large cities.[2] The favored solution, obtaining an adequate supply of "pure and wholesome water," was right but for the wrong reason. While pure water for drinking and sanitation would not *directly* eliminate the disease, it would eliminate the breeding grounds for the *carriers* of the disease. After the 1798 epidemic, therefore, concerned New Yorkers intensified their efforts to establish an adequate water supply. While the city had been considering such a project since 1774[3], it took the stimulus of the

---

[2]Nelson M. Blake, *Water for the Cities: A History of the Urban Water Supply Problem in the United States* (Syracuse: Syracuse University Press, 1956), 5-8, 44-45.

[3]For the twenty-five year debate, see *Minutes of the Common Council of the City of New York, 1784-1831* (New York: City of New York, 1930), 1:198-200, 213-214, 354-355; 2:63, 135, 137, 225, 307, 314, 347, 420, 484, 486-487. There is an excellent discussion of this early effort in Blake, *Water for the Cities*.

epidemic to finally move the various governmental bodies to action.

In light of subsequent events, one of the most interesting aspects of the founding of the Manhattan Company was the bipartisan support the effort received at both the state and local levels. Though the Manhattan Company later was to become a Republican power in the state, there was no hint of this at the time of its founding. Pure water for New York City seemed to be of such overriding public benefit that both Federalists and Republicans endorsed it. For example, both Alexander Hamilton and Aaron Burr, those perennial political rivals, worked for the project. According to Harold C. Syrett, it is "highly unlikely" that Burr would have received a charter for the company without the support of Hamilton and other prominent Federalists.[4]

The debate over a water company quickened with the actions of Dr. Joseph Browne in the summer of 1798. Browne, a physician and engineer, also was Aaron Burr's brother-in-law and may have been working in concert with Burr. Browne submitted a detailed memorandum

---

[4]The best treatment of the founding of the Manhattan Company is a two-part article in the *Political Science Quarterly*. Beatrice Reubens, "Burr, Hamilton, and the Manhattan Company. Part I: Gaining the Charter," *Political Science Quarterly*, 72 (December 1957): 578-602. Reubens, "Burr, Hamilton, and the Manhattan Company. Part II: Launching a Bank," *Political Science Quarterly* 73 (March 1958): 100-25. My page numbers refer to the reprint in the CMB Archives which combines both articles. See also Blake, *Water for the Cities*, 49-54. Harold C. Syrett, ed., *The Papers of Alexander Hamilton* (New York: Columbia University Press, 1975), 22:446-451.

to the New York City Common Council recommending the establishment of a private water company with a capital of $200,000. The core of Browne's proposed solution involved transporting water from the Bronx River. The source of the water was not a minor point; it later became an important issue in the history of the Manhattan Company.[5]

Browne's memorandum and other water supply proposals were referred to a special committee of the Common Council. While the committee accepted much of Browne's proposal, it rejected the idea of a private water company. The Common Council concurred with the committee, deciding to push for a municipal water company. The Common Council thereupon petitioned the state legislature for the necessary legal authority and financial resources.[6]

Burr's subsequent actions lend credence to the belief that he had ulterior motives all along. According to Syrett and others, Burr planned from the beginning to use the Manhattan Company to break the Federalist monopoly on banking in New York City. In their view, Burr seized upon the bipartisan issue of improved water supply to gather allies for a private company with the hidden purpose of engaging in banking. The Common Council's change in Browne's plan would have been alarming to Burr, therefore, because a municipal water works

---

[5]For Browne's memorandum, see *Proceedings of the Corporation of New York to Supply the City With Pure and Wholesome Water With a Memoir of Joseph Browne, M.D.* (New York, 1799).

[6]*Minutes of the Common Council*, 2:486-487, 490.

could not be redirected toward banking. If Burr at this point was only interested in improved water supply, it would not have mattered if the city had a public or private company. It became clear, however, that a private company mattered greatly to Burr.

As was the normal routine, when the Common Council's petition reached Albany it was referred to a committee of the thirteen assemblymen representing the City of New York, of whom Burr was a leader. Though Burr pressed the committee to recommend a private water company, the committee was leery about ignoring the stated preference of the Common Council. The committee agreed, therefore, that Burr should return to the city and ascertain the view of the Common Council toward a private water company.[7]

A caution is in order at this point. It would be incorrect to think that the issue of public vs. private control of internal improvements was resolved in the minds of most people. While later experience in New York and other cities made clear that municipal water systems were the better option, in 1799 the course was not so clear. For one thing, there was a strong feeling that the state should not increase its debt by the large amounts necessary for internal improvements. Also, previous experience with government control of turnpike construction in New York State had shown the

---

[7]*Journal of the Assembly of the State of New-York*, 1799, p. 123. Burr also was to address a second disputed bill, one dealing with drainage and sewage.

waste, corruption, and inefficiency such an arrangement could spawn. Therefore the shift from a public to a private project would not have been an immediate cause for alarm.

Burr returned before the Common Council with a committee of six prominent citizens equally divided between Federalists and Republicans. In addition to Burr and Hamilton, the other committee members were: John Murray, President of the Chamber of Commerce; Gulian Verplanck, President of the Bank of New York; Peter H. Wendover, President of the Mechanic Society; and John Broome, a New York City merchant and prominent Republican politician. The committee expressed concern that the bill for a municipal water company might not pass the state legislature and requested the flexibility to change the bill if necessary.[8]

Burr's formation of this committee was a master stroke of political operation, for it showed bipartisan support for his position. As it turned out, the key person in getting the Federalist Common Council to reverse itself was Alexander Hamilton. He submitted a signed statement to the Common Council on behalf of the committee of six. Hamilton stated that the legislature's approval of the present plan was "Problematical" because of the finances involved. He estimated that it would cost one million dollars to supply the city with water. "The Amount of the revenue to result

---

[8] *Minutes of the Common Council*, 2:514-515.

from the supply of the Water must be for some time uncertain," Hamilton continued, "and under this uncertainty extensive loans on this basis [a low interest rate] ought not to be counted upon. To raise what may be wanted by taxes to carry on the enterprise with vigour might be found so burthensome on the Citizens as to occasion the operation to languish." He believed the "final Success of the object" would be better promoted by permitting the capital "to be created by the voluntary contributions of individuals."

Hamilton also foresaw another potential problem with a municipal water works. Based upon previous projects, there was some question about the ability of the Common Council and its part-time representatives to provide proper ongoing management to a project of this magnitude. Hamilton instead recommended a private company with the city recorder serving as an *ex officio* member of the board of directors and with the city as a stockholder.[9]

Two days later the Common Council adopted Hamilton's recommendation, stating that it would "be perfectly satisfied if the objects in View are pursued in any Way that the Legislature may think proper by which their fellow Citizens may be benefitted in the most easy, safe and effectual method, and the Charter rights of the City

---

[9]Hamilton's statement to the Common Council is enclosed in a letter to Mayor Richard Varick dated February 26, 1799, *Hamilton Papers*, 22:508-11.

remain inviolate."[10]

This was not the end of Hamilton's efforts, however. He also prepared a memorial to the state legislature on behalf of a number of citizens of the city. The memorial stated that some citizens had become "alarmed lest a difference of Opinion" about the best means of providing water "should prevent any law being passed on the subject." While professing no desire to interfere with the original plan for a municipal water works, the memorial presented an "alternative" in case that plan should not be approved. The alternative was the same as the one presented to the Common Council: a private corporation with the city as a major shareholder.[11]

Burr returned to Albany armed with the Common Council resolution and a number of petitions recommending a private water company. He did not, however, immediately introduce the Manhattan Company bill. Rather, he waited until after the legislature had resolved a related sewage and drainage bill for New York City. Burr wanted to see if the legislature would approve sufficient public financing of the related venture. If it did not, Burr would be able to argue that the legislature likewise would not approve sufficient funding for a municipal water company, thereby leaving a private

---

[10]*Minutes of the Common Council*, 2:517-520.

[11]Memorial to the Legislature of the State of New York, February-March, 1799, *Hamilton Papers*, 22:515-6.

company as the only alternative. Burr was correct in his initial assumption, for the legislature passed the sewage bill without providing any financial provisions for its execution.[12]

The Assembly passed the Manhattan Company bill on March 28th, less than twenty-four hours after it was introduced.[13] From there it went to the Senate, which was less under Burr's direct control. In order to shepherd the bill through the Senate, Burr enlisted the support of several key Federalists, the most prominent of whom was Samuel Jones, Sr. Jones, a lawyer dubbed "the father of the New York Bar," was the state comptroller as well as a state senator. The bill was referred to a special committee of three chaired by Jones, whose stature was such that his support would virtually guarantee passage. Jones' committee held the bill for two days and then reported favorably on it to the Senate. The Senate, in turn, approved the measure on March 30th.[14]

Once approved by both houses, the bill next had to go to the Council of Revision. This body was created by the New York Constitution of 1777 to review all bills passed by the legislature

---

[12]For more on the related bill, see Reubens, "Burr, Hamilton," 24-26.

[13]*Journal of the Assembly of the State of New York*, 22nd sess., 2nd meeting, 263.

[14]*Journal of the Senate of the State of New York*, 22nd sess., 2nd meeting, 109-10, 118.

for conflicts either with the Constitution or the public good. The Council consisted of the Governor, the Chancellor, and the judges of the Supreme Court. A two-thirds majority of each house was required to override the veto of the Council.[15]

It was in the Council of Revision that the bill faced its most serious challenge. A Republican judge, John Lansing, raised serious objections to a "surplus capital clause"[16] which Burr inserted at the last moment. Lansing was outvoted, however, when Chancellor Robert R. Livingston (a Republican and the largest single stockholder in the proposed company) joined forces with Federalist Judge Egbert Benson. Benson's vote was later to come back to haunt him, as he bore the brunt of much of the Federalist outrage and lost a chance to run for governor. The lesson of the entire chartering process, as Beatrice Reubens pointed out thirty years ago, was that "without Federalist help, Burr could not have achieved his legislative triumph."[17]

---

[15]The Council of Revision continued to exist until 1821, when a new state constitution abolished it. Reubens, "Burr, Hamilton," 32n.

[16]I will discuss this clause in detail below.

[17]Reubens, "Burr, Hamilton," 34. Sidney I. Pomerantz went even further, claiming that "Responsibility for the passage of the Manhattan Company charter must be placed squarely on the Federalists." According to Pomerantz, Burr made clear his intended uses of surplus capital. Federalists supported the plan because they, too, stood to gain economically from the new company. Viewed in this way, the Federalists' attacks on Burr had the political

But what exactly *was* Burr's legislative triumph? Simply put, three key elements in the Manhattan Company's charter made it a business corporation unlike any of its contemporaries.[18] First was the large capital authorized for the company, two million dollars. Of the twenty-six banks chartered in the United States before 1800, only three had authorized capital equal to or greater than that of the Manhattan Company: the Bank of North America ($2 million), the Bank of Pennsylvania ($3 million), and the Bank of the United States ($10 million). The average capital of the other twenty-two banks was $502,273.[19] By way of comparison, the largest capitalization for a textile factory in New York State before 1811 was $250,000, while the

motive of defeating the Republicans in the next election. "The artful political maneuvering that had made Burr the arch-conspirator in the Manhattan Company affair was so skillfully executed that historians to this day have uncritically accepted the accusations heaped upon him in the bitterness of an election campaign." *New York, An American City, 1783-1803: A Study of Urban Life* (New York: Columbia University Press, 1938), 187-91. A legal historian recently has discussed the implications of the Federalists' actions: "Federalist legislators either were duped, bribed, or convinced to vote for a project that its sponsors intended to use for ends entirely distinct from the purposes stated in the charter: a direct and manifest violation of standard republican principles and an important event in the evolution of the business corporation form." Hartog, *Public Property*, 149.

[18]"Act Incorporating the Manhattan Company [hereafter MC]," 1799. The charter can be found in the microprint edition of *Evans' American Bibliography*. See also *New York Laws*, 22nd sess., ch. 84.

[19]Bray Hammond, *Banks and Politics in America From the Revolution to the Civil War* (Princeton: Princeton University Press, 1957), 144-145.

average was approximately $100,000.[20]

The second major feature of "this extraordinary charter" (to quote a contemporary),[21] the feature which made banking possible, was the so-called "surplus capital" clause:

> *And be it further enacted*, That it shall and may be lawful for the said company, to employ all such surplus capital as may belong or accrue to the said company in the purchase of public or other stock, or in any other monied transactions or operations, not inconsistent with the constitution and laws of this State or of the United States, for the sole benefit of said company.

Undoubtedly, the majority of the legislators who voted in favor of the charter expected the Manhattan Company to use this clause to invest any funds not immediately needed for the water works. When asked about this clause by a Senate committee, however, Burr did state that he intended the company to be able to establish "a Bank or an East India Company" since furnishing the city with water would not sufficiently remunerate the shareholders.[22] The financial return to shareholders was not an idle concern. The Manhattan Company needed to raise a great deal of money from subscribers in order to

---

[20]Ronald E. Seavoy, "The Origins of the American Business Corporation, 1784-1855: New York, the National Model" (Ph.D. diss., University of Michigan, 1969), 74.

[21]Nicholas Fish to Arthur Noble, February 13, 1800, Record Group 1, Box 1, Chase Manhattan [hereafter CMB] Archives, New York, New York.

[22]Quoted in Joseph S. Davis, *Essays in the Earlier History of American Corporations* (Cambridge: Harvard University Press, 1917; reprint, New York: Russell & Russell, 1965), 2:101.

accomplish its purpose. Unless investors thought they would make a sufficient return on their investment, they would avoid (and thus doom) the project.

Burr and his Republican associates quickly exploited the power of the surplus capital clause. It became the lever for prying open the Federalist monopoly over banking in New York City. At the time of the founding of the Manhattan Company, both of the other banks in the city -- the Bank of New York and the local branch of the Bank of the United States -- were controlled by Federalists. The establishment of the Manhattan Company expanded the capital available to those with Republican political leanings. For these reasons, Hamilton subsequently regretted his part in the chartering of the Manhattan Company. Referring to Burr, he said "I have been present when he has contended against Banking Systems with earnestness....Yet he has lately by a trick established a *Bank*, a perfect monster in its principle; but a very convenient instrument of *profit and influence.*"[23] Bray Hammond, one of the leading banking historians, stated the point even more forcefully. "Aaron Burr's ruse was more than just a trick," according to Hammond. "It was a minor

---

[23]Hamilton to James A. Bayard, January 16, 1801, *Hamilton Papers*, 25:321. Pomerantz was similarly harsh in evaluating the Manhattan Company: "Economic manipulators had taken advantage of a genuine civic movement to launch a profit-making undertaking that not only thwarted a plan for a publicly-owned utility but frustrated the program to secure an adequate supply of pure water." *New York*, 284.

revolution, economic and political. It illustrates the larger revolution which in the country as a whole was changing the disciplined and restricted economy of the eighteenth century into the dynamic, complex, *laisser faire* economy of the nineteenth century."[24]

The third unusual feature of the charter, the perpetual life of the corporation, assumed even greater significance because of the freedom given the company in the area of finances. Judge Lansing of the Council of Revision stressed this in his objection to the Manhattan Company's charter. Because no one could know how the Manhattan Company would use its surplus capital, Lansing emphasized that the situation "peculiarly requires the application of the policy which has heretofore uniformly obtained: that the powers of corporations relative to their money operations, should be of limited instead of perpetual duration."[25] Lansing was right about previous practice, as I have illustrated in chapter one. Furthermore, by requiring banks and other financial institutions to apply for charter extensions every twenty or thirty years, the state maintained some control over this important function. In the case of the Manhattan Company, control by re-charter would be noticeably missing in the

---

[24]Hammond, *Banks and Politics*, 156. See also Seavoy, "Origins," 59-60.

[25]*Minutes of the Council of Revision*, April 2, 1799, Record Group 1, Legal Size Files, CMB Archives.

future.[26]

Taken as a whole, the Manhattan Company's charter was remarkably free. It was a radical departure from previous corporate charters, especially those in the financial area. As such, it engendered fear among the political adversaries of Burr. "I challenge any man," went a typical comment, "to produce an act of incorporation, that ever passed in any civilized country, which conferred power so entirely without definition, limitations, or control."[27] This unique act of incorporation would be a continuing source of controversy throughout the next half century, with the Manhattan Company trying to protect its charter rights and opponents trying to invalidate the far-reaching document.

The Manhattan Company Charter: The Continuing Controversy

The Manhattan Company's charter offered great possibilities because of its surplus capital clause. As chapter three will show, Burr and the other leaders of the company tried to augment the "surplus" capital by spending as little as possible on the water works. This increased the funds available for such profitable enterprises as banking and insurance.

---

[26]For example, in 1829 New York State was not able to force the Manhattan Company to join the Safety Fund System, despite a law suit I will discuss below.

[27]New York *Commercial Advertiser*, May 1, 1799.

There was one problem, however, with the Manhattan Company's charter. Embedded in the charter was an important restriction. Within ten years of its incorporation, the Manhattan Company was required to "furnish and continue a supply of pure and wholesome water, sufficient for the use of all such citizens dwelling in the said city, as shall agree to take it on the terms to be demanded by the said company." If the company did that not meet this condition, the corporation would be dissolved.[28]

The requirement that the Manhattan Company furnish a sufficient supply of water placed the charter of the company, as well as its profitable banking business, in jeopardy. Throughout the period of this study, and even into the twentieth century, the Manhattan Company took great pains to defend its viability as a water company. This defense included efforts to modify or clarify the original charter of the company.[29]

Less than a year after its founding, the Manhattan Company was interested in amending its charter. The Board of Directors of the company approved a resolution presented by Burr to petition the legislature for a modification of the charter. The company was

---

[28]"Act Incorporating the Manhattan Company." See also Reubens, "Burr, Hamilton," 26.

[29]In chapter three I will discuss the other side of the company's defense, trying to prove that it indeed was furnishing a sufficient supply of pure and wholesome water

willing to confine its powers to: water supply; banking; buying and selling annuities, stocks, and bills of exchange; and insurance. The company also was willing to limit its issuance of notes to three times its capital, the standard present in most bank charters. In return for these concessions, the company wanted its elections to last for more than one day and, more importantly, wanted permission to hold real estate by mortgage or in payment of outstanding debts. The directors appointed a committee of three to prepare an application to the legislature embodying these points. There is no record, however, that the application ever was submitted.[30]

At the same time that the Manhattan Company was contemplating its future role, its opponents were taking steps to insure that there would be no similar charter fiascoes. On April 11, 1804 the state legislature enacted a restraining law to prevent the formation of any additional Manhattan Companies. By this act, the state restricted banking powers to corporations specifically chartered for that purpose.[31] The effect of the restraining law was to make

---

[30]MC Minutes, 1:67 (March 10, 1800). Unless otherwise noted, all Manhattan Company records are found in the CMB Archives, Record Group 1.

[31]Other states also had troubles with "back door banking." For example, the first bank west of the Alleghenies was chartered in 1802 as the Kentucky Insurance Company. There was no mention of banking in its charter, as a way of circumventing agrarian opposition. While the company insured river boats and cargoes, it also had a profitable discount business. Similarly, the Miami Exporting Company of Cincinnati was chartered in 1803 ostensibly to

possession of a bank charter in New York after 1804 a "political privilege rather than a public service franchise."[32] This did not change until 1838 when a general incorporation statute, the so-called "free-banking act," separated the granting of bank charters from the politics of the state legislature. The supporters of the Manhattan Company in 1804, however, were able to insert a clause in another bill then under consideration to prevent the restraining act from applying to the company.

Also beginning in 1804, the Manhattan Company took serious steps to have its charter amended. The particular points of concern were: an extension of the time for supplying the city with adequate water, recognition as a bank, and permission to transfer its water works to the city without endangering its banking operations.

One idea was to merge the Manhattan Company with the State Bank located in Albany. DeWitt Clinton drafted a memorial to the New York State Legislature in March, 1804 outlining the advantages of such a connection. As part of the merger, the Manhattan Company proposed

---

transport farm products to New Orleans. However the company soon established a profitable banking business. See Hammond, *Banks and Politics*, 159, 168-170.

[32]Seavoy, "Origins," 93. For a discussion of these 1804 bills and their implications, see The People v. the President and Directors of the Manhattan Company, 9 Wendell, 390-391 (1832). The text of the restraining can can be found in *New York Laws*, 27th sess., ch. 117. See also Hammond, *Banks and Politics*, 159 and Seavoy, "Origins," 60, 92.

limiting the duration of its charter to fifty years, provided that the time for furnishing New York City with water was extended to twenty-one years. The company also asked permission to "sell or lease the Water Works without affecting their Charter in any other respects."[33]

The Manhattan Company continued to explore this merger for a year. By February 1805 a committee was negotiating the merger and the modification of the Manhattan Company's charter. The detailed instructions the board of directors prepared for this committee are such a clear expression of the company's views at this time that they are worth quoting at length:

> The Manhattan Company is distinguished from other Banking Institutions -- 1st in the extent of its power, 2nd its indefinite duration. To secure the retention of the first object, it is necessary that the State Bank should be *annexed* to the Manhattan Company & that the law constituting it [the State Bank] should be repealed after this annexation. With regard to our unlimited duration, this is to be understood in a qualified sense, that is, if a sufficient supply of water is brought into the City in ten years after our charter. If we can retain the indefinite duration and get rid of the restriction, it will be a great point gained. At all events [the directors explained to the committee,] you must extend the period of supplying the City with water and enable us to disencumber ourselves from the obligation by investing us with the right of selling the water works. And if you are compelled to limit the period of our Corporate existence, we wish you to keep the time as extended as possible, not less than fifty years.[34]

---

[33]Draft of a Memorial to the Legislature, March 1804, DeWitt Clinton Letterbooks, 16:246-248, Columbia University, New York, New York. It is unclear whether or not this memorial ever was sent.

[34]MC Minutes, 1:167-168 (February 6, 1805).

At the same time, the Manhattan Company was involved in a negative effort: trying to block the chartering of the Merchant's Bank. While the company certainly feared competition with its resulting loss of revenues and the political threat posed by the existence of another Federalist-controlled bank in the city, the company's fears also extended to its own charter situation. Therefore the directors of the Manhattan Company instructed a committee, of which DeWitt Clinton was a member, to assess the ·prospects of the Merchant's Bank. If it looked like the bank would be successful in receiving a charter, the committee was to try "in the last resort" to get an extension of the Manhattan Company's time for providing water and also "to obtain some explicit recognition of the Company as a Bank."[35]

Because of the politics involved, it was not easy for the Manhattan Company to achieve its triple objective of extended time, sale of the water works, and recognition as a bank. Over the next

---

[35]MC Minutes, 1:182 (February 26, 1805). For a fuller discussion of the politics involved with the chartering of the Merchants Bank, see Syrett, ed., *Hamilton Papers*, 25:203-8. The original intention of the 1804 restraining act was to prevent the Merchants Bank from continuing to operate without a charter as it had since 1803. As a political compromise, however, both the Merchants Bank and an unincorporated Republican-controlled bank in Albany were exempted from the restraining act. Only at a later date was the restraining act used as a weapon against the Manhattan Company. For more on Clinton's opposition to the Merchant's Bank, see Dorothie Bobbe, *DeWitt Clinton*, Empire State Historical Publication 11 (Port Washington, New York: Ira J. Friedman, Inc., 1933), 114-16.

two years activity continued. For example, the Clinton letterbooks contain a draft of a committee report to the Common Council recommending that the city apply to the legislature for permission to purchase the Manhattan Company's water works.[36]

It was not until 1808, however, that the issue finally was resolved. By that time the Manhattan Company was nearing the end of the ten-year period mandated in its charter for supplying New York City with an adequate supply of pure and wholesome water. As chapter three will discuss in greater detail, there was a legitimate question whether or not the water the company supplied was either "sufficient" or "wholesome." Therefore the charter of the company was in real danger.

The Manhattan Company decided to petition the New York State Legislature for an amendment to its charter permitting the transfer of its water works to the city. The key person in advancing this petition was DeWitt Clinton, a Manhattan Company director who also was mayor of New York City. Clinton had an obvious conflict of interest, holding leadership positions on both sides of the issue. There was a further conflict of interest since Clinton also was a state senator and a powerful figure in the Legislature.[37]

---

[36]Clinton Letterbooks, 16:408-12, Columbia University.

[37]For more on Clinton's conflict of interest, see Blake, *Water for the Cities*, 103-104. Clinton remained on the Manhattan Company board until 1813. In 1816 he sold his Manhattan Company

In late February the Manhattan Company appointed James Fairlie as its agent to go to Albany and work toward the charter revision. The board gave him the following instructions, an earlier draft of which can be found in the DeWitt Clinton Letterbooks:

1st. It may be objected that our charter is unlimited in its duration. We are willing, if better cannot be obtained, to have it limited to *fifty years*, and as a last concession to *thirty years*, provided the bill which accompanies this becomes a law.

2nd. With regard to the admission of the State as a Stockholder in the Institution: We have no objection that the State shall become a Stockholder to the amount of one thousand additional shares to be created.[38]

After Fairlie reached Albany and assessed the situation, he wrote to the directors of the Manhattan Company suggesting that they prepare a new petition requesting an extension of the time allotted for suppling New York City with water. The directors prepared a memorial for the legislature, but instructed Fairlie "to consult with Mr. Clinton and Mr. Emmett" before presenting it. The gist of the memorial was that the company had done all that was humanly possible

---

stock in order to raise cash for personal reasons, thereby ending his association with the company. On Clinton's role in New York City's intellectual life, see Thomas Bender, *New York Intellect: A History of Intellectual Life in New York City from 1750 to the Beginnings of Our Own Time* (New York: Alfred A. Knopf, 1987), 51-54. For a less favorable view of Clinton's role in the political sphere, see Howard L. McBain, *DeWitt Clinton and the Origins of the Spoils System in New York*, Studies in History, Economics and Public Law 28, no. 1 (New York: Columbia University Press; reprint, New York: AMS Press, 1967).

[38]MC Minutes, 1:254 (February 23, 1808). For the earlier draft, see Clinton Letterbooks, 16:400-401.

with the springs on the island. Henceforth it would be necessary to bring water from upstate via aqueduct, "which will require considerable time to erect."[39]

Throughout the entire legislative process, Clinton kept the Manhattan Company directors informed. This correspondence offers insights into the legislative process in early nineteenth century New York. It also documents the extent of Clinton's political support for the Manhattan Company. When the charter revision passed the Senate, Clinton wrote to President Henry Remsen that "the bill fixes the interests of the Company on a firm and solid basis." In particular, Clinton was pleased with the provision extending the life of the company after it transferred its water works to the city. "As that will not in all probability expire until most of us have bid adieu to this transitory world, we must leave our example as a lesson to posterity to imitate us in supporting the cause of republicanism which is certainly intimately connected with the prosperity of our institutions."[40]

On March 21st the Manhattan Company bill passed the Assembly, but not before an amendment to tax the company for the support of the schools "was got rid of." Clinton assessed the importance of the

---

[39]MC Minutes, 1:260 (March 14, 1808).

[40]Clinton to Remsen, March 16, 1808, Clinton Papers, Folder 3 New York Public Library [hereafter NYPL].

bill, which now went to the Council of Revision for final action. "Let me now tell you and the Board," he wrote to Remsen, "that nothing but a singular concurrence of circumstances and let me add not a little good management could have carried us through so triumphantly. The Bank is now placed on ground from which she may look down upon her enemies and put them at defiance. The twenty years [really thirty years] limitation attaches only when *the sale takes place* at it is in all conscience long enough."[41]

The charter amendment passed the Council of Revision four days later "without any opposition." The major points of the law were:

1.   The Manhattan Company could transfer its water works to the City of New York without affecting any of its rights or powers.

2.   After the transfer, the company could use its *entire* capital in the way that the original charter permitted it to use its surplus capital.

3.   The company was granted an additional ten years during which it had to supply the city with pure and wholesome water.

4.   Once the transfer of the water works was made, the company would exist for thirty additional years.

---

[41]Clinton to Remsen, March 21, 1808, ibid.

5.   The State of New York had the right to subscribe up to 1,000 shares of the company's stock over the next ten years.   The capitalization of the company would be increased by $50,000 to cover this subscription.[42]

Clinton's final assessment of the revised charter was that "the interests of our institution are now secured on a strong foundation and I most cordially congratulate you and the other gentlemen of the Board on this happy result."[43]

As with so many other episodes in the history of the Manhattan Company, political considerations were as important to the re-chartering as economic ones.   DeWitt Clinton's roles as politician and bank director blurred throughout this entire incident.   What would be unacceptable behavior in terms of modern standards of conflict of interest was commonplace in nineteenth century America. In fact, the political nature of the banking franchise made such conduct not only common, but necessary.   The connection between politics and banking is further illustrated by a subsequent court

---

[42]A copy of the revised charter can be found in the MC Minutes, 2:1-5 (March 21, 1808). The capitalization of the Manhattan Company remained at $2,050,000 until 1918 when it merged with the Bank of the Metropolis and the capital stock was increased by $450,000. For more on the history of the company's capitalization, see "Dividends Paid, Miscellaneous Memos," Record Group 1, Box 2, CMB Archives.

[43]Clinton to Remsen, Record Group 1, Box 1, CMB Archives. For more on Clinton's role, see Bobbe, *Clinton*, 131-3.

Daniel Ludlow, c. 1798, first president of the Manhattan Company. *(Courtesy of the Chase Manhattan Archives.)*

challenge to the charter of the company.

The People vs. the President and Directors of the Manhattan Company

In 1828 New York State had forty incorporated banks, the charters of thirty-one of which would expire within the next few years. There was a problem with these renewals, however, because the 1821 state constitution now required a two-thirds majority for the approval of charters. With the factious nature of New York politics, it was unlikely that all these banks would receive the required two-thirds vote in the legislature. The banks were receptive, therefore, to a new approach.

As I will discuss in greater detail in chapter four, a new approach emerged in 1829 in the form of the "Safety Fund System." According to this plan, banks would make annual payments into a safety fund which then would be available to pay the debts of any failed participating banks. While the banks might not have agreed to join voluntarily, most had no choice because of their expiring charters: the state would only grant new charters to banks that joined the Safety Fund System.[44]

---

[44]For general information about the Safety Fund System see Fritz Redlich, *The Molding of American Banking: Men and Ideas* (New York: Hafner Publishing, 1947; reprint, New York: Johnson Reprint Company, 1968), 1:88-94. Hammond, *Banks and Politics*, 352. Ronald E. Seavoy, *The Origins of the American Business Corporation, 1784-1855: Broadening the Concept of Public Service During Industrialization* (Westport: Greenwood Press, 1982), 120-21. Stephen Allen Memoirs, NYPL, 116.

In order for the Safety Fund to work, it was crucial that all banks participate. However two banks, the Manhattan Company and the Dry Dock Bank, had perpetual charters and appeared to be beyond the reach of the state. Rather than concede this point, the state attorney general filed a suit in State Supreme Court against the Manhattan Company seeking to invalidate its charter. According to the suit filed in October 1830, the Manhattan Company was engaged in banking operations without proper legislative authorization.[45]

This case merits detailed discussion because it centered on the nature of corporate charters in general, as well as the Manhattan Company's charter in particular. At the heart of the state's case was the view that

> A corporation is an artificial body -- a creature of the legislature; it has no powers but such are given to it, either at the time of its creation or subsequently, or as are incidental to those granted; it can have no capacities other than such as are necessary to carry into effect the purposes for which it was established, and no power is to be conceded to it by *implication* but such as is indispensable to the accomplishment of the main object of its creation; and when the mode of exercising its power is prescribed, such mode cannot be departed from.

The attorney general's point was that the Manhattan Company "usurped the banking privileges" which it exercised. "No such power

---

[45]Most of this section is based upon the published trial account which can be found in 9 Wendell 351-394. The case was decided in October, 1832. For comments on the case, see Seavoy, "Origins," 136-137; Hammond, *Banks and Politics*, 154; and Blake, *Water for the City*, 124-135.

is conferred by their charter and no one reading the act can believe it was the intention of the legislature to confer it. If it exists it was obtained by fraud."

In addition, according to the attorney general, the 1804 restraining act forbade the exercise of banking powers except by corporations specifically chartered for that purpose. The Manhattan Company, therefore, was acting in violation of this restraining act.

The state also took issue with the company's surplus capital clause, which I already have discussed in some detail. The state argued that "surplus" capital implied an amount left over once the main object of the act had been accomplished. Since the Manhattan Company was established to supply pure and wholesome water for the City of New York, by definition it could have no "surplus" until the city was so supplied.

Finally, the state argued that since the company had not fulfilled the condition on which its charter depended, the company had forfeited its corporate privileges and should be disbanded. The suit explained this alleged failure as follows:

Although a great number of citizens dwelling in the city of New-York, had at all times since the passing of the act of incorporation *been willing and desirous* to agree for and take from the president and directors of the Manhattan Company a supply of pure and wholesome water sufficient for the use of such citizens on such reasonable terms as should be demanded by the company, *yet the president and directors of the company had not at any time since the passing of the act of incorporation furnished or continued a supply of water sufficient for the use of all such citizens dwelling in the said city as were willing and desirous to agree for and take the same.*

The Manhattan Company's attorneys offered arguments against all of the state's positions. In regard to the "usurpation" of banking powers, the defense presented voluminous evidence of the state government's own recognition of the banking franchise of the company. They pointed out that the state purchased 1,000 shares of Manhattan Company stock in 1809 "and from that time until now have been partners with the defendants and [have] participated in the profits of the banking business." As a shareholder, the state received regular dividends and voted in the annual election of directors. The defense also cited numerous instances when the state either deposited money with the company or borrowed funds from the same. "Can it now be permitted to the state to say that the [banking] power claimed by the defendants does not exist?"

The defense then turned to the 1804 restraining statute, which limited banking to corporations specifically chartered for that purpose. They pointed out that a provision in another another law passed during the same session[46] expressly exempted the Manhattan Company from the restraining act. Since this "saving clause" never was repealed, the defense argued that the exemption of the Manhattan Company still was in effect and could not be arbitrarily abridged by the state.

---

[46]It was a bill incorporating the Friendly Union Society of Albany, which passed the legislature April 10, 1804, the day before the restraining act.

On the question of whether or not the capital devoted to banking was "surplus," the defense argued as follows:

> It cannot be said that the company could not employ their surplus capital in banking until after they had supplied the city with water; their capital was \$2,000,000; by the original act of incorporation, they had 10 years with which to supply the city with water, and this limitation by the act of 1808, was extended for 10 years longer. During this period of 20 years, they were not obliged to permit their capital to lie unemployed; and whatever sum was unapplied to the operation of bringing water into the city, was surplus capital, within the meaning of the act ... [T]he legislature knew at the passage of the act of 1808, that the company were employing their capital in banking operations, and ... they recognized their so doing as a proper and legitimate exercise of their powers.

Finally, the defense turned to the purported non-supply of water. They argued that the state did not name even *one* person who had requested that the company supply him or her with water and who subsequently was dissatisfied with the company's response. How could the state say that the supply of water was inadequate when it had no specific complaints to buttress its allegations?

The State Supreme Court weighed these arguments and issued its decision in October, 1832. The verdict was a major victory for the Manhattan Company, affirming the right of the corporation to continue operating under its landmark charter.

In dealing with the question of "usurped" banking powers not authorized by the state legislature, the court relied heavily on the 1808 amendment to the Manhattan Company's charter, in particular the extension of the corporation's existence after the sale of its water works to the city. As the court reasoned, "If it had no powers, either under the original or supplementary act, except as a water company, why prolong its existence for 30 years? In the event of its transferring all the rights and duties which belonged to it in that character, why add 1000 shares to its stock and authorise the state to become a stockholder to that amount?" The court concluded that the entire act clearly demonstrated the legislature's understanding that after the transfer of its water works, the Manhattan Company was "still to remain an efficient corporation, with a capital of more than two millions of dollars and engaged in operations of so profitable a character that it was desirable for the state to become interested in its stock." The inference from this act was "irre-sistable" [sic] to the justices: the legislature understood that the Manhattan Company was using capital not invested in the water works for banking operations. Rather than "manifesting any disapprobation of such proceeding, one of the principal effects of the act was to authorize and enable [the Manhattan Company] to employ the *whole*, instead of *a portion* of their capital in that manner."

In terms of the 1804 restraining act, the justices agreed with the Manhattan Company that it had been specifically exempted from the provisions of the act. Furthermore, the restraining act spoke in terms of *future* corporations, not those in existence in 1804. "There was nothing therefore in its terms," the justices concluded, "which interfered with or prohibited the continuance of accustomed business." In keeping with the common view of incorporation, the justices reaffirmed that the legislature could not arbitrarily change the terms of a preexisting corporate charter. "Corporations are creatures of the legislature," they stated. "It gives or withholds such powers as it pleases; but whatever it gives, either expressly or according to the legal construction of the terms employed by it, it has not the constitutional right to withdraw or essentially to modify or impair."

As to whether or not the Manhattan Company could have a "surplus" before it fully supplied the city with water, the justices again sided with the company. The "complete fulfillment" of the water works "duty" was not necessary in order to have a surplus. Rather, any sums which "might remain ... unemployed" would be surplus capital within the meaning of the charter. The company, in turn, had the right to employ these funds in "monied operations."

Finally, the court turned to the alleged non-supply of water by the Manhattan Company. The justices chided the attorney general for not having named at least one person who had requested water from the Manhattan Company and had been refused service. "How could the defendants supply water to those of whose wish to take it they were ignorant?" It was necessary for the state to present specific names so that the defendants could "come to trial prepared to controvert or explain the fact." The state's failure in this regard permitted the Manhattan Company to avoid the whole issue of the adequacy of its water supply.

That the Manhattan Company achieved so complete a victory in this court case is a tribute to the work of DeWitt Clinton during the first decade of the century. The exemption of the company from the 1804 restraining act, the implied recognition of the banking functions of the company in its 1808 charter amendment, and the participation of the state as a shareholder in the company all were key factors in the court's decision. If the Manhattan Company had had less astute politicians advancing its cause early in its life, its charter probably would have been struck down in 1832.

The lesson of the Manhattan Company's exceptional charter was not lost on nineteenth century New Yorkers. While the legislature occasionally combined banking with other functions,[47] it never again gave a corporation of any type, including not-for profit corporations, carte blanche in the financial area.[48] Other states

---

[47]In 1812 the New York Manufacturing Company, which was formed to produce iron and brass wire, also was granted banking powers. This was to encourage investment in the manufacturing efforts. Similar hybrids were the Chemical Bank (1824) and the Dry Dock Bank (1825). See Seavoy, "Origins," 75-77; and Hammond, *Banks and Politics*, 161.

[48]The following letter contains a poignant example: "I went to Albany yesterday," wrote the general counsel of the newly-established United Negro College Fund in 1944, "and submitted the Certificate of Incorporation ... to the Corporation Bureau of the Secretary of State's Office. The gentleman whom I spoke to ... made only one comment: he objected to any reference to 'trusts' in the purpose clause of the Certificate of Incorporation. I had rather expected that this objection would be made, since the Secretary of State is very scrupulous against the exercise of any trust powers by a corporation which is not organized as a trust company under our

followed suit and were similarly careful when granting charters.[49]

Once the courts reaffirmed the Manhattan Company's right to engage in banking, the company retained its liberal charter even after it abandoned the water business. As the next chapter will detail, the Manhattan Company and the City of New York failed to reach agreement on the transfer of the water works. As a result, the city constructed its own water works, the Croton system, which became fully operational in 1842. The Manhattan Company thereafter curtailed its water operations but did not abandon them for many decades. In order to protect its charter, the Manhattan Company pumped water from a well to a holding tank at Reade and Centre Streets each day until 1923.[50]

Furthermore, the Manhattan Company retained its unique charter through all of its twentieth century mergers, including the one with the much larger Chase National Bank in 1955. At that time, press reports likened the merger retaining the charter of the smaller institution to "Jonah swallowing the whale." As late as 1956, Coburn and Middlebrook, a financial service, still could marvel, "This is a

---

Banking Law." Arthur B. Brenner to Frederick D. Patterson, March 18, 1944, Frederick D. Patterson Papers, Box 1, Folder 16, United Negro College Fund Archives, New York, New York.

[49]For more information, see Hammond, *Banks and Politics*, 613; and Blake, *Water for the City*, 75.

[50]For a picture of this tank at the turn of the century, see the *New York Times Illustrated Magazine*, April 2, 1899.

fabulous charter."[51]   Only in 1965 did the Chase Manhattan Bank surrender the original Manhattan Company charter and receive a national banking charter instead.   One cannot help but wonder, in this day when banks are becoming involved in insurance, brokerage, and other financial services, how powerful and free to act Chase Manhattan would be if it still operated under its 1799 charter permitting it to use capital in any "monied transaction" not forbidden by law.

Conclusion

Even though the Manhattan Company had a structure which should have permitted it to operate freely, it never could escape public scrutiny.   Furthermore, the *structure itself* was subjected to a number of attacks, culminating in the 1832 court decision quoted above.   Not only were the Manhattan Company's leaders astute in *securing* a charter, they were skillful in *defending* it as well.

This brief investigation of the Manhattan Company's founding and charter illustrates two points to which I will return.   First, the Manhattan Company was involved in politics and influencing government from the moment of its creation.   This was necessary because the company had to protect the unique charter which permitted

---

[51]The report, entitled "The Chase Manhattan Bank: A Unique Charter," is quoted in Reubens, "Burr, Hamilton," 50n.

its profitable banking business to operate. Second, the Manhattan Company was on the cusp of the change of corporations from quasi-public bodies to private institutions. As a corporation, the Manhattan Company had one "public" division (the water works) and one more "private" division (the bank). Throughout its entire history the Manhattan Company would struggle with the question of how best to balance these two elements. As subsequent chapters will show, the balance sometimes was precarious and often was subject to public criticism.

CHAPTER THREE

MANAGING THE WATER WORKS

> Various Institutions have been chartered for the purpose of bringing Water into the City, but none have as yet ever complied with the main object of their Charters, so far as the public was interested; and the Committee remark that similar incorporations of private individuals whether they propose at their commencement to furnish pure and wholesome water or pure and first quality gas, are soon found to have an eye only to the profits of their incorporations and the public suffer under the monopolies.[1]

Supplying nineteenth century New York City with water would have been a difficult task under any circumstances: the population was increasing at a faster rate than the technological and engineering expertise needed to carry out such a project. But in the case of the Manhattan Company, supplying the city with water was combined with the equally formidable task of establishing and maintaining a major financial institution. There was bound to be tension and conflict as the Manhattan Company pursued these two diverse objectives, especially since the public's expectations and desires often were different than those of the company's management.

---

[1]Report of the Committee on the Fire Department, March 16, 1829, *Minutes of the Common Council of the City of New York, 1784-1831* (New York: City of New York, 1930), 17:722-23.

An engraving of the Manhattan Company's reservoir on Chambers Street. *(Courtesy of the Chase Manhattan Archives.)*

This chapter will explore how the Manhattan Company managed its water works from 1799 until the city's own Croton System was fully operational in the 1840s. In managing the water works, the Manhattan Company had to balance both internal and external factors. Internally, the officers and directors had to determine the amount of energy and resources to devote to each of the principal operating units, keeping in mind the previously-discussed charter clauses tying the company's continued existence to the furnishing of an adequate water supply for the city. Externally, the structure and strategy of the corporation were affected dramatically by the social and political environments. The Manhattan Company was subject to intense public scrutiny because of the visibility and importance of each of its units. In the case of the water works, this public review forced the company a number of times to change the way it managed its operation. As the next two chapters will show, this is similar to what happened with both the bank in New York City and the upstate branches.

As a way of analyzing the water works and exploring the interplay between internal and external influences on management, I will discuss the following topics: water in New York City before the Manhattan Company; the company's initial decisions on the nature and structure of its water works; the different phases in the management of the water works and why the company found it necessary to make such changes; the threat posed by other private water companies and how the Manhattan Company responded to these challenges; and the agitation for a municipal water system and its effect upon the Manhattan Company. As this chapter will make clear, far from operating its water works in isolation, the Manhattan Company actually operated it in a fish bowl.

Water in New York City Before the Manhattan Company

During most of the colonial period, New York City was so small that there was no need for a massive "water works" project. Public wells and pumps were the extent of municipal involvement in this area. In 1658, for example, the Dutch of New Amsterdam dug a public well in front of a fort located just south of present-day Bowling Green. After the English took control of the city, they dug six more wells "for the public good."[2]

As the population of the city increased, however, it became apparent that other water supply arrangements were necessary. As early as 1748, New York's well water was considered so bad that even horses balked at drinking it.[3] By the 1770s, most of the wells in the lower part of the city were contaminated to such an extent that the water was not drinkable. The exception was a large well in

---

[2]Nelson M. Blake, *Water for the Cities: A History of the Urban Water Supply Problem in the United States* (Syracuse: Syracuse University Press, 1956), 12.

[3]Ibid., 13.

Chatham known as the "Tea Water Pump." A cottage water supply industry grew around this pump, as enterprising cartmen mounted hogshead barrels to their vehicles and delivered the water directly to houses. These carters became known around the city as "Tea Water Men" and carried on a thriving private enterprise.[4]

The first major effort to improve the water supply situation in New York City came in the 1770s. Christopher Colles, an Irish-born engineer, proposed to the Common Council in April, 1774 that he "Erect a Reservoir and ... Convey Water thro' Several Streets of the City." The Common Council studied the plan and approved it in July of the same year. One month later the Common Council sampled the water from the well Colles dug, pronounced the water "of a very good Quality," and instructed Colles to proceed with the project. The Council also issued notes valued at 2,500 pounds to finance the effort. In order to supervise this project, the Common Council appointed a committee of eight members to "assist in making Contracts, purchasing Materials, auditing Accounts &c." The presence of three members was to be sufficient to transact business.[5]

---

[4]Stephen Allen, "Manuscript History of the New York Water Works," 1:23. Stephen Allen Papers, New-York Historical Society [hereafter NYHS], New York, New York. Allen, Mayor of New York and one of the leaders of the movement for a municipal water works, will be discussed again later in this chapter.

[5]*Minutes of the Common Council of the City of New York, 1675-1776* (New York: Dodd Mean & Co., 1905), 8:26-27 (April 22, 1774); 40-41 (July 21, 1774); and 47-49 (August 25-29, 1774).

Colles worked on the water project through 1776. During this time the Common Council appropriated an additional 9,600 pounds for the project, bringing the total to 12,100 pounds.[6] The well and reservoir were on high ground north of a fresh water pond known as the Collect. The well was thirty feet in diameter and located near where the city prison known as the "Tombs" now stands. The reservoir had a capacity of 20,000 hogsheads and was erected on the east side of Broadway, between Pearl and White Streets. It was completely covered, in keeping with the belief at the time that sunlight was harmful to drinking water. Perhaps the most interesting part of Colles' project, however, was the steam engine he built to pump water from the well. This was one of only three steam engines in existence in the colonies before the revolution, the other two being used in mines.[7] Though Colles successfully pumped water, the revolutionary

---

[6]The additional appropriations (in pounds) were as follows. Dates and pages refer to volume eight of the *Minutes of the Common Council*.

Amount	Date	Page
500	October 25, 1774	67
1,000	December 7, 1774	67
900	February 20, 1775	78
600	May 30, 1775	93
2,600	August 2, 1775	100
2,000	January 5, 1776	121
2,000	March 5, 1776	131

Blake incorrectly gave the total appropriation as 11,400 pounds. *Water for the Cities*, 16-17.

[7]Louis C. Hunter, *Steam Power: A History of Industrial*

war prevented him from completing the system of distribution pipes. All that remained of his system after the war was a well and a large number of unpaid bills. In fact, Colles did not settle his claims against the city until 1788, when he accepted 150 pounds and signed a release.[8]

Almost ten years passed between the suspension of Colles' water project in 1776 and the next round of agitation for an improved New York City water supply system. In April 1785 Samuel Osgood proposed to the Common Council that he supply the city with water. The Common Council appointed a committee to confer with Osgood. Nine months later, Chancellor Robert R. Livingston also submitted a proposal for supplying the city with water.[9]

Power in the United States, 1780-1930 (Charlottesville: University Press of Virginia, 1985), 3-4.

[8]*Minutes of the Common Council of the City of New York, 1784-1831* (New York: City of New York, 1930), 1:348 (January 16, 1788). For more on Colles' project, see Blake, *Water for the Cities*, 16-17; George William Edwards, *New York as an Eighteenth Century Municipality, 1731-1776*, Studies in History, Economics and Public Law, No. 178 (New York: Columbia University Press, 1917; reprint, New York: AMS Pres, 1968), 138-41; Allen, "History of the Water Works," 1:22; "Stephen Allen Memoirs," 163, New York Public Library [hereafter NYPL], New York, New York; and Sidney I. Pomerantz, *New York, An American City, 1783-1803: A Study of Urban Life* (New York: Columbia University Press, 1938), 279-80. In 1784 Colles unsuccessfully asked the New York State Legislature to charter a company to remove navigational obstructions from the Mohawk River. See Joseph Stancliffe Davis, *Essays in the Earlier History of American Corporations* (Cambridge: Harvard University Press, 1917), 2:157-58.

[9]For Osgood, see *Minutes of the Common Council*, 1:129

With two proposals in hand, the Common Council took a number of actions. First, it commissioned an engineer to "survey and give his Opinion on the Reservoir and Engine" of Colles' water works. Second, it invited the submission of sealed proposals for supplying the city with water. It is interesting to note that the original closing date for the submission of proposals was to be January 1, 1787. However Chancellor Livingston, who already had submitted a proposal, asked for a sooner closing date. Eventually the Common Council agreed to a closing date of April 20, 1786.[10]

By April 19th the Common Council had received three sealed bids. Before opening the bids, the council asked the aldermen to report the "Sense of the Citizens in their respective Wards" on the subject of supplying the city with water. The Aldermen reported that they had conferred with many citizens and it appeared to be the majority opinion "that the Corporation [the city] ought not to grant the Privilege of supplying the City with Water to Individuals; but that the same ought if possible to be undertaken by the Corporation." As a result, the Common Council decided not to open the bids at that time. Instead, it ordered the aldermen to return to their constituents, more fully ascertain their views, and submit them

---

(April 5, 1785). For Livingston, see ibid., 194 (January 30, 1786).

[10]For the survey, see ibid., 195 (January 30, 1786). For the discussion of the proposals, see ibid., 198-200 (February 15, 1786). This also is discussed in Blake, *Water for the Cities*, 44.

in writing to the Common Council. If the public wished the city to undertake the project, the Common Council wanted the public to realize "that the monies necessary for the Purpose should be raised by a Tax on the citizens."[11] Though there is no record of these written reports, one can surmise that there was inadequate support for the new taxes necessary for a municipal water works.

The next few years were quiet in terms of formal proposals for water supply, though there is some evidence that the populace continued to press the Common Council for action. For example, in 1788 the Common Council received a petition signed by "a great number of Inhabitants" outlining "the inconveniences which arise from the present Mode" of water supply. The petition asked the Council to improve the present situation by adopting Colles' plan or any other which "shall appear most expedient." In the best bureaucratic tradition, the petition was referred to a committee and never heard from again.[12]

During the 1790s the movement for improved water supply came to a head. The Common Council received numerous proposals for supplying the city with water, including one from Christopher Colles and another from Nicholas Roosevelt, who later was involved in the

---

[11]*Minutes of the Common Council*, 1:213-214 (April 19, 1786).

[12]Ibid., 1:354-355 (February 27, 1788).

Philadelphia water supply system.[13] It also was during this time that Dr. Joseph Browne submitted a plan proposing to use the Bronx River as a water source. But as chapter two indicated, it ultimately took the impetus of a yellow fever epidemic to spur the government, and such key politicians as Aaron Burr and Alexander Hamilton, to action.

It was clear by 1799 that informal water supply efforts no longer would suffice for New York City. It was necessary to have both a dependable supply and a system for conveying the water to individual homes. With the chartering of the Manhattan Company, the public expected both of these objectives to be realized. As a result, even though the Manhattan Company was "private," it never would be far from the public gaze. Indeed, a large segment of the population still was not convinced that the privilege of supplying the city with water should have been granted to anything but a municipal agency.[14] As a result, there was a great interest in the

---

[13]Ibid., 2:63 (February 17, 1794); 135 (March 30, 1795); 137 (April 7, 1795); 225 (March 21, 1796); 307 (December 5, 1796); 314 (December 28, 1796); 347 (May 15, 1797); 420 (February 12, 1798); and 484 (December 12, 1798). See also Blake, *Water for the Cities*, 45.

[14]"By the first years of the nineteenth century there had emerged a consensus that at least some activities ought to be the exclusive responsibility of city government. Street construction and nuisance abatement stand out as tasks over which the corporation managed to assert largely unchallenged monopolistic control. But other areas remained more controversial, and debate over whether a particular service ought to be publicly or privately provided shaped New York City's political life throughout the first decades of the

initial water supply decisions which the Manhattan Company would make. Depending upon one's view of the company and its central role, these decisions would either prove the worst fears or justify the highest hopes of the public.

The Manhattan Company Water Works: Initial Decisions

As the directors of the Manhattan Company began to organize the water works, they faced three key decisions: What would be the source of the water? How would it be pumped, if that proved necessary? And how would the water be distributed to individual homes? While these decisions obviously were crucial for the design of the water works, they also were crucial for the structure of the entire company. Clearly the nature of the water works would affect the amount of surplus capital available for other endeavors.

One of the first board actions was to appoint a committee of three members, Samuel Osgood, John B. Coles, and John Stevens, to "report with all convenient speed" the best measures for supplying the city with water.[15] The committee presented a lengthy written

---

nineteenth century." Hendrik Hartog, *Public Property and Private Power: The Corporation of the City of New York in American Law 1730-1870* (Chapel Hill: University of North Carolina Press, 1983), 147. For a discussion of water supply and the Manhattan Company, see ibid., 148-50, 224-5.

[15]Manhattan Company [hereafter MC] Minutes, 1:1 (April 11,1799). Unless otherwise noted, all Manhattan Company records are found in the Chase Manhattan [hereafter CMB] Archives, New York, New

report six days later which focused primarily on possible sources of water. As the committee saw it, there were two principle options: transport water from the Bronx River to the north, or pump water from a well located near the Collect. The Bronx River project probably was the option most of the public expected the Manhattan Company to pursue. This was, after all, the initial proposal of Dr. Joseph Browne to the city before the Manhattan Company was established. The anticipation of such a large-scale project made the company's capitalization of two million dollars seem reasonable.

As the committee analyzed the situation, however, the Bronx River option seemed less attractive. In the first place, the closest part of the Bronx River was still fourteen miles from the city. Furthermore, one of the most commonly-discussed methods of transporting the water, by open canal, had a problem which seemed "insufferable:" in the winter, the water in the canal would be "congealed by frost," thereby interrupting the supply to the city.

Another Bronx River option, the one proposed by Browne, was to dam the river and divert it into the Harlem River. According to Browne, gravity and water pressure would be sufficient to carry the water from the Harlem River to the city without pumps. The committee concluded that this power would be "incompetent to the purpose," especially when the demand was greatest. One suggestion for

---

York.

increasing water pressure was to also dam the Harlem River. However, the project then would become very complex. "Before an undertaking of so expensive a nature is gone into," the committee concluded, "a minute and thorough investigation, both as to the probable expense as well as of its being adequate to the purpose will be indispensably necessary." Such a study would delay supplying the city with water. Moreover, once the study was completed, the committee estimated that it would take two years to construct the Bronx River system.

Turning to the use of a well near the Collect, the committee concluded that the company could construct a steam engine "sufficiently large to give an adequate supply for all culinary purposes for 12,000 to 15,000 dollars. The annual expense of working which would probably be under two thousand dollars." One major advantage, therefore, of a well and steam pump was that the cost would be "of no great moment." But the committee also stated a second advantage: since the project was much less complex, the company would be able to supply water to each household before the winter. The board of directors agreed with the committee report and requested more information about "the best mode of procuring a supply of water from sources in the vicinity of this City."[16]

Ultimately the Manhattan Company decided it was easiest to use Colles' old well and reservoir, which still were city property. The

---

[16]MC Minutes, 1:7-10 (April 17, 1799).

board sent a committee to the Common Council to discuss three options with the city: selling the land outright, giving the company a perpetual lease, or letting the company "occupy" the grounds until they could determine the quantity and quality of water available. The Common Council agreed to the third option.[17]

With these actions, the Manhattan Company set the course for its future development. Clearly most of the $2 million capitalization would not be devoted to the water works, but to the "other monied transactions" authorized by the company's charter. As a result, for the next half-century the Manhattan Company would be hounded by the question of whether or not it was devoting sufficient resources to supplying the city with water. Later sections of this chapter will illustrate how the company answered this question at different times in its history.

On the positive side, the Manhattan Company's initial decision guaranteed that the city would have *some* water in a short period of time. Nelson Blake, the preeminent historian of urban water supply in the United States, concluded that while the Manhattan Company's efforts may not have been ideal, they were better than nothing. Blake pointed out that transporting water from Westchester to the city challenged the abilities of the best engineers a generation later. Blake doubted that such an ambitious project as the one

---

[17]*Minutes of the Common Council*, 2:543-544 (May 13, 1799).

Soon after its charter was obtained, the Manhattan Company began the installation of a water system for New York. This panel commemorates the laying of the first water mains which were wooden logs bored through the center to provide a pipe. In the background is the Old Federal Hall at Wall and Nassau Streets. Alexander Hamilton, one of the founders of the company, stands to the extreme right. With him is Oliver Wolcott, first president of the Merchants Bank, established in 1803, which merged with the Bank of Manhattan Company in 1920. *(Courtesy of the Chase Manhattan Archives.)*

proposed by Browne could have been carried out in 1799.[18] Blake also made an important point which will merit repeating several times throughout this study: the Manhattan Company's water supply efforts must be judged in terms of the early nineteenth century, not by standards of fifty or one hundred years later.

It is important to keep this point in mind as one looks at the second major decision the Manhattan Company faced: how to transport water to individual houses. While today metal pipes are universal in the United States, they were not widely used in 1799. The most common option was to use wooden water pipes made out of bored saplings. Since these pipes easily rotted and leaked, they were a constant source of trouble for all water works using them. Nevertheless, wooden pipes were the main option available. As Joseph S. Davis concluded, "Here, as so often, economic progress waited on technical advance."[19]

Despite the technical problems, the Manhattan Company did consider metal pipes. The company concluded, however, that metal pipes would be seven times more expensive than wooden ones.[20] The

---

[18]Blake, *Water for the Cities*, 62, 56.

[19]Davis, *Essays*, 2:248.

[20]"Report of the Manhattan Committee: Being a Report on the Best Mode of Procuring a Supply of Water From Sources in the Vicinity of the City and the Probable Expense Thereof" (New York: 1799). This can be found in the CMB Archives and the NYPL.

board therefore empowered the Water Committee to contract for as many pine logs as were necessary and to have the same bored. A subsequent newspaper advertisement specified that the logs needed to be of yellow or white pine and measure between twelve and fourteen feet long.[21] While it is difficult to ascertain motive, in the case of the pipes for water distribution it does not appear that the Manhattan Company was purposely withholding capital in order to better endow the banking operation. Rather, the company was employing the best technical means then available to solve the problem.

This is in marked contrast to the situation with the third major decision the company faced: how to raise water from the well. The initial committee report, already cited regarding the source of water supply, discussed at great length the amount of water a *steam engine* could pump. Nowhere in the early discussions is there a hint of using anything but a steam engine to pump water. As Christopher Colles' earlier project had shown, steam engines were the state of the art in water supply technology.

On June 10, 1799, the Manhattan Company authorized its water committee to negotiate a contract with Nicholas Roosevelt for the purchase of a steam engine. Roosevelt, a prominent manufacturer of

---

[21]MC Minutes, 1:14 (May 6, 1799). New York *Journal*, May 8, 1799. The CMB Archives has a number of sections of wooden water pipe.

steam engines who eventually became Benjamin Latrobe's brother-in-law, supplied engines to the Philadelphia water works. At this same meeting the board approved building a reservoir with a capacity of one million gallons to hold the water raised by the pump. Water would go from the reservoir, through the wooden distribution pipes, to individual houses.[22]

One week later, the board of directors changed its mind, voting to rescind the resolution authorizing a contract with Roosevelt. Instead, the board instructed the water committee to take whatever measures were necessary to raise 250,000 gallons per day by means of pumps worked by horses.[23] While there is no explanation for this change, it is possible to speculate on the reasons. One possibility is that there was some problem with Roosevelt's meeting of the contract terms. This seems unlikely, however, because only one week separated the two board actions: Roosevelt would not have had time to even begin work on the project, no less encounter problems with it.

A more likely reason for the board's change of heart was the desire to conserve as much capital as possible. While one can use the technological limitations of the time to justify the company's

---

[22]MC Minutes, 1:29 (June 10, 1799). For more on Nicholas Roosevelt, see Blake, *Water for the Cities*, 27.

[23]MC Minutes, 1:31 (June 17, 1799). The CMB Archives has artists' illustrations of these early horse-drawn pumps.

decision not to transport water from the Bronx River, such technological arguments do not apply in the case of steam engines. By choosing horse-drawn pumps, the Manhattan Company took a short-term approach to the problem, opting to save money *now* to the possible long term detriment of the city and its inhabitants.

An interesting assessment of the company's efforts to this point was provided by Joseph Browne, the engineer who a year earlier had proposed transporting water from upstate and who then was serving as the first superintendent[24] of the Manhattan Company's water works. "If the founders of the Manhattan Company do really expect that one half of the City is to be supplied with water in the Course of this Summer and Fall," Browne wrote to Burr, "they will certainly be disappointed. But I expect and hope that enough will be done to satisfy the Public and particularly the Legislature that the Institution is not a speculating Job, but an undertaking from whence will result ... incalculable advantage to the City of New York." Browne then noted that since only one or two men at a time can dig a well, "It might ... have [had] the appearance of inaction and subjected the undertaking to ridicule. But the progress we shall shortly make will be the best answer to such impertinence." But

---

[24]The Manhattan Company Minutes often spell superintendent as follows: superintendant. For the sake of consistency, I will use the preferred modern spelling.

This panel shows the horse-powered water pump of the Manhattan Company, which once stood at the present corner of Reade and Centre Streets and which was in operation from 1800 to 1803. John Stevens, the engineer, is the central figure in the picture. At the right stands Samuel Osgood, a prominent citizen of that day. Both were original stockholders and directors of the Manhattan Company. At the left appears John Browne, superintendent of the water works. *(Courtesy of the Chase Manhattan Archives.)*

perhaps the most interesting part of the letter was Browne's view of the company's decision to use horse-drawn rather than steam pumps. He considered the best means of raising the water to be "a question of calculation only." In his opinion, "The company can never be unsound for economizing their capital." As long as the less expensive solution does the job, "it appears to me the Company will never be found fault with for making [the decision]."[25]

The last sentence of Browne's letter, in particular, is somewhat surprising. Based upon his efforts prior to the Manhattan Company, Browne would be the last person one would imagine as a supporter of the company's decisions to save money on its water works. For the person who proposed the most grandiose of all water supply plans -- and whose influential writings were instrumental in securing a $2 million capitalization for the company -- now to favor economizing, was a radical change of mind. Perhaps Browne was converted to the view that banking was a better use of the company's capital. Or, perhaps Browne came to realize that supplying the city with water was a much more difficult proposition than anyone had anticipated beforehand. Whatever the case, it is hard to believe that this longtime supporter of improved water supply would make a capricious decision.

---

[25]Joseph Browne to Aaron Burr, July 7, 1799, Reel 4, Frames 528-530, Burr Papers Microfilm, NYHS.

By the summer of 1799, therefore, the management of the Manhattan Company had made three key decisions which would effect the entire course of its corporate existence. The company chose to secure a water supply from wells in the city rather than upstate rivers, to use horse rather than steam power to pump the water, and to distribute the water to individual homes through wooden rather than metal pipes. Subsequent phases in the management of the water works often involved rationalizing these initial decisions and modifying them as necessary in the face of public pressure. While the structure basically was set, the company changed strategies over the next forty years in response to external stimuli.

Phase One: Superintendent, 1799-1811

For its first twelve years, the Manhattan Company's water operation was managed by a "superintendent," an employee of the Company. During this time, a "water committee" of the board of directors also was actively involved in the daily management of the water works. The following people served as superintendent of the water works: Joseph Browne, 1799-1803; Caleb Leach, 1803-1806; and John Fellows, 1806-1811.

While the superintendent and the water committee faced a number of important issues during these years, I will focus on three issues which were central to the nascent water works: implementing the water supply plans, dealing with the city government, and handling complaints from the company's customers.

The first part of implementing the water works was to set up a financing system. In doing so, the board of directors treated the water works as a distinct subsidiary. The water works had its own set of books,[26] with the board of directors appropriating lump sums of money which the water committee and superintendent spent. In the first five years of the water works' existence, the board of directors appropriated the following amounts:[27]

Date	Amount
April 17, 1799	1,000
July 16, 1799	1,000
August 20, 1799	1,000
August 27, 1799	5,000
November 28, 1799	12,000
April 16, 1800	10,000
June 30, 1800	10,000
August 7, 1800	10,000
October 13, 1800	10,000
April 20, 1801	10,000
July 20, 1801	20,000
March 31, 1802	10,000
July 8, 1802	10,000
January 23, 1804	30,000
October 16, 1804	15,000
	155,000

---

[26]The Water Works Ledger, 1799-1821, is preserved in the CMB Archives. The ledger contains the following accounts: Manhattan Bank; real estate; water revenue; reservoir; capital stock; profit and loss; Barker Smith & Co.; superintendents and other employees (various names); expenses of raising water; Manhattan Company; wells and pumps; pipes of conduit; contingent expenses; lateral pipes; cash; and notes receivable.

[27]These appropriations are documented in the Manhattan Company's Journals for the dates listed.

As the above shows, the board of directors appropriated larger sums at more frequent intervals as time went on. This reflected both the increasing expenses of the water works and also the growing independence of the unit within the Manhattan Company.

In addition to appropriating funds, the board of directors issued official "regulations" for the water works covering such issues as price and method of service. While such regulations were common for water companies, the Manhattan Company once again was unusual in that its charter permitted the company *alone* to set the rates for water service. In most other charters, the water companies had to secure governmental approval of proposed rates. This is similar to the situation with modern utilities.[28]

The key points in the regulations the Manhattan Company issued were:[29]

1. People wishing to receive water had to apply personally or in writing. The superintendent then would send a worker to tap the main water pipe closest to the requestor's house. Only authorized workers could tap the main pipes.

---

[28]Perhaps one way to understand public opinion toward the Manhattan Company's water works would be to further extend the analogy of modern utilities. Imagine the public outcry if a Con Edison or a Long Island Lighting Company could set its own rates.

[29]For the full regulations, see MC Minutes, 1:55-56 (November 11, 1799).

2. The recipient was responsible for the purchase and installation of the "lateral pipes" which brought water from the main pipe to the house. The company recommended lead pipes[30]

3. Recipients were asked to guard against "wasteful consumption." They also were prohibited from supplying water to neighbors.

4. The minimum charge for a house would be five dollars per year, payable quarterly. This rate was guaranteed for five years. Certain businesses which used a great deal of water, such as stables and taverns, had to apply for special rates. Ships would be supplied at the rate of twenty cents per barrel of water.

These regulations are of more than antiquarian interest. Many of the points outlined above would later become the focus of disagreements between the Manhattan Company and its water customers. For example, the responsibility of citizens to notify the company that they wished to receive water became one of the key points in the 1830 court case against the Manhattan Company which I discussed in chapter two. Furthermore, in times of diminished or interrupted

---

[30]Blake pointed out that lead distribution pipes were common in water works from ancient Rome to modern Philadelphia and London. Lead was used because it was highly malleable and easily joined, even though authorities had been warning for centuries about possible health dangers. *Water for the Cities*, 253.

water supply, the division of responsibility for "main" vs. "lateral" pipes became a source of tension between the company and its customers. Once again, the unusual freedom that the Manhattan Company had to organize and structure its divisions became a point of contention in daily operations.

With the financial and organizational questions somewhat resolved, Joseph Browne, the first superintendent, turned his attention to the physical plant of the water works.[31] His immediate concern was the design and building of a reservoir for the pumped water. During 1799 the company originally planned for a reservoir with a capacity of one million gallons. By April 1800, however, the board of directors changed its mind and instead ordered a reservoir with a capacity of approximately 100,000 gallons. Nelson Blake attributed these scaled down plans to "considerations of economy," meaning that the company was trying to save capital in order to invest it in the banking operation. Blake probably is right

---

[31]Browne was hired at a salary of $1,500 per year. See MC Minutes, 1:26-31 (May 29-June 17, 1799). The board forced him to resign in 1803, when they learned that he also had accepted the position of Street Commissioner for the City of New York. Ibid., 131-132 (August 1, 1803). After this, Browne continued to lease the lot on which he had lived as superintendent because he had built and operated a "bath house" on the property. By 1807 Browne was behind on his rent payments, was overdrawn at the bank, and "had gone into one of the U.S. territories to reside." Since the board could not locate Browne, they seized the bath house to settle his debts. Thus ended the saga of one of the key players in the early history of New York water supply. See ibid., 135 (November 28, 1803); 136 (December 5, 1803); 227 (January 5, 1807); and 233-234 (July 9, 1807).

in this assessment. Even the smaller reservoir, however, was an imposing structure of flagstone, clay, sand, and tar. Decorating the front were four doric columns and a reclining figure of Oceanus, the Greek mythological figure associated with water. Oceanus remained the corporate symbol of the Manhattan Company until well into the twentieth century.[32]

In the area of pumps, it became apparent within a year or two that the company's economizing was a failure. Since the horse-drawn pumps were not able to supply enough water, it became necessary to consider steam engines once again. In 1801 John Stevens, one of the leaders in the field, offered to build a steam engine on terms "evidently so very advantageous" that he did not "expect to meet the least hesitation" on the part of the board of directors. As with most projects involving the expenditure of funds on the water works, however, the board did hesitate. Stevens' only explanation was that the board thought the project would "prove abortive," thereby involving Stevens "in ruin" and the "Board in embarrassments." Stevens therefore offered to demonstrate the superiority of his engine by installing one, at his own expense, next to the horse

---

[32]MC Minutes, 1:15-16 (May 8, 1799); 26 (May 29, 1799); 48 (August 27, 1799); 62 (December 23, 1799); 66 (March 3, 1800); 73 (April 25, 1800); 75 (May 9, 1800); 89 (May 21, 1801). *Minutes of the Common Council*, 2:561 (July 22, 1799); 694 (January 5, 1801). Blake, *Water for the Cities*, 58-59. For a description of the corporate seal, see MC Minutes, 1:16 (May 8, 1799).

pumps. The board agreed to the test, with the understanding that the company did not "hereby engage to make a purchase thereof, but are at liberty to order the same to be removed whenever they think proper."[33]

While no details of the test remain, it must have been successful, for eight months later the board authorized a committee composed of the president and two directors to purchase one or two steam engines for the water works.[34] In February, 1803 the board finally purchased the test steam engine, authorized the construction of a second steam engine capable of pumping one million gallons in a twenty-four hour period, and decided to sell the horses which were still used for the pump.[35]

In a sense, it took the Manhattan Company four years to finalize the initial design of its water works. If the company's main interest had been using capital for water supply, it would have opted for steam engines in 1799. The four year delay, however, created a great deal of ill-will between the company and the publics it served. After such an inauspicious start, it is doubtful that the company ever could have regained the confidence of the public.

The City of New York, in particular, quickly came to distrust

---

[33]MC Minutes, 1:93-94 (September 4, 1801).

[34]Ibid., 1:102 (May 3, 1802).

[35]Ibid., 1:126-127 (February 8, 1803).

the Manhattan Company and entered into an adversarial relationship with it on many points. Most of the disagreements stemmed from the Manhattan Company's charter. As noted above, the Manhattan Company could set its own rates for water service. In addition, the company was not required to provide free water for use at fires or to repair streets damaged by the laying of water pipes. These clauses were atypical for water company charters at the time and led to constant tension between the city and the company.[36]

The condition of the city streets was the first issue to come to the fore. In July 1801 the Common Council appointed a committee to confer with the Manhattan Company about the poor condition of the pavement. The situation remained unresolved, however, for over two years. Finally, in November 1803 three commissioners appointed by a justice of the Supreme Court to assess damages reported that the company owed the city $6,881.14. The Manhattan Company rejected this amount, with the result that the controversy continued for another nine months. Finally both sides agreed to the findings of a new arbitration panel which fixed the damages at $5,500.[37]

---

[36]For more on these clauses see Blake, *Water for the Cities*, 50-51. Beatrice Reubens, "Burr, Hamilton, and the Manhattan Company," *Political Science Quarterly*, 72, no. 4 (December 1957): 578-607, and 73, no 1 (March 1958): 100-25, reprint of both issues in the CMB Archives.

[37]For this ongoing dispute, see MC Minutes, 1:95 (September 24, 1801), 95-96 (October 1, 1801), 137 (December 26, 1803), 137-138 (December 29, 1803), 138 (January 12, 1804), 139 (January 23, 1804),

There was a similar disagreement in 1806 over how much the city should pay for water the Manhattan Company furnished to it. Once again the parties could not resolve the dispute and the matter was referred to arbitration. Eventually the city agreed to pay the company $1,244.43 to settle the issue.[38]

Not all matters required arbitration, however. The city and the company were able to reach an understanding about furnishing water for fighting fires. The Manhattan Company permitted fire companies to use water free of charge, even though they drew much water and often wasted it once the fire was out. The original practice was to tap directly into the wooden water main in the street. In order to repair the main, a wooden plug was driven into the pipe. According to some sources, this is the origin of the term "fireplug."[39]

By 1807 this ad hoc practice of tapping water mains no longer

---

144 (April 12, 1804), 144-145 (May 7, 1804), 149 (August 16, 1804). *Minutes of the Common Council*, 3:6 (July 6, 1801), 29 (September 22, 1801), 34 (October 5, 1801), 248 (March 28, 1803), 326 (July 1, 1803), 333-334 (July 6, 1803), 355-356 (July 25, 1803), 400 (November 24, 1803), 445 (January 16, 1804), 453 (January 23, 1804), 454 (January 30, 1804), 493 (April 9, 1804), 494-496 (April 16, 1804), 507-508 (May 7, 1804), 591 (August 20, 1804), 619 (October 22, 1804); 4:20 (June 24, 1805). See also Blake, *Water for the Cities*, 60.

[38]*Minutes of the Common Council*, 4:181 (April 21, 1806) and 4:255 (July 28, 1806).

[39]Blake, *Water for the Cities*, 61. *Water for Old New York* (New York: Chase Manhattan Bank, no date), found in the CMB Archives, Record Group 1, Box 1.

was sufficient to meet the city's needs. The Common Council, therefore, negotiated with the Manhattan Company to obtain water "on reasonable terms" for fighting fires. The company eventually placed approximately 150 wooden fire hydrants throughout the city. Even with these hydrants, the Manhattan Company's supply often was inadequate for fighting fires. Local companies, therefore, still resorted to bucket brigades from nearby pumps or the rivers on either side of Manhattan Island.[40]

Throughout this period, the Manhattan Company's relations with the city can best be described as strained. It quickly became apparent that the company would not immediately solve the city's water supply needs. The most popular solution, the transfer of the water works to municipal control as authorized by the Manhattan Company's 1808 charter revision, never was completed. Increasing dissatisfaction with the Manhattan Company's supply of water led, in turn, to public second-guessing of the events of 1799. As the quote at the beginning of this chapter indicates, by the 1830s there was a strong feeling that the city should retain control over certain basic services rather than entrusting them to private enterprise[41] The

---

[40]On the fire hydrants, see *Minutes of the Common Council*, 4:614 (November 2, 1807); MC Minutes, 1:236-237 (November 9-12, 1807); and Blake, *Water for the Cities*, 61. See also *Water for Old New York*.

[41]On the closely related issue of sewage and waste water disposal, see Joanne Goldman, "The New York City Sewer System,

City of New York, having surrendered a basic municipal responsibility to a private company in 1799, never appeared to forgive the Manhattan Company for running the water works its own way.

Despite this dissatisfaction, it took the anti-Manhattan Company forces three more decades to organize enough support to create a municipal alternative to the Manhattan Company. In the interim, the city government and the company would be faced with a number of issues -- street repair, water for cleaning the streets, and water for fighting fires -- which would be recurring sources of annoyance and tension. For better or worse, the two entities were joined in a union of mutual distrust.

The company experienced a similar tension with other customers of the water works. While there were complaints about the quantity and quality of water from the time of the founding of the company, the problems intensified between 1808 and 1811. The complaints

---

1800-1866: The Evolution of a Technological and Managerial Infrastructure," unpublished paper delivered at the 1988 Annual Meeting of the Organization of American Historians. Goldman made an important point about the development of the city's sewer system which also relates to the ability of the Manhattan Company to meet the technological problems of water supply early in the century: "... there is an inherent link between the technology incorporated into the urban infrastructure and the management of city services. Simply stated, the skills, perspectives and goals of the administrative body charged with delivering municipal services must be compatible with the technology required to design, construct and maintain the urban infrastructure. This constraint largely determines the rate of development and the nature of technology-intensive city services." For a fuller discussion of municipal vs. private responsibilities, see Hartog, *Public Property*, 147-50.

ultimately forced the Manhattan Company to change the way it managed the water works. This was a clear case of structure being changed by external pressures.

The basic problem was that by 1808 many of the wooden water mains were partially or completely blocked. In the words of Superintendent John Fellows, "the Obstructions [in the pipes] became very alarming, and considerable expense was incurred to remove them." As the supply of water became less dependable, more and more subscribers refused to pay their bills. This led to a crisis at the water works and a complete reassessment of the operation by the board of directors.

Most of the blockages were caused by the roots of poplar trees, which worked their way into the joints of the pipes. Fellows realized that the only true solution to the "evil" was the "extirpation of the tree."[42] But since this would require the ripping up and replacement of all the company's pipes, it was not a course of action the board of directors was anxious to approve.

The complaints grew worse by the middle of 1809. In May the board received complaints from "several citizens stating that they were not receiving sufficient water." As a result, the board appointed a committee of four members plus the president "to

---

[42]Report by John Fellows to the President and Directors of the Manhattan Company, June 7, 1810, Manhattan Company Records, NYHS.

ascertain how far the preceding complaints were well founded" and to give "such direction" to the superintendent "as would prevent similar complaints in [the] future."[43] As so often happened in the history of the Manhattan Company, it took a public outcry to force the board of directors to focus more closely on the day-to-day operations of the water works.

The committee reported its findings to the board of directors one month later. They told how they had met frequently with the superintendent and had impressed upon him the necessity of furnishing adequate water. Most interesting was the committee's proposal to the superintendent that "in order to ascertain the number and justice of the complaints for water [the company] insert an advertisement in the papers, calling on the inhabitants who were subscribers for the water *to state their complaints in writing, and leave them at the Bank.*" It is important to note that the committee did not propose having the complaints sent to the water works. Because of the "earnest request" of the superintendent, however, the committee delayed the advertisement until a new main pipe could be laid. But even this new pipe did not solve the water supply problem. The superintendent did try clearing the pipes by inserting a hose into the pipes and using the suction created by a fire engine to dislodge

---

[43]MC Minutes, 2:44 (May 15, 1809).

the blockages. This was only moderately successful.[44] The president concluded by reporting that he had made "enquiries concerning a person more suitable to conduct the water works department than the present superintendent." Among those he contacted were Benjamin Latrobe, the superintendent of public buildings in Washington, and John W. McComb, Jr., the superintendent of the new city hall in New York.[45] Despite this recommendation, there was no immediate change in the management of the water works.

Complaints continued to mount over the next two years. Superintendent Fellows wrote a lengthy report in 1810 to Manhattan Company President Henry Remsen responding to a number of specific complaints. One concerned plumbers sent to stop a leak at a the house of a woman who was out of town. Since the plumbers could not

---

[44]Another interesting approach was the offer received later from a Virginia company to furnish "Stone ware Pipes for the purpose of conveying Water." Apparently word of the Manhattan Company's difficulties extended far to the south, for this manufacturer had heard that the Manhattan Company "met with much trouble, disappointion [sic] & expense" in using wooden pipes. The proposed stoneware pipes were to be glazed inside and out with "Common Salt" for "sweetness & durability." Though the manufacturer claimed that another water company ordered 6,000 feet of pipe, there is no record that the Manhattan Company ever did. S.R. Bakewell & Co. to Henry Remsen, November 9, 1810, Manhattan Company Records, NYHS. The Manhattan Company again considered "earthen conduit pipes" in 1813. At that time the contractor of the water works reported that similar pipes had failed in London because they could not withstand high pressure and were apt to burst in winter. MC Minutes, 2:180-181 (May 31-June 3, 1813).

[45]The committee report can be found in MC Minutes, 2:48-50 (June 19, 1809). See also "Report by John Fellows," June 7, 1810.

reach the leak, they shut off the water "agreeably to the uniform orders of the Water Committee, without respect to persons." Fellows dealt with a second complaint, concerning a frozen pipe, by pointing out that "several hundred" pipes were in the same condition, often "closed by frost for four or five weeks" during the winter. The final complaint concerned the high fees charged by the plumbers, a common complaint even to this day. Fellows promised to "do every thing in my power to procure the plumbing work done cheep [sic] as possible."[46]

In addition to inadequate quantity, poor quality continued to be a problem. One of the more graphic expressions of this is found in an 1810 letter from Henry B. Livingston to Remsen. "When last in the City of New York altho' in the Winter Season, I found nothing so disagreeable as the water," wrote Livingston. "Even in the most elevated parts," he continued, "this impurity I perceive has been increasing with the Population." If the trend continued unchecked, he predicted it would render "a great part of [the] inhabitants ... prey to epidemical diseases." Livingston believed disease would eventually arise "from the Inhabitants Literally in their water drinking a proportion of their own evacuations, as well as that of their Horses, Cows, Dogs, Cats and other putrid liquids so

---

[46]John Fellows to Henry Remsen, March 6, 1810, MC Records, NYHS.

plentifully dispensed in the different yards, streets, and alleys of that City not to mention the cemeteries, another great source of corruption."[47] Granted that Livingston's letter most likely was referring to wells and pumps other than those of the Manhattan Company, and also granted that Livingston wrote this letter hoping to supply the city with water from upstate rivers, it still is a powerful indictment of the condition of New York's water ten years after the founding of the Manhattan Company.

While a committee of the Manhattan Company refused to take action on Livingston's proposal, it did agree with much of what he had to say. The committee admitted that the Manhattan Company's water system was "very deficient" in addition to being unprofitable. The company supplied "but a small proportion of the inhabitants" with water, and even that water "is not given with such regularity or certainty as to make it advantageous or desirable to those who receive and pay for it." In addition, the water being conveyed "will continue to become more impure and unwholesome until the whole system is improved or abandoned which in the opinion of your Committee ought not to be much longer delayed."[48] This was a startling private admission from a company which publicly was trying to present a

---

[47]Henry B. Livingston to Remsen, April 11, 1810, MC Records, NYHS.

[48]MC Minutes, 2:74-75 (April 30, 1810).

favorable image to the city and its inhabitants.

The result of these water supply deficiencies was a rebellion on the part of the company's customers. The non-payment of water bills became more widespread as this period came to a close. In the words of a later report, customers "pretty generally refused to pay for the water," thereby reducing the revenue generated by the water works. While the superintendent admitted that the water supply was not "regular," he thought that the inhabitants "out to pay for it notwithstanding, as they were never charged for the water as much as they ought to have been."[49]

This crisis led the board to appoint a special committee to study the state of the water works and report a plan for the "better management" of the division.[50] It was obvious by 1811 that the low-cost water works which the Manhattan Company designed in its first few years was inadequate to the task of supplying a rapidly-expanding city. The task now facing the company was twofold: to improve the physical plant of the system, and to change

---

[49]Ibid., 4:98-104 (April 12, 1821); 2:115-116 (August 15, 1811).

[50]At about the same time, Manhattan Company president Henry Remsen requested details about London's water companies from a contact in England. Remsen's friend prepared a packet of information, including engineering drawings, and forwarded it to Remsen in "the Admiralty letter bag for greater security." Daniel Dulany to Remsen, April 6, 1812 and July 2, 1812, Remsen Papers, NYPL.

the management of the works so it would be more responsive to the public and more accountable to the board. To accomplish this would require a radical change of direction.

Phase Two: Contractor, 1811-1821

The Manhattan Company committee charged with recommending changes in the water works proposed as the best option the "renting" of the entire operation to an individual or company. If this was not possible, they recommended using an independent "contractor" to raise and distribute water at the Manhattan Company's expense. Instead of paying the contractor a salary, he would receive "a percentum allowance on the income or revenue." The committee believed this arrangement "would stimulate the contractor to great exertion, as every cent expended in raising and distributing the water and in repairing the pipes, or lost by not being seasonably collected, more than ought to be expended or must be lost (some loss being unavoidable) would be a diminution of the allowance to the Contractor." The company placed an advertisement for a contractor in the newspaper, received three bids, and selected a person identified only as "F. Huguet." The new contractor agreed to work on a fifteen percent commission. Unlike the previous superintendents, however, Huguet was not permitted to live rent-free in the company's "house" on Chambers Street. Instead the house would be rented and the water office moved to Read Street, directly opposite the pump house.[51]

During the ten years that Huguet was contractor of the water works, two major issues had to be addressed. The first, naturally, was the repair of the physical plant so that the company would better meet the needs of the populace and deflect public criticism. The second issue involved the degree of freedom and independence the contractor would have in managing the water works. As I already have shown, the management of the company preferred to commit monetary and other resources to the banking operations. How would the board of directors balance this preference with the charter-mandated requirement of supplying pure and wholesome water? Similarly, how much independence would the board *really* give the contractor?

Once Huguet assessed the state of the water works, he saw two problems: the well, pumps, and pipes were in disrepair; and the revenue was much below what it should be. He tried to correct both situations.

In April 1812, Huguet submitted an ambitious plan for improving the water works. He wanted to fence the yard, install one or two "cisterns" next to the reservoir, build a new boiler, add another steam engine, and enlarge the engine house. All of these improvements may seem obvious today except for the cisterns. They

---

[51]MC Minutes, 2:117-128 (October 31, 1811); 129 (November 11, 1811).

were intended to "receive the water before it passes into the Reservoir, in order that it may settle, by which means the Reservoir and pipes will be in great measure kept free from the gravel, etc. pumped out of the well."[52] This appears to have been a much-needed improvement.

Upon the recommendation of the Water Committee, the board of directors agreed to install the fence, build two wooden cisterns, add another steam engine, build a copper boiler, and enlarge the engine house.[53] The board also agreed to let Huguet build a small blacksmith shop next to the water works to facilitate repairs to the "small pieces of machinery."[54] In addition, Huguet devoted a great deal of time and money to improving the company's distribution pipes. It is unlikely that the Manhattan Company would have spent so much money on the water works had it not been for the pressure of public criticism.

As one would expect, the cost of these extensive improvements far exceeded the income of the division. As a result, there was no "net revenue" out of which Huguet was supposed to receive his commission. The board, therefore, agreed in 1813 to grant Huguet an

---

[52] Ibid., 2:144 (April 20, 1812).

[53] Ibid., 2:144-146 (April 29, 1812); 155-157 (June 8, 1812). For the copper boiler, which came later, see ibid., 3:23-25 (August 5-8, 1816).

[54] Ibid., 2:167-168 (October 19, 1812).

"allowance" of $1,000 per year, which was increased by $500 the following year. While the allowance was intended to be a temporary measure until the water works were "complete and *productive,*" that status never was reached. The contractor continued to receive an allowance until 1821.[55]

In addition to improving the physical plant, Huguet tried to increase the revenue of the water works. He did this by raising existing fees, looking for new sources of income, and improving collection practices.

At the same time that the board of directors approved Huguet's extensive building plans, it approved a general increase in rates for water.[56] In addition, certain other groups which were heavy users of water, such as leather tanners, received even greater increases. This led the tanners to protest that their prices were "quite high enough" and ought not to be raised. Huguet responded that the increase was a "trifling rise" which was "just" because the tanners used approximately one-fifth of all the water pumped by the company. The Board apparently backed Huguet.[57]

In terms of new sources of revenue, Huguet once again rekindled

---

[55] Ibid., 2:173-174 (January 25, 1813); 4:98-104 (April 12, 1821).

[56] Ibid., 2:144-146 (April 29, 1812).

[57] Ibid., 2:155-157 (June 8, 1812); 205 (April 21, 1814).

the argument with the City of New York over who should pay for water used in fighting fires. Huguet reported to the board of directors his opinion that the Manhattan Company had a "claim" on the city for water used at fires. Two weeks later, the Common Council asked the city's chief engineer and comptroller to "make enquiry and report as to the right of the Corporation" to use Manhattan Company water at fires. Two years later the Common Council was still considering this matter. At that time Huguet sent a letter to the Common Council "stating the terms upon which the Manhattan Company would give the use" of the water.[58] While there is no record of the ultimate resolution of this point, it is interesting that the Manhattan Company would pursue for so long such a controversial source of additional revenue. Even if the city agreed to pay for the water used in fighting fires, the bad feelings generated would more than offset the increased revenues.

Huguet also worked to regularize the collection of water fees. First, he served notice on subscribers that since the water works had been greatly improved, subscribers would not be permitted to withhold payments. As long as the company kept the main pipes filled with

---

[58]MC Minutes, 2:138 (January 4, 1812). *Minutes of the Common Council*, 6:785 (December 16, 1811); 7:11 (January 20, 1812); 7:718 (April 4, 1814). During this period the Manhattan Company was charging the city $100 per year for supplying water for public buildings. In 1816, the company charged the city an additional $100 for the alms house and jail. See ibid., 8:320 (October 9, 1815); 8:532 (May 27, 1816).

water, he stated, subscribers would be expected to pay. Freezing or other problems with the smaller lateral pipes, which were considered to be the property and responsibility of the homeowner, were not sufficient grounds for non-payment of fees.[59]

The last piece in Huguet's puzzle was securing additional staff to regularly collect water fees. When the water works began, there was one person who served as both clerk in the office and collector of revenue. "This opened a door for the commission *of frauds*," in the words of a later report, "as [the clerk] received applications for water and entered them in a Book kept for that purpose, made out the Collection Book, and collected the revenue."[60] The functions of clerk and collector subsequently were separated; this was the situation Huguet inherited. The custom was for the collector to receive a commission of five percent of revenues. In order to temporarily speed matters, the board of directors approved the hiring of one or more collectors who would receive a commission of seven and one-half percent. This appears to have solved Huguet's short-term problem and completed his reorganization of the water works.[61]

Once these changes were made, the next major question was how the board of directors would control this energetic and qualified

---

[59]MC Minutes, 2:179-180 (May 13, 1813).

[60]Ibid., 4:98-104 (April 12, 1821).

[61]Ibid., 2:139-140 (February 20, 1812).

independent contractor. Would the board divorce itself from the day-to-day management of the water works? Would the board place greater emphasis on its water committee? Though the board wished to focus on banking and other non-water activities, was it wise to entrust to a non-employee the function upon which all other corporate privileges rested?

It is easy to answer the first two of these questions. Once the board approved the structural and other changes outlined above, it seldom concerned itself with the water works. For the rest of this period, there are very few references to the water works in the directors' minutes. In those few cases when the board *did* discuss the water works, the matter usually was referred to the water committee for further study and action. An example came in 1815 when Huguet reported that the wooden planks lining the reservoir were badly decayed and needed replacing. Instead of authorizing the improvement, the board referred the letter to the water committee "to give such directions to Mr. Huguet on the subject as should be proper."[62]

A further example of the independence of the contractor is found in the entries in the Water Works Journal for 1817-1821, which survives in the Chase Manhattan Archives. Not only did the water

---

[62]Ibid., 2:257 (October 9, 1815). For other examples, see ibid., 4:12-13 (January 24-27, 1820).

works pay for such things as pine logs and their transportation,[63] they also paid directly for the staff in the water office as well as for various day laborers.[64] The payment of staff salaries, in particular, was a departure from other Manhattan Company practices. In terms of the bank, the board of directors authorized salary payments each quarter. The complete list of employees (including the lowest level clerks, messengers, and porters) was voted on and recorded in the minutes of the board.

In addition to staff salaries, another indication of the independence of the water works was the way it handled finances on property. As the journal documents, the water works paid the taxes on the property it used and collected rent from tenants. For example, in 1819 they paid the city $188.16 for property taxes on the reservoir, engine house, three other houses, and a lot. They also collected $43.00 for rent on one of the houses.[65] Finally, as one

---

[63]For example, they paid Herman Rainsworth $408 for 204 white pine logs. Water Works Journal, July 2, 1817. Two years later, they paid Peter Persalls $20 to raft 333 logs from "State prison" to Manhattan Island. Ibid., June 12, 1819.

[64]An example of the water works office is J.S. Gardner, who received one month's salary of $29.16. See ibid., September 25, 1819. Payments to day laborers are scattered throughout the volume. One example is the $41.75 paid to Thomas P. Browning for stopping leaks in pipes. The entry is followed by a two-page listing of fifty-seven locations where Browning stopped leaks. Ibid., January 14, 1819.

[65]For the taxes, see ibid., February 17, 1819. For the collection of rent, see ibid., August 28, 1819.

would expect, the journal also records an occasional unusual expense, such as the $1.30 spent for "Spirits for [the] workmen in [the] Engine House, Sundry times."[66]

Taken as a whole, it is obvious that the board of directors abdicated its control over the contractor and the water works. The board was very happy to focus on the banking operations and leave the water works to its own devices. This was possible because the contractor period was a relatively quiet one in terms of public agitation for other sources of water. As long as things appeared to be going smoothly, the board was content to leave well enough alone.

It was only after Huguet's death in 1821 that the board realized that all had not been going well.[67] At that time the board appointed a committee to examine the water works and recommend any necessary changes. The committee investigated the water works and uncovered a number of problems with the independent contractor system.

In one case the contractor disregarded the instructions of the water committee and even lied to them. The committee had "suggested"

[66]Ibid., September 20, 1818.

[67]For a reference to Huguet's death, see MC Minutes, 4:92 (March 12, 1821). Almost a year earlier the board was informed that Huguet's health prevented him from performing his duties. See ibid., 4:28 (April 13, 1821) and 4:34-35 (May 8, 1820). It is not clear if Huguet was sick constantly over the intervening months, or if he recovered and then died suddenly.

to the contractor that he stockpile wood for fuel during the summer when it was cheapest to purchase (five dollars per cord). Huguet's "answer was (if he was not misunderstood) that he had already done so; but it appears through his accounts (recently audited) that wood has been purchased during the late winter at eight dollars per cord," sixty percent higher.

As far as the books were concerned, the board of directors later learned that the collector had not balanced the water revenue ledger since 1814. The board correctly noted that "this examination and proof is the only check the Company and their Superintendent have on the Collector of Water Revenue." Furthermore, the collector was in the practice of taking out his commission *before* depositing and accounting for the revenue. Both of these instances showed poor management on the part of the contractor.[68]

In addition, Huguet was involved in two instances of questionable ethics, if not outright fraud. First of all, he had "been in the practice of selling ashes, and pocketing instead of accounting for the same." The committee concluded that the amount of money involved "must have been considerable," judging by the amount of wood consumed. The second instance involved the "lateral pipes,"

---

[68]Ibid., 4:168-172 (June 6-13, 1822). It is important to note, however, that the non-balancing of accounts was a perennial problem in nineteenth century America. As the next chapter will show, the company's banking operations also faced this problem.

which were supposed to be the responsibility of the company's customers. It turned out that Huguet had a side business in this area: "he has bored the lateral pipes, purchased and sold on his own account, with the Machinery of the Company." The committee could not determine how much this cost the company, since Huguet "used his own augers, and the boring was made when the [steam] Engine was in ordinary use."

The committee concluded its report by recommending a number of changes in the management of the water works. Because of the importance of these recommendations, they are worth repeating at length:

First. That the Superintendent should neither receive nor expend any monies.

2nd. That he should make no contracts, nor purchases, nor repairs, except trifling repairs, without consulting the Water Committee, or an officer of the Bank who may be designated by the Board.

3rd. That having received the assent of the Committee, or such officer, he may proceed to make his Contracts, Purchases & Repairs, but shall give orders on the Committee or such officer for payments to be made, having first examined the bills of accounts, and certified them to be correct.

4th. That the contingent accounts of the Office, such as wages to the workmen, &c. &c. shall be paid in like manner.

These changes did away with the independent contractor and returned control of the water works to a Manhattan Company employee. Unlike the earlier phase, however, the superintendent now would be under much tighter control. To reiterate this fact, the committee recommended "that the President or Cashier should frequently visit the works, and that they should so manage their business in the Bank, as to allow of this without detriment to said business."[69] Perhaps by 1821 the officers and directors of the Manhattan Company finally learned two truths: that the water works would not manage itself; and that even if it *could* manage itself, it was much too visible to the populace to be left alone.   These points would become increasingly evident over the next two decades.

Other Private Water Companies

No sooner had the management of the Manhattan Company resolved the water works' internal problems, than it again faced faced threats from without.   The inadequacy of the Manhattan Company's water supply led to a number of attempts at establishing other private water companies during the 1820s.   At stake, once again, were both the charter and the profits of the Manhattan Company. As with the complaints of 1809-1811, the company tried to improve its water service enough to assuage the public and diffuse its critics.   Such reassurances, however, were much more expensive in the 1820s than in earlier decades.

One alternative to the Manhattan Company was the plan advanced by Robert Macomb in 1819 to transport water from Rye Pond to the city

---

[69]The full committee report can be found in the MC Minutes, 4:98-104 (April 12, 1821).

within two years. Macomb asked the Common Council for no money, only permission to dig up the streets to lay pipes. The Common Council agreed to this request, conditioned upon Macomb's ability to fill a reservoir with water. More important in terms of the City's experience with the Manhattan Company were two other requirements the Common Council placed on Macomb: he must be willing to sell his water works to the city after forty years "at any time when required," and the city would retain the right to regulate the rates charged for water. Existing records do not indicate why Macomb's project never was implemented. Interestingly enough, Macomb also was working the other side of the street, offering to purchase the Manhattan Company's water works or to serve as "agent" of the company.[70]

A more serious water supply effort took place while Stephen Allen was Mayor of New York from 1821 to 1824. Allen was a prominent Jeffersonian and Jacksonian politician, though a member of the artisan class rather than the merchant and professional elite of the city. During the 1830s and 1840s he served as commissioner of the Croton Water Works, indicating his continuing interest in the problem of water supply for the city. In addition, Allen was familiar with banking, the Manhattan Company's other main endeavor. Allen served

---

[70]*Minutes of the Common Council*, 10:503 (August 9, 1819); 11:15-16 (March 6, 1820). MC Minutes, 4:12-13 (January 27, 1820).

on the board of directors of the Mechanics Bank from 1810 to 1826 and was president of the Tradesmen's Bank from 1826 to 1829. Allen also had an active personal life: he fathered seven children by his first wife, nine by his second wife, but none by his third wife. Allen's third marriage, however, took place when he was seventy-two years old. Perhaps the increasing agitation for water supply alternatives to the Manhattan Company under Allen's leadership was as much an indication of the shifting of power away from the old merchant elite as it was a response to the company's inadequate supply of water. In any case, there were a number of serious challengers to the Manhattan Company over the next few years.[71]

The first of these was the New York and Sharon Canal Company, which received a New York State charter in 1823. This company's plan was to build a canal from the Housatonic River in Connecticut to either Mt. Pleasant or Manhattan. The State of Connecticut chartered a company to build a canal from the Housatonic to Sharon, on the New York border; the New York charter was to cover the rest of the project. The canal was supposed to combine "the double object of navigation and supplying the City with water." The Common Council

---

[71]For a discussion of Allen and his role in the artisan class, see Thomas Bender, *New York Intellect: A History of Intellectual Life in New York City, From 1750 to the Beginnings of Our Own Time* (New York: Alfred A. Knopf, 1987), 86-87. See also Blake, *Water for the Cities*, 109ff; and "Stephen Allen Memoirs," 140-67, NYPL.

was a strong supporter of the project and petitioned the state legislature to charter the company. While the canal company never succeeded, it was, in the words of Nelson Blake, "a complicating factor in the water situation for the next six or seven years."

This was especially true in 1825. At that time the Sharon Canal Company responded to the threat posed by another private water company (to be discussed below) by petitioning the legislature for an amendment to its charter. In order to attract investors to finance the water works, the canal company requested authorization to engage in banking. Surprisingly enough, the request was supported by a majority in the state senate; it fell short, however, of the two-thirds approval then needed to amend corporate charters. The New York and Sharon Canal Company remained on the scene even after this setback. In 1830 it again contacted the Common Council "in relation to a modification of their Charter to enable the Corporation of New York to pursue their plans for the supply of the City with water."[72]

An even more serious threat than the Sharon Canal Company was another private endeavor, the New York Water Works Company. Beginning in 1824, the state legislature considered chartering the New York Water Works Company to bring water into the city from

---

[72]*Minutes of the Common Council*, 12:767-771 (March 10, 1823); 13:168 (July 14, 1823); 18:668 (April 19, 1830). Also Blake, *Water for the Cities*, 109-113.

upstate. Throughout the year, the Manhattan Company opposed the charter in every way it could: by appointing two committees "to remonstrate against the passage" of the act; by sending three "memorials" to the legislature; by selecting an agent to represent the company in Albany; and by "conversing" with the legislators from the city. The Manhattan Company hoped to impress upon the legislators "the great injury that would be done" to the company "by an act so unjust, after they had expended so large a sum under their Charter which was an undoubted pledge to them of the *Exclusive* privilege to supply the City with Water [emphasis added]." Somewhat amusing in terms of the charges leveled against the Manhattan Company early in its existence was the company's concluding point that "the present applicants were mere speculators."[73]

Also at the end of 1824, the directors of the Manhattan Company again considered transferring their water works to the city. The directors *unanimously* concluded that the "wisest course" was for the company to sell the water works to the city or to reach "some other understanding." As in the past, the sale never took place.

---

[73]The quotes are from MC Minutes, 5:25 (December 24, 1824). See also ibid., 4:253 (March 29, 1824); 5:5-6 (July 26-28, 1824); and 5:19 (October 28, 1824). The Common Council also was concerned about the new private company, though primarily because the company would be able to dig up the city's street at will. They passed a resolution asking the legislature to guard and protect New York City's corporate rights. *Minutes of the Common Council*, 15:326-327 (February 14, 1825).

These discussions are of particular interest, however, because they were held at the same time the Manhattan Company was railing against the "injustice" of chartering another water company.[74]

As it became apparent in 1825 that the New York Water Works Company stood a good chance of receiving a corporate charter, the Manhattan Company tried one last tactic: a personal appeal for help from President Henry Remsen to DeWitt Clinton. As will be recalled, Clinton's efforts were crucial to the success of the Manhattan Company's charter amendment in 1808.[75]

Remsen began by informing Clinton of the company's recent unsuccessful efforts to sell the water works to the city. He blamed the failure of the discussions on Mayor Stephen Allen. "If there had been a different man presiding in the Corporation [New York City] at that time," Remsen wrote, "who would or could have stated and explained matters properly to that Body, a transfer of the Company's right and water property might have been made to the Corporation on such terms" as would have made the operation profitable "even if they had reduced the present rates 20 to 50 percent." In Remsen's opinion, no "private Company or Companies can, perhaps for a Century, make it a profitable business."[76]

---

[74]MC Minutes, 5:26 (December 29, 1824).

[75]See chapter two on the charter of the Manhattan Company.

[76]There clearly is an underlying issue at work in this

Remsen then went on at length to defend to Clinton the quality of the Manhattan Company's water. Some citizens, he said, were concerned about a sediment left after the water was boiled, because it resembled "putty, paint or white lead, which (if that had been the case) would have rendered it poisonous." According to Remsen, the Manhattan Company had the sediment tested and determined that it "was composed of lime and soda." In an attempt to show the safety of the sediment, the engineer doing the testing mixed it with copper and oil to make a paint, and spread the result on a doorway. There is no word whether New York City residents were reassured or revolted by the fact that the residue in their tea kettles made a suitable base for paint.[77]

Clinton responded a few weeks later. In a somewhat testy letter, he chided the management of the Manhattan Company for not transferring its water works to the city. "When I was associated with you in the direction of the Manhattan Company," he wrote, the transfer of the water works was in the best interest of the company, "and this idea was expressed in the law of 1808." Clinton rather

---

letter, namely Remsen's disdain for Allen's perceived lack of education and perhaps intelligence as well. This is an indication of the tension between the elite of the "old guard" and the leaders of the increasingly-powerful mechanic and artisan elements. See Bender, *New York Intellect*, especially chapter two, "Patricians and Artisans," 46-88.

[77]Henry Remsen to DeWitt Clinton, February 10, 1825, DeWitt Clinton Letterbooks 13:18, Columbia University.

bluntly told Remsen, "Your capital is not sufficiently extensive for the combined operations of banking and supplying the City with Water." If the company pursued the water works to "the needful extent, your banking facilities would be impaired if not destroyed."[78] This exchange of correspondence sheds an interesting light upon Clinton's earlier involvement with the company. It shows that Clinton really *was* serious about transferring the water works to the city in 1808 and that his exertions were not just an insincere effort to shield the banking operation from public attack.

Despite the Manhattan Company's best efforts, the New York Water Works Company received a charter on March 24, 1825. At first investors flocked to the new company, making it a concern to the Manhattan Company. It soon became apparent, however, that the charter was deficient in several key respects, the most important of which was the company's inability to take upstate land and water rights by condemnation. The New York Water Works company unsuccessfully tried to amend its charter in 1826 to correct these deficiencies. When the charter was not amended, investors concerned about the ability of the company to achieve its objectives withdrew their financial support. The directors of the new company, therefore, voted in 1826 to abandon the project. The following year

---

[78]Clinton to Remsen, March 10, 1825, ibid., 21:426-7.

they liquidated the company and surrendered the charter.[79]

Though today these private water works may not appear to have been much of a threat to the Manhattan Company, at the time the Manhattan Company took them quite seriously. The company responded to their challenge by trying to improve its public image and by spending significant amounts of money upgrading the water system.

In 1823 the Manhattan Company issued what now would be called a "fact sheet" on the extent of its water works. This document, in a question and answer format, was titled "Queries to the Superintendent." It described the system as follows: 691,200 gallons of water pumped each day by two 18 horsepower steam engines; reservoirs with a capacity of 132,696 gallons; twenty-five miles of pipes suppling over 2,000 houses; and 155 fire hydrants provided free of charge to the city.

The "Queries" also contained a number of interpretations with which others could disagree. For example, the superintendent said the present capacity would enable him to supply an additional 11,520 houses. The water, he maintained, was pumped "perfectly clear," with the reservoirs constructed in such a way that impurities could not pass into the pipes of conduit. According to the superintendent, the

---

[79]For more on the New York Water Works Company, see Blake, *Water for the Cities*, 113-118. The Common Council continued to receive proposals for supplying the city with water even into the 1830s. See *Minutes of the Common Council*, 19: 34, 209, 239, 307, 646.

Manhattan Company's water was "considered wholesome. I drink it," he said, "and have experienced no unwholesome effects from it, nor have I ever heard of any. The water appears as pure and clean as any I ever saw."[80]

Another part of the company's public relations campaign was a "Memoranda Relative to the Manhattan Water Works," also published in 1823. This document related how the company spent over $400,000 on its water works "presuming that their chartered rights could not be impaired, directly or indirectly." It also talked about the free water the company provided for fighting fires, which had "saved an incalculable amount of property from being burnt." In terms of shareholders, the company pointed out that in addition to the state, "a considerable number of Shares are also owned by Trustees, Guardians, Widows, and Children, who, in making this investment, have relied on the continuance of the Charter inviolate." The document reaffirmed the company's intention to "leave no mean[s] untried" in its search for better water. Finally, in an appeal to the patriotic spirit, the company reminded the citizenry that "before and during the late war" it had made loans to the state "to a very large

---

[80]"Queries to the Superintendent of the Manhattan Water Works and his Answers Thereto," March 5, 1823, Record Group 1, Legal Size Files, CMB Archives. Remsen included these "Queries" in his letter to DeWitt Clinton (noted above) trying to enlist his support for the company.

amount."[81]

A year later the company still was trying to improve its public image. The superintendent placed an advertisement in the newspapers extolling the water works and appealing for additional subscribers. By that time the superintendent had markedly decreased his estimate of how many additional houses he could supply with water, now saying he could handle 1,000 more. He still maintained, however, that the "quality of the water is as good as can be found" and that the customers would receive it "clearer and in better order than heretofore." So certain was the company of this that it would "GUARANTEE to those who subscribe for the water, a regular supply at all seasons of the year."[82]

The Manhattan Company also responded to the threat of other private water companies by making major improvements to its own operations. One part of this was a search for additional sources of water. The Manhattan Company, however, did not look to bring fresh water from upstate rivers. Rather, it followed a theory then popular and only later discredited: that drilling a well deep into the bedrock of the island would release a new and unlimited supply of fresh water. This theory is a further indication that the debate

---

[81]In the CMB Archives, the "Memoranda" is printed on the reverse of the "Queries."

[82]New York *Emerald*, June 10, 1824.

over the solution to the city's water problems was far from over. As late as the 1820s the issue went beyond public vs. private control to a disagreement over the best source of water for the city.

The Manhattan Company, therefore, contracted with Levi Disbrow, a successful driller, to sink a deep well at the corner of Bleecker Street and Broadway. Beginning in 1825, Disbrow bored for water on the Manhattan Company's property. By 1832 the well reached a depth of 442 feet; it ultimately cost the company over $12,000.[83]

In order to transport this water, the Manhattan Company began replacing its wooden pipes with ones made of cast iron. The pipe situation finally had become intolerable. For example, the residents of Liberty Street asked the Common Council to construct a drain to carry off water from a spring in the ground and leakage from the Manhattan Company's pipes.[84] Beginning in 1827, the company systematically replaced its pipes. By 1832 the company had spent

---

[83]For Disbrow's project, see MC Minutes, 5:40 (May 5, 1825), 5:161 (November 5, 1829), 5:197 (January 31, 1831), 5:199 (March 3, 1831), 5:200 (March 14, 1831); MC Journal 9 (April 18, 1831), 10 (July 9, 1840); and Blake, *Water for the Cities*, 113, 119-122. In 1833 Disbrow and a partner proposed forming a private Rock Water Company with a capital of $2 million, one-half to be invested in water works and one-half in banking. See Blake, 137. It is important to note that despite the furor over the Manhattan Company's combined operations, individuals continued to try to combine banking with other functions. This also happened in the next few decades with railroads.

[84]*Minutes of the Common Council*, 12:774 (March 17, 1923).

approximately $80,000 on this effort.[85]

During this time, the company also spent money on its real estate and related buildings. In 1831 the company spent almost $17,000 purchasing at auction the property adjacent to the existing water works. This gave the Manhattan Company a complete square lot fronting on Chambers, Cross, and Read Streets. In 1838 the company purchased three more lots on Cross Street at a cost of over $33,000.[86] Finally, from 1835 to 1836 the company paid over $30,000 for an iron holding tank and building at Bleecker Street and Broadway.[87]

Taken as a whole, the Manhattan Company's exertions from 1825 to 1838 resulted in a major capital commitment of over $170,000. This is an impressive amount, particularly in light of earlier efforts. Clearly the threat of other private water companies, as well as the municipal system to be discussed in the next section, influenced the allocation of resources by the management of the Manhattan Company. In this as in other aspects of the company's

---

[85]See MC Minutes, 5:105 (September 3, 1827), 5:107 (October 8, 1827), 5:141 (January 29, 1829), 5:198-199 (February 21, 1831); MC Journal 7 (December 30, 1828), 8 (December 31, 1829), 9 (June 30, 1832); and Blake, *Water for the Cities*, 122.

[86]MC Journal 8 (March 9, 1831), 10 (January 23, 1838).

[87]MC Minutes, 5:333 (April 27, 1835), 5:338 (June 23, 1835); MC Journal 10 (June 30, 1836, June 28, 1837). The actual cost of the tank was $32,130.12.

The Manhattan Company's water reservoir, which is depicted in this panel, was erected on Chambers Street about 1800. The figures in the panel are not portraits but merely characteristic citizens of the period. The figure of Oceanus, which appears over the reservoir, was incorporated as a symbol in the original seal of the Manhattan Company. *(Courtesy of the Chase Manhattan Archives.)*

operations, the city and state environments had a profound impact upon the strategies of the Manhattan Company's leaders.

The 1830s: Municipal Water Supply

As I have already shown, the Manhattan Company and the City of New York had a tumultuous relationship. There were recurring arguments over repairing city streets and supplying water for fires.[88] There also were numerous attempts to transfer the Manhattan Company's water works to the city. While some people were motivated solely by the desire to improve water supply, others were convinced that the supply of water was a municipal responsibility which never should have been transferred to a private company. In their opinion, private companies were "soon found to have an eye only to the profits of their incorporations, and the public suffer under the monopolies."[89]

In chapter two I discussed the early efforts to transfer the Manhattan Company's water works to the city, culminating in the 1808 charter revision. In the years following 1808, the issue remained

---

[88]Examples of the continuing controversy over street repair and damage caused by the Manhattan Company's water works can be found in MC Minutes, 4:209 (May 22, 1823) and *Minutes of the Common Council*, 10:12 (September 7, 1818), 14:713 (August 15, 1825), 17:521 (December 15, 1828), 539-540 (December 22, 1828). For fires, see ibid., 17:300 (July 14, 1828), 18:604 (March 15, 1830).

[89]The quote is from the "Report of the Committee on the Fire Department," ibid., 17:722-723 (March 16, 1829).

alive. In 1816 the Common Council formed a committee to consider an application to the state legislature for a municipal water works. Nothing came of this effort.

In 1821 the Common Council appointed a committee to ascertain "the best and most practicable means" of supplying the city with pure and wholesome water. The committee was authorized to "procure any plan drawings, surveys, estimates and calculations" which may be required.[90] The committee reported four months later that they had visited Rye Pond and the Bronx River, but could not yet determine the feasibility or cost of the proposed project. They recommended, and the Common Council approved, $500 for an engineer to survey "the whole line of country between this city and the lakes forming the principal source of the river Bronx."[91] As Stephen Allen later recalled, the urgency of the situation was reinforced by a yellow fever epidemic which afflicted the city from July to October of 1822.[92] But even with the recent experience of disease and the constant pushing of the city's energetic mayor, the 1820s ended without a municipal water system.

By the time the issue again came to a head in the 1830s, both the city government and the public had some basis for comparison with

---

[90]Ibid., 12:168-169 (December 24, 1821).

[91]Ibid., 12:309-311 (April 1, 1822).

[92]"Stephen Allen Memoirs," 140-141, NYPL.

the experience of other cities. The inadequacy of water supply was not just a New York City problem; rather, it was a fact of life in all the rapidly growing major cities of nineteenth century America. It is important, therefore, to briefly look at how other cities faced this problem and what influence, if any, their experiences may have had upon the principals in New York.

The London example was the one most often used by opponents of private water companies. London had eight private water companies which, instead of competing, divided the city into monopolistic districts. Much of London's drinking water was taken from the Thames into which 139 common sewers discharged. In addition to an inadequate supply, the populace was upset because water rates were unregulated and arbitrarily fixed. The water companies exerted so much political influence, however, that reform was impossible.[93]

Philadelphia, on the other hand, was the model to which most New Yorkers pointed. In 1792 the State of Pennsylvania chartered the Delaware and Schuylkill Canal Company and gave it ten years to complete a canal which also could transport water. The city did not wait ten years for the private company, however. In 1799 Philadelphia broke ground for its own water system, which was completed in 1801. As with the Manhattan Company, Philadelphia used wooden conduit pipes and experienced major problem with them.

---

[93]Blake, Water for the Cities, 140.

Interesting in terms of the Manhattan Company's statements about the unprofitable nature of water supply is the fact that the Philadelphia water works did not show a profit until 1830. In that year there were 10,000 customers receiving 2 million gallons of water per day. Even the Philadelphia situation, which was considered a "great success" in Blake's words, soon proved inadequate. By 1850 the city's consumption was 5 million gallons per day.[94]

Baltimore also had a relatively successful water works, even though it was under private control. The Baltimore Water Company was founded in 1804 but did not receive a charter until four years later. In order to avoid a Manhattan Company situation, the charter specifically prohibited the company from engaging in banking. The Baltimore company was mildly profitable, paying annual dividends of three percent for its first twenty-four years. The Baltimore Water Company enjoyed a monopoly in the city for fifty years, even though its water supply never was adequate. Blake attributed this to the fact that the Baltimore company invested more capital in its works and made greater efforts to extend its services than did companies in other cities. Perhaps as a "reward for virtue," the stockholders of the company were given liberal compensation when the municipality acquired the private water company in 1854.[95]

---

[94] Ibid., 18-43, 89.

[95] Ibid., 69-77, 219, 256.

Boston's experience was similar to New York's in that there was a long struggle over private versus public control of the water system. The Boston Aqueduct Company, a private effort, was chartered in 1795. The company paid no dividends for its first twelve years and over the next thirty years its annual dividends averaged less than four percent. As with the Manhattan Company, the Boston Aqueduct Company regularly received public criticism. A major fire in 1825, which destroyed fifty-three buildings and caused over $500,000 in damages, started a debate over a more adequate supply of water. As in New York City, where there was an argument over whether water should come from the nearby Bronx River or the more distant Croton River, Boston also had two options, the Spot Pond and the Long Pond. As Boston's population increased, the nearby Spot Pond became less attractive, though it took twenty years before a final decision was made through a public referendum. Boston broke ground on its Cochituate Aqueduct in 1846 and completed it two years later. The aqueduct was fourteen miles long, half the distance of the Croton Aqueduct. In 1851 Boston purchased the property and rights of the original private aqueduct company for only $45,000, a mere token payment much below what was paid in Baltimore.[96]

Though there are many more examples I could detail,[97] the

---

[96] Ibid., 67, 172, 193, 197, 211, 215, 218.

[97] Brief comments on some of the other cities are as

trend in nineteenth century America already should be clear.
Although private water companies were the norm early in the century,
city after city turned to municipal water works. By 1860, only
fifty-eight percent of the 136 American water works were private,
with most of the private companies located in smaller communities.
Of the sixteen largest cities in 1860, only four (New Orleans,
Buffalo, San Francisco, and Providence) still had private water
systems.[98]

New York City, therefore, was part of a larger trend in turning
from private to municipal water supply. Similarly, the city's
experience with inadequate supply and unregulated private enterprise
was mirrored elsewhere. While the Manhattan Company obviously was at
fault in these matters, understanding the wider universe of

---

follows: **Cincinnati** organized a private company in 1820 which
pumped water from the Ohio River first by horse and then by steam.
The city purchased the system in 1839. **New Orleans** began a
municipal water works in 1811 and completed it in 1822. The
municipal system was so inadequate, however, that in 1833 the
legislature chartered a private company which four years later began
supplying the city with water pumped from the Mississippi River.
Cleveland waited twenty years for a private company and then
decided in 1854 to build its own works and pump water from Lake
Erie. In **Chicago**, a private company was chartered in 1836 and
began to serve customers in 1842. The water was pumped by steam
engine from Lake Michigan. In 1854 the city contracted to purchase
the private water works, though the transfer did not take place for
several years. Eventually the water was improved by extending the
intake tunnel two miles into the lake. These and other examples can
be found in Blake, *Water for the Cities*, 265-267.

[98]Ibid., 77, 267.

nineteenth century water supply helps put these shortcomings in perspective.

In the 1830s, the movement for a public water system in New York City finally reached fruition. There were serious negotiations between the company and the city several times during the decade. In 1833 the Manhattan Company offered to transfer all its water rights to the city and to accept compensation determined by arbitration. While the city appointed a committee of six to negotiate with the company, nothing came of this effort.[99]

In 1836 further serious discussions took place. These discussions are worth recounting in some detail because they illustrate the problems encountered in a transfer of the water works and how quickly a deal could turn sour. In March 1836 an internal Manhattan Company committee estimated the value of the water works as well as the "Rights and Privileges of the Company as regards the Supply of the City with Water." The directors of the company reviewed this estimate and offered to lease the water works to the city. The lease was to run for fifty or ninety-nine years with the option to renew, and was to be at a minimum rate of $20,000 per year.[100]

---

[99]MC Minutes, 5:264 (April 1, 1833), 279 (October 3, 1833). Blake, *Water for the Cities*, 144-145.

[100]MC Minutes, 6:11 (March 7, 1836).

Over the next three days, the Manhattan Company had two meetings with representatives from the city. The company offered to lease the water works for $21,300 per year plus a rate of six percent per year for any real estate and reservoir improvements the company would have to make to "accommodate" the city. Negotiators for the city stated that these terms were too expensive and offered instead to pay $16,000 per year plus the six percent additional charge on improvements. Surprisingly, the Manhattan Company board agreed to lease the water works for twenty-one years at an annual fee of $16,000 plus six percent interest on any sums the company would spend on improvements.[101]

In the next few days, the company sent copies of its proposed lease for review by two attorneys, one of whom was Benjamin F. Butler, the New York University Law School founder who had successfully defended the company in the 1830 suit discussed in chapter two. The Manhattan Company directors also unanimously approved the preparation of a resolution to be submitted to the city finalizing the lease. The transfer appeared to be all but certain. But suddenly, three days later, the Manhattan Company board unanimously voted to rescind "all the Resolutions heretofore passed respecting the Leasing of the Water Works to the Corporation."[102]

---

[101]Ibid., 6:11-12 (March 10, 1836).

[102]Ibid., 6:12-13 (March 14-17, 1836).

The negotiations fell apart as quickly as they had begun. While there is no record of the reasons for this reversal, subsequent events lead to the surmise that it involved the question of *leasing* the water works.

Seven months later, the negotiations again picked up steam. The Common Council inquired whether the company was willing to "dispose" of its water works. The company responded that it was willing to do so "on fair and equitable terms." A number of meetings thereafter took place between representatives of the city and the company. The board of directors ultimately agreed to the sale of the water works, but wanted the value of the operation determined through arbitration by "five or seven respectable disinterested individuals." The city, however, did not want arbitration, preferring, instead, to offer a specific purchase price. Once again, promising discussions for the transfer of the water works never reached completion.[103]

Naturally these discussions did not occur in isolation. At the same time that the city was negotiating with the company, it was moving toward building its own water supply system. Spurring the

---

[103]Ibid., 6:26 (October 17, 1836), 27 (October 20, 1836), 28 (October 27, 1836), 28 (October 31, 1836), 36-37 (January 26, 1837). Similar discussion in 1839-1840 also ended unsuccessfully. See ibid., 6:189-195 (August 17- September 8, 1840). As I pointed out in chapter two, the Manhattan Company never did transfer its water works to the city. The company continued to pump water every day until 1923.

city were two major threats to nineteenth century urban existence, fire and disease. In 1828 fire losses in the city totaled over $600,000. By 1831 the city government itself supplied some water for fighting fires from a reservoir on 13th street, but this was far from adequate. The following year, New York City was visited by the worldwide cholera epidemic. The disease claimed 3,500 lives and cost the city government $110,000 in direct expenses. Though the city's water supply generally was not blamed for the epidemic, there was a widespread appreciation that a more abundant supply of water would help keep the city clean and avoid future epidemics.[104]

As in the case of the Manhattan Company, which was founded in the wake of an epidemic, the fire and health problems in the city led the public to support improved water, no matter what the cost. The voters approved the Croton plan on April 16, 1835. According to Nelson Blake, the resulting water supply system was "one of the most notable public works of the nineteenth century." When completed, Croton Dam was 270 feet long and fifty feet high. Behind it formed a lake five miles long covering 400 acres. Water went from the dam to the Harlem River via thirty-three miles of masonry aqueducts. The water then crossed the river on a "High Bridge" 1,450 feet long with arches 100 feet above the surface of the river. After the river,

---

[104]On these matter, see *Minutes of the Common Council*, 17:300 (July 14, 1828), 18:487 (January 25, 1830), and Blake, *Water for the Cities*, 120-124, 131-133.

seven-and-a-half miles of masonry conduits and iron pipes carried the water to a "receiving reservoir" at Yorkville (capacity 150 million gallons) and a "distributing reservoir" at Murray Hill (capacity 20 million gallons).[105] In 1833 the estimated cost of the project was $5 million. The final cost of the Croton system, however, was $10.3 million, with the city actually incurring debt of almost $13 million.[106] In some ways this vindicated the original officers and directors of the Manhattan Company: transporting water from upstate was far more difficult and expensive than anyone had imagined in 1799.

Conclusion

Based upon the evidence presented in this chapter, it is not fair to say that the Manhattan Company completely neglected its water works. While it is true that the initial decisions on the design of the water works largely were based on the desire to conserve capital for banking, the city's experience with the Croton System four decades later indicates the technical problems the Manhattan Company also would have faced transporting water from upstate. To ignore the

---

[105]The receiving reservoir was between 79th and 86th streets and 6th and 7th avenues. The distributing reservoir was on the present site of the main branch of the New York Public Library (between 40th and 42nd streets, and 5th and 6th avenues).

[106]See Blake, *Water for the Cities*, 142-171.

second factor is to see only one side of the coin.

At many times in its history, the Manhattan Company did realize that its water works needed improvement and took steps to correct the situation. For example, the company tried different methods of managing the water works in the hopes of making the operation more efficient and responsive. The directors moved from tight control over a superintendent, to loose control with a contractor, and back to even tighter control after 1821. The company made these changes in an attempt to respond to the concerns of the public, especially the customers of the water works.

In addition to management changes, the company made significant improvements to its water works. Granted many of these improvements were centered around times of great pressure on the Manhattan Company -- non-payment of fees by subscribers, the threat of other private water companies, agitation for a municipal supply of water, etc. Nevertheless the company did try to improve both the source (Disbrow's deep well) and the delivery system (wooden and then iron pipes). Particularly telling are the expensive improvements the company made after the Croton plan was approved in 1835. If the company's main purpose was doing as little as possible for the water works, why would it have spent over $60,000 on improvements once the Croton System was a foregone conclusion?

While the Manhattan Company obviously could have done better with water supply, in light of most previous writings about the company it is somewhat surprising to see that they did *anything* in this area. Similarly, realizing that other municipalities faced the same problems of public versus private control and an increasingly inadequate local source of water supply, helps put the New York situation in perspective.

This is not to say that the Manhattan Company should be applauded for all its water supply efforts. Without regular public outcry and the fear of having its charter invalidated, the company probably would have devoted fewer resources to the water works. As the next two chapters will show, banking remained the company's top priority. But it is important to state, in the interests of fairness, that the Manhattan Company was not evil incarnate in the area of water supply. Rather, the leaders of the company were individuals trying to balance complex obligations and multiple constituencies. They had to deal with such groups as state and local politicians, small property owners, and merchants and other business leaders. It is more than a simple tale of good versus evil.

CHAPTER FOUR

MANAGING THE MANHATTAN COMPANY'S
BANK IN NEW YORK CITY

> The people have learnt that they can put
> down Monied Monopolies. This is a lesson
> which they will be slow to forget. Our State
> is literally groaning under the accumulating
> power of these MONOPOLIES. Industry and
> enterprise, at every turn we take, are
> cramped and trammeled by INCORPORATED
> COMPANIES. Our Statute Books are filled with
> CHARTERS conferring advantages upon the *few*
> at the expense of the *many*. Our whole
> course of Legislation, for the last ten
> years, has tended to make the *"rich richer
> and the poor poorer."*[1]

As I already have discussed, nineteenth century corporations
were considered to be public franchises. State legislatures granted
corporate status, and its accompanying benefits, as a way of
encouraging activities thought to advance the "public good." Early
corporations were extremely visible and, therefore, subject to
intense public scrutiny.

With the Manhattan Company, the nature of its water works as a
franchise was obvious. The state gave the company broad powers in
recognition of the difficult water supply task it faced. For almost
half a century, both the government and the public expected to see
progress commensurate with the powers granted. The Manhattan

---

[1]Albany *Evening Journal*, November 18, 1834, p. 3.

Company's halfhearted water supply efforts, however, led to regular public criticism and calls for other water supply options, both private and public. Dissatisfaction with the Manhattan Company's use of its water supply franchise eventually led the city government to return this important public function to itself through the Croton project.

The public service nature of *banking*, the Manhattan Company's second major operation, is not always so obvious to modern Americans. We are not accustomed to thinking of banks as public utilities; rather we consider them to be private enterprises. In the nineteenth century, however, the franchise nature of banking was clearer. At that time, banks supplied much of the circulating currency for the expanding Republic through the issue of bank notes. The presence or absence of banks, therefore, could have a profound effect upon the economic development of an area.[2]

---

[2]For more on the franchise nature of bank charters, see Ronald E. Seavoy, *The Origins of American Business Corporations, 1784-1855: Broadening the Concept of Public Service During Industrialization* (Westport: Greenwood Press, 1982). Seavoy also discusses this in his doctoral dissertation, "The Origins of the American Business Corporation, 1784-1855: New York, The National Model," (Ph.D., diss., University of Michigan, 1969). See also Fritz Redlich, *The Molding of American Banking: Men and Ideas* (New York: Hafner Publishing, 1947; reprint, New York: Johnson Reprint Company, 1968), 1:8. In Redlich's words, the common people came to regard "a bank rather in the light of a benevolent than ... a money making institution and as possessing recognized special claims on public and legislative favor and therefore bound to accommodate the public."

Furthermore, in New York State the issue of banks and incorporation assumed political importance. I have discussed already how Burr and the Republicans used the Manhattan Company's "surplus capital" clause to break the Federalist monopoly over banking in New York City. This, however, was just the beginning of the link between banking and politics in New York State. For the next fifty years, banking policy, especially the granting of corporate powers, was a constant source of partisan conflict.[3]

In the midst of this maelstrom, the Manhattan Company tried to manage its banking operations in New York City. As with the water works, the company's managers could not ignore the social and political environment in which the bank found itself. The Manhattan Company regularly had to adjust policies and procedures to meet the demands of the changing climate. Strategy and structure were directly influenced by environmental pressures.

In order to explore these relationships, I will divide this chapter into three main sections: initial decisions on the use of surplus capital and the structuring of operations; the period of Henry Remsen's leadership, 1799-1826 (Remsen was one of the earliest

---

[3]The classic treatment of the link between politics and banking is Bray Hammond's *Banks and Politics in America From the Revolution to the Civil War* (Princeton: Princeton University Press, 1957). The partisan nature of policy toward banks also is discussed in Lee Benson, *The Concept of Jacksonian Democracy: New York as a Test Case* (Princeton: Princeton University Press, 1961), 86-109.

professional bankers in the United States); and the post-Remsen period with its decline in managerial expertise and major public investigation of the Manhattan Company's operations in 1840.

Initial Decisions

The major initial decision the founders of the Manhattan Company faced was how to use the "surplus" capital of the company. With such a liberal charter in hand, the directors had many possibilities. There were numerous "monied operations" not forbidden by law: for example, banking and finance, and insurance of various kinds.

It is important to keep in mind, however, what I already have discussed in chapter three. At the same time the Manhattan Company was deciding what to do with its surplus capital, it was determining the nature and extent of its water works. Furthermore, this was not a one-time occurrence. Throughout the next forty years, the two areas of water supply and banking would be intertwined in the daily affairs of the company. Public perception and dissatisfaction in one area often would affect the other. For example, there is some evidence that the well-publicized 1840 investigation of the Manhattan Company's bank turned the tide of opinion against the city's proposed purchase of the water works. Though in this chapter I will be separating water from banking, in reality this seldom was the case.

Even before the Manhattan Company had a bank, it had cash to safeguard. Therefore the earliest decision on the use of capital was to deposit "all monies" paid to the corporation in the two existing city banks, the Bank of New York and the local office of the Bank of the United States. The money was split evenly between the two banks.[4]

Having resolved the short-term situation, the board of directors appointed a committee to consider "the most proper means of employing the capital of the company" and to report "the different objects to which it may be advantageously applied." It is interesting that Aaron Burr, the originator of the surplus capital clause, was not appointed to this committee.[5] One week after the committee began its deliberations, however, Burr introduced a resolution, which the directors approved, recommending that the committee also consider "the several objects of marine insurance and foreign commerce."[6] The "also" in the resolution would seem to imply that the committee already was considering other uses of capital, most likely banking.

On May 15th, the board considered the report of the committee

---

[4]Manhattan Company [hereafter MC] Minutes, 1:2-5 (April 11-15, 1799). Unless otherwise noted, all MC records are located in the Chase Manhattan [CMB] Archives, New York, New York.

[5]Ibid., 1:11 (April 17, 1799). The committee members were Brockholst Livingston, William Edgar, and John B. Church. Though Burr was not on the committee, he had influence through Church, who was his brother-in-law.

[6]Ibid., 1:13 (April 24, 1799).

on the use of capital. The board ultimately resolved that the surplus capital of the company should "be employed in discounting proper securities." In order to promote this objective, the company was authorized to establish "an office of discount and deposit."[7] While no record exists of the board's debates, it is clear that the decision was not unanimous. One director, William Laight, felt so strongly about the matter that he resigned his position with the company. Laight stated that the Manhattan Company's decision placed him in a situation where "delicacy and duty" required him to "make a prompt election." Since Laight also was a director of the New York Branch of the Bank of the United States, he thought it "improper" to "hold an office of similar import in any other institution whose object is pointed to the same end and whose mode of producing the same effect may possibly contravene each other."[8]

The Laight incident raises a number of interesting questions. If it was obvious from the start that the Manhattan Company was going to engage in banking, why did Laight wait until the middle of May to resign? Was it because the committee on the use of capital kept the subject of banking a secret, even from the directors, until it

---

[7]Ibid., 1:18 (May 15, 1799). While in the next section I will define "discount" more formally, suffice it to say at this point that the primary difference between a "discount" and a "loan" is the time when the borrower pays the interest.

[8]The letter from Laight to the board of directors is found in Ibid., 1:19 (May 16, 1799).

presented its report? Or, if the idea of banking was known to the directors, did Laight stay on the board in the hope of convincing a majority to vote against the proposal? Unfortunately, the detailed records needed to answer these questions do not survive.

Before returning to the office of discount and deposit, the main use of the Manhattan Company's surplus capital, I first will discuss insurance and other uses of capital. By late June 1799, Burr was growing impatient at the lack of action in the area of insurance. He introduced a resolution, which the board approved, requesting the capital committee to report "with all convenient speed" specific plans "for the sale of annuities and for insurance of houses and goods against risk from fires."[9]

As it turns out, the committee's speed was less than "convenient:" the committee did not report until late September. Even at that late date, the general report was referred to another committee to develop a "specific plan for carrying the same into effect."[10] It was not until November 1799 that the directors voted to "open an office for the sale of annuities at five percent and for the insurance of lives." At the same meeting the directors authorized a committee to investigate insuring houses and goods against fires. The board of directors, however, abruptly cancelled

---

[9] Ibid., 1:32 (June 24, 1799).

[10] Ibid., 1:51 (September 3, 1799).

the investigation of fire insurance one month later.[11]

The Manhattan Company did proceed with life insurance and annuities. Though the records of this activity are slim, some documentation exists. In March 1800, the company published tables covering these two areas.[12] One year later, Henry Remsen answered a request for information about the rate the company would charge to insure someone traveling to the West Indies. Remsen wrote that the risk associated with the area would result in a surcharge for the person insured. In the actuary's opinion, the premium would "be too high ... to be paid by the intended assuree, but not more than the company ought in justice to receive."[13] As late as 1803, the main journal of the Manhattan Company shows an entry for life insurance payments.[14] For at least three or four years, therefore, life

---

[11]Ibid., 1:57 (November 18, 1799), 61-62 (December 17, 1799).

[12]Ibid., 1:68-70 (March 10-31, 1800).

[13]Henry Remsen to Hez. Perkins, February 20, 1801, CMB Archives.

[14]MC Journal No. 1, December 31, 1803. The Manhattan Company was not the only corporation which combined banking and insurance. For example, the Pennsylvania Company for Insurance on Lives and Granting Annuities, which was established in 1809, continued to use its original name until 1947, even though it long since had abandoned insurance and confined itself to banking. Its new name was the First Pennsylvania Banking and Trust Company. See Hammond, *Banks and Politics*, 195. As I pointed out in chapter two, it is an interesting flight of historical fancy to speculate on the insurance possibilities which today's Chase Manhattan would have if it had not surrendered the original Manhattan Company charter in 1965.

insurance and annuities were a minor use of the company's surplus capital.

Banking, however, soon became the primary use of the company's capital. Once the board authorized the establishment of the office of discount and deposit in May 1799, quick action followed. Two weeks later the company bought a building on Wall Street from one George Scriba for $30,000.[15] The company also printed abstracts of the board's proceedings in the local newspapers as a way of keeping the public informed and encouraging business.[16]

In August the board approved a series of twenty-one regulations for the office of discount and deposit. Among the key regulations were:

1. Discounts would be made twice per week, on Mondays and Thursdays. The interest rate was set at six percent, and the discounted bills or notes were not to run for more than sixty days. There was to be a three day grace period on repayment.

2. Bills or notes offered for discounting had to be

---

[15]MC Minutes, 1:27 (May 29, 1799). For the actual payment, see MC Journal No. 1, December 4, 1799.

[16]For example, the New York *Spectator* of May 29, 1799 contains abstracts of the board's proceedings on April 11th, 17th, and 29th; and May 6th, 8th, 15th, and 16th.

delivered the day before "discount day." At least seven directors had to be present to act on discounts; their decision had to be unanimous.

3.   The company's books were to be balanced twice per year, in preparation for the payment of dividends.

4.   A committee of three directors would examine the cash each month, compare it to the ledger balances, and report any differences to the board.

5.   Performance bonds had to be posted by the cashier ($25,000); first teller ($5,000); second teller ($4,000); and bookkeepers and runners ($3,000 each).[17]

The Manhattan Company's Office of Discount and Deposit opened for business on Tuesday, September 3, 1799. As one would expect, the company withdrew its funds from the Bank of New York and the branch of the Bank of the United States and placed them in its own bank. The new office quickly assumed the trappings of a bank: the first Manhattan Company bank notes totaling $348,000 were issued on October 26th; the first committee to examine the company's cash was appointed in November; and loans and discounts were acted upon from the

---

[17]The full text of the regulations can be found in the MC Minutes, 1:40-43 (August 13, 1799). See also the minor change in the regulations the board made on August 27, 1799 (page 49). Henry Remsen's performance bond as Cashier, dated September 11, 1799 is preserved in the CMB Archives. There also is the bond of assistant clerk William Ireson, which was co-signed by Aaron Burr. Record Group 1, Legal Size Files, CMB Archives.

beginning.[18]

Leading the new bank were two key individuals, Daniel Ludlow and Henry Remsen. Ludlow, president of the Manhattan Company from 1799 to 1808, was descended from King Edward I of England. He received his first business experience in the Amsterdam countinghouse of his maternal grandfather, Daniel Crommelin. Ludlow came to own the largest importing business in New York City; he was known around town for his handsome horses and carriages. Though Ludlow was a Tory during the Revolution, Thomas Jefferson thought enough of Ludlow to appoint him Navy Agent for New York in 1801. As president, Ludlow was not deeply involved in the day-to-day workings of the bank, leaving this, instead, to the professional bankers. Ludlow, however, did bring an air of respectability to the fledgling bank and attracted merchants and other wealthy individuals as customers.[19]

Henry Remsen was one of the first professional bankers in America. Born in 1762, he began his career as an associate in his father's importing business. Remsen served as John Jay's secretary

---

[18]For the withdrawal of the Manhattan Company's funds, see MC Minutes, 1:47 (August 20, 1799). For the first issue of bank notes, see MC Journal 1, October 26, 1799. The first examination committee is found in MC Minutes, 1:58 (November 25, 1799). For a sample loan, $2,000 advanced to the Cayuga Bridge Company, see MC Journal 1, November 28, 1799.

[19]For biographical information about Ludlow, see Hammond, *Banks and Politics*, 152, 161; "Manuscript History of the Manhattan Company," by the Brearly Service Organization, April 2, 1930, Record Group 1, Box 1, CMB Archives.

in the 1780s and then spent two years as chief clerk in the State Department under Thomas Jefferson. In 1792 Remsen was appointed First Teller in the New York Branch of the Bank of the United States.[20] Remsen served as Cashier of the Manhattan Company from 1799 to 1808 and president from 1808 to 1826. During this time he established professional practices and built the bank into a major financial institution.

The Remsen Years, 1799-1826

It is important to remember that banking in 1799 was much different than modern banking, primarily because of a the lack of precedents and proven procedures to guide managers and directors. Even procedures which we may take for granted, such as endorsing a check, only evolved after a great deal of trial and effort. Therefore the first generation of professional bankers, Henry Remsen and his contemporaries, had a profound impact upon the course of banking's development in America.

In terms of the Manhattan Company, the experience with banking was similar in many ways to that of the water works. In both cases,

---

[20]For biographical information, see Remsen Papers, New York Public Library [hereafter NYPL]; Remsen Papers, New-York Historical Society [hereafter NYHS]. The CMB Archives contains a 1792 letter of reference from Thomas Jefferson. The Remsen Papers in the NYPL (Box 1, Folder 9) contain a 1784 letter of reference from Charles Thomson to John Jay and the 1792 letter appointing Remsen as First Teller.

the government and public closely watched the developing enterprise and periodically criticized the company.[21]   Also, in both cases, what one might consider to be "internal" matters became the focus of public investigations. In 1840, for example, the Manhattan Bank was roundly criticized in public for its loan procedures and its internal controls over cash.

Henry Remsen played a key role in establishing the Manhattan Company's policies and procedures. In order to understand his contributions, as well as the shortcomings of his successors which led to the 1840 public investigation, I will divide this chapter into the following sections: internal controls over tellers and accounts; loan and discount policies; relationships with governments at all levels; and dealings with other banks in the emerging national financial system. Once again internal and external, public and private, were intimately connected in the history of the Manhattan Company.

In these and other areas, the Manhattan Company generally followed the management progression outlined by Fritz Redlich in his pioneering study forty years ago. In the early years, according to Redlich, bank management was most often by the full board of directors. Gradually bank boards delegated their management: first

---

[21]I already have discussed some of these cases in chapter two, particularly the 1830 suit against the Manhattan Company's banking operations.

to temporary committee's; then to standing committees (by the 1820s); and finally, by the 1830s, to the officers, the president and cashier.[22] Though the Manhattan Company also experienced this progression, Remsen's professional expertise accelerated it. After Remsen left the company, however, there were problems: the management system which permitted Remsen a great deal of latitude also gave such latitude to his less-prudent successors.

In the early 1800s there were few standard internal controls over such things as overdrafts, forgeries, employee differences, and thefts. The Manhattan Company, as with other banks, used trial and error in developing procedures to prevent losses. Though the Manhattan Company became a recognized leader in these efforts, it never was completely successful during the period of this study. Up to 1842 and beyond, losses both large and small continued to be quite common.

The overdrawing of accounts was one such recurring problem. Under Remsen, the Manhattan Company tried many different solutions.

---

[22]Redlich, *Molding*, 1:18-19, 55-59. See also Alfred D. Chandler, Jr., *The Visible Hand: The Managerial Revolution in American Business* (Cambridge: Belknap Press, 1977), 41. J.S. Gibbons, *The Banks of New York, Their Dealers, the Clearing House, and the Panic of 1857* (New York: D. Appleton, 1859; reprint, New York: Greenwood Press, 1968). The Gibbons book is a unique source because it describes in detail the duties of all bank employees as of the late 1850s.

At the root of the problem was faulty communication between the bookkeepers, who maintained "dealer" (customer) accounts, and the paying tellers, who gave cash to the customers. To try to improve communications, the board in 1802 ordered the bookkeepers to supply each teller with a list of habitual overdraft offenders. The tellers, in turn, were instructed to check this list before paying checks. At the same time, the cashier was to notify customers with overdrawn accounts that they were expected the make the accounts "good" and that future overdrafts would force the bank to close their accounts.[23]

Beginning in 1805, the board tried to place greater responsibility on the tellers and bookkeepers for preventing overdrafts. The board decided that the employees "and their sureties" would be responsible for any overdrafts. Later in the year the directors requested to see at each meeting a list of overdrafts and the tellers who paid the checks. In December 1806 the board resolved that losses due to overdrafts would "be made good by the Teller" unless he was "exonerated from his liability by the Board." By the end of 1806, the bank's total losses from overdrawn accounts and protested bills reached $91,419.90. These losses were too big for the directors "to pass them over in silence." The Manhattan Company also formed a committee to confer with the other banks to

---

[23]MC Minutes, 1:111-112 (September 23, 1802).

adopt regulations to prevent overdrafts.[24]

Though the board did not remain silent, problems with overdrafts continued into the next decade. In 1811 the board again addressed the situation, but this time in a way that indicates the relative power of the officers and directors. The board passed a resolution authorizing the *president and cashier* to close the accounts of "all persons, without discrimination" who overdrew their accounts. Furthermore, the officers were authorized to do this "without consulting the Board." During the discussion of the resolution, the president and cashier noted that "checks of directors had been presented when there was not money to pay them." Also, "some of the best dealers" had overdrawn their accounts. Closing the accounts of directors and good dealers "would not only produce ill will against the officers of the Bank, but might also prove injurious to the Institution." Remsen stated his position that "no check, by whomever it might be drawn, ought to be paid, if there was not sufficient money in the Bank to pay it when it was presented, but he was decidedly opposed to the vesting either in the President or Cashier of a Bank, the excessive power of closing accounts, unless they were dangerous or doubtful accounts." It is interesting that on this issue, the officers were not enthusiastic about accepting a

---

[24]Ibid., 1:162 (January 28, 1805), 194 (July 1, 1805), 222-223 (December 9, 1806), 226-229 (January 5-12, 1807), 232 (June 18, 1807).

responsibility the board wished to delegate to them. In fact, six months later the directors changed the above procedure so that the officers would only *present information* on overdrafts to the directors on the next discount day "with such observations as may appear to either of them [the president or cashier] proper to be made, in order that the Board may have the means of deciding with promptness and propriety."[25]

Even this did not put an end to the problem of overdrafts. In 1816 the bank tried charging interest on the overdrawn amount until it was repaid. A year later, the directors had to remind the tellers and bookkeepers that they expected "frequent communications" between them to prevent overdrafts. The board also ordered that each teller and bookkeeper receive a "certified copy" of the 1811 and 1817 resolutions dealing with overdrafts. As a further warning, the board in 1822 ordered that $250 per year be deducted from the salary of the first teller, and half that amount from the salary of a bookkeeper, until an overdraft was repaid. As late as 1836, however, the first teller still permitted a company to overdraw its account by almost $22,000.[26]

The Manhattan Company had more success controlling the

[25]Ibid., 2:106-107 (February 1811), 130 (November 14, 1811).

[26]Ibid., 3:24 (August 8, 1816), 36 (December 5, 1816), 62-63 (August 25, 1817), 147 (January 28, 1822), 177 (August 4, 1822); 4:30-31 (November 21, 1836).

counterfeiting of checks than it did the overdrawing of accounts. In fact, the Manhattan Company was one of the leaders in this area. In 1806 the directors ordered that the person cashing a check should "endorse his or her name thereon." If the person could not write, the teller was instructed to "note on the back of the check the name and description of such person in summary manner." The key point, however, was the sending of this resolution to the other banks in the city "for the purpose of ascertaining whether they will not concur in so salutary a measure." From this time forward the endorsement of checks became common practice. The Manhattan Company further refined procedures in 1816 by requiring "all the persons composing a house or firm" to write their names "in the signature book." Obviously the increase in the number of customers was making it difficult for bank employees to know personally everyone associated with the various firms. Fritz Redlich summarized well these and related developments. "The use of checks ... increased parallel with the growth of demand deposits; but [even as late as 1832] the check was still in its infancy."[27]

Also in their infancy were internal controls over tellers and

---

[27]Ibid., 1:224 (December 29, 1806); 2:16 (October 20, 1808); 3:24 (August 8, 1816); Redlich, *Molding*, 1:51. For other references to counterfeiting, see MC Minutes, 1:72 (April 16, 1800),1:104-105 (July 1, 1802), 2:12 (August 8, 1808), 2:68 (February 1, 1810), 2:90 (October 25, 1810), 2:185 (August, 1813), 4:30 (April 24, 1820), 5:18 (October 18, 1824).

their cash. As a contemporary wrote, "New modes of error are turning up every day. No Teller has ever yet reached the end of them, and never will, while the firm of Cunning, Carelessness & Co., does half the world's business."[28] Throughout this period, the Manhattan Company regularly appointed committees of directors to count the tellers' cash. Often these committees found large differences in the accounts. In 1807 the differences stood at $5,057.61.[29] Between 1807 and 1826 the tellers' cash showed total differences of $23,978.15.[30] In 1824 the Board of Directors tried to determine who was responsible for these large losses. The cashier, Robert White, sought to remove himself from blame by stating that the "President [Henry Remsen] was responsible for the Clerks and everything else." At a subsequent meeting Remsen countered that "he thought the Cashier should take some responsibility, that he spoke as a Director not as the President, but there was no Director to second him."[31] This was an unusual situation, since in most other banks the Cashier was directly responsible for the clerks and the president

---

[28]Gibbons, *Banks of New York*, 172.

[29]MC Minutes, 1:226 (January 5, 1807).

[30]MC Journal No. 6, June 29, 1826. See also MC Minutes, 1:225-226 (December 31, 1806), 2:56 (August 28, 1809), 2:59-60 (October 19, 1809), 3:185 (March 15, 1819), 5:16-17 (October 4, 1824), and 5:89 (January 11, 1827).

[31]Ibid., 5:1-2 (July 3, 1824), 16-17 (October 4, 1824).

was largely a figurehead. Apparently Remsen's long experience in banking made him the key person in supervising the clerks.

As serious as were these errors in handling cash, even more alarming were outright thefts by tellers. During the Remsen years, the Manhattan Company experienced one major incident. In 1803 one of the bookkeepers, Benjamin Brower, substituted one Saturday for an ill receiving teller. At the end of the day he stole $10,000 and quickly left the city. Brower was apprehended in Boston two months later; ultimately the Manhattan Company recovered all but $877.60 of the stolen funds.

The Manhattan Company found out later that Brower was involved in another fraud. In addition to his duties as a Manhattan Company bookkeeper, Brower worked part-time for another person, David Lydig, who happened to be a Manhattan Company customer. As it turned out, Brower's bank responsibilities included keeping the ledger in which Lydig's account was located. Brower's second fraud involved depositing only part of Lydig's money in the bank, keeping the rest for himself. As a result, Lydig's account was overdrawn on the bank's books. Lydig refused to pay the overdraft, arguing that "money intended to be deposited in the Bank and delivered to any officer of the Bank, amounted to a deposit." The Manhattan Company eventually compromised with Lydig in 1810.[32]

---

[32]For Brower's theft, see ibid., 1:132 (September 1, 1803),

In all of these cases -- overdrafts, forgeries, employee differences, and thefts -- the management of the Manhattan Company, despite its best efforts, had difficulty controlling the situation. One might think that such a litany of problems would lead the board of directors to lose confidence in the bank managers, especially Henry Remsen. On the contrary, the board retained Remsen and even increased his authority in another area, the lending of the bank's funds.

Early banks dealt with a number of different credit instruments. In general, they fell into two broad categories: "real" paper and "accommodation" paper. Real paper consisted of promissory notes or bills of exchange generated in actual business transactions. These were short-term loans based on the sale of merchandise and therefore were considered to be relatively "safe." By way of contrast, accommodation loans were not based on a specific business transaction. Rather, they were advances of capital often for investment purposes. Technically, accommodation loans were granted for short periods of time. However regular renewal became the norm, creating, in effect, a long-term loan. Because there were

---

132-133 (September 8, 1803), 133 (October 17, 1803), 133-134 (October 27, 1803). Also MC Journal No. 1, May 28, 1805; Remsen to William Edgar, September 22, 1803, November 11, 1803, Edgar Papers, Vol. 8, NYPL; Remsen to Chancellor Lansing, January 13, 1806, Remsen Papers, Box 1, Folder 10, NYPL. For the Lydig affair, see MC Minutes, 2:86-87 (July 19, 1810).

no business transactions supporting accommodation loans, they were considered riskier than real paper. Commenting on the lengthening terms of accommodation loans, Bray Hammond concluded that "the tradition of short-term credit continued to be held in pious respect and bankers liked to pretend that they were faithful to it."[33]

When nineteenth century banks extended credit, it was one of two types: deposit credit or banknote credit. Deposit credit is the type with which we are familiar today: a person deposits money into an account and gradually expends it by checks. With banknote credit, a borrower received the loan amount in the form of notes issued by and redeemable for specie at a particular bank. These bank notes tended to circulate as currency, thereby preventing a wide circulation of specie. As Fritz Redlich said, "the lending of funds in the form of bank notes became the essential feature of American banking from the outset. For decades to come, in America banking was synonymous with note issue and one cannot understand the contemporary

---

[33]Hammond, *Banks and Politics*, 192. For a further discussion of the differences between real and accommodation paper, see Gibbons, *Banks of New York*, 59-60, 215. Redlich, *Molding*, 1:10-11. Naomi R. Lamoreaux, "The Structure of Early Banks in Southeastern New England: Some Social and Economic Implications," *Business and Economic History*, 2nd ser. 13 (1984): 173. Donald J. Adams, *Finance and Enterprise in Early America: A Study of Stephen Girard's Bank* (Philadelphia: University of Pennsylvania Press, 1978), 102, 122-123. Thomas C. Cochran, *200 Years of American Business* (New York: Basic Books, 1977), 33. J. Van Fenstermaker, *The Development of American Commercial Banking, 1782-1837* (Kent, Ohio: Bureau of Economic and Business Research, Kent State University, 1965), 45-47.

sources before the Civil War unless this specific American meaning of the term 'banking' is kept in mind."[34]

In the nineteenth century, the lending of a bank's funds also had political overtones. As will be recalled, one of the reasons Burr and other Republican leaders surreptitiously established a bank was the fact that Federalists held a monopoly over New York City's banking resources. The Manhattan Company, therefore, was intended to supply capital to emerging Republican business interests.[35]

Because of the centrality of the loan function, most early bank boards retained tight control over the process. The Manhattan Company was no exception. The common practice was for the entire board to vote on each loan or "discount."[36] Most banks designated

---

[34]Redlich, *Molding*, 1:12. For the difference between deposit and banknote credit, see Seavoy, *Origins*, 55-56; and Adams, *Finance and Enterprise*, 1-2. Banks also issued two types of notes: "demand" notes (payable on demand), and "post" notes (payable on a specified later date). See Redlich, *Molding*, 1:13; Fenstermaker, *Development*, 32-33. For an example of this difference in the Manhattan Company's records, see Journal No. 1, June 9, 1803. In this case, the post notes were payable "three days after date." The Manhattan Company also was involved in embryonic investment banking through the practice of "loan contracting," which really involved setting up an investment syndicate. See Redlich, *Molding*, 2:304-333; Adams, *Finance and Enterprise*, 114.

[35]For more on the political nature of New York banks and their policies, see Lee Benson, *The Concept of Jacksonian Democracy: New York as a Test Case* (Princeton: Princeton University Press, 1961), 86-109. Alvin Kass, *Politics in New York State, 1800-1830* (Syracuse: Syracuse University Press, 1965), 95-97.

[36]"Discounts" and "loans" are virtually the same. The former differs from the latter in that the borrower pays the interest

two discount days per week, with the unanimous consent of all directors present necessary to approve a loan. In effect the board of directors, composed mainly of merchants, passed on the credit-worthiness of other merchants.[37]

The Manhattan Company gradually moved away from this practice of full board approval of all discounts. In 1807 the directors decided that two negative votes, rather than just one, would be required to veto a discount. In 1821 they delegated loan decisions to a "Standing Committee" of the board. And finally, in 1824 the directors permitted the "President and Cashier ... to discount and make loans on what they deemed good security."[38]

This last action was a radical departure from previous standard policies: it almost totally divorced the directors from the lending

---

at the beginning of the loan, rather than over the loan's entire term. See Adams, *Finance and Enterprise*, 199-201.

[37]See "Regulations for the Office of Discount and Deposit" in the MC Minutes, 1:40-43 (August 13, 1799). See also Hammond, *Banks and Politics*, 74-75; Gibbons, *Banks of New York*, 26-48.

[38]MC Minutes, 1:231 (March 5, 1807); 4:119 (July 12, 1821); 4:257 (April 22, 1824); and 6:145-147 (January 27, 1841). For other changes in the discount policy, see ibid., 1:49 (August 27, 1799); 1:75 (May 9, 1800); 1:192 (June 17, 1805); 1:223 (December 22, 1806); 1:230 (January 26, 1807); 2:9 (May 16, 1808); 2:157 (June 8, 1812); 2:166 (September 14, 1812); 2:214 (July 21, 1814); 2:215 (August 15, 1814); 2:232-244 (April 12, 1815); 2:260 (October 19, 1815); 3:8-9 (March 14, 1816); 3:67 (November 17, 1817); 3:72-73 (December 8, 1817); 3:141 (September 19, 1818); 4:18 (February 28, 1820); 4:161 (April 22, 1822); 4:173 (June 20, 1822); 4:210 (June 5, 1823). For a sample discount entry, see Journal No. 1, June 25, 1804.

of bank funds. This change also gave a great deal of authority to the officers of the bank. With officers as responsible and careful as Henry Remsen, the board's trust was well placed.[39] But with people of a lesser caliber, the bank could be in a very precarious position. If this was combined with a tight money situation requiring the bank to call in a large number of questionable loans, the result could be disaster and public ridicule. This is precisely what occurred at the Manhattan Company following the Panic of 1837.

This is not to say that the Manhattan Company never called in loans before 1840. Whenever credit became tight, the company decreased its outstanding loans, usually by requiring a percentage reduction in each accommodation loan at the time of next renewal. From time to time the company also raised the interest rate on new discounts. Most times the public took these actions in stride. In fact, there is one case where the customer apparently took the situation better than did Remsen. In 1822 Augustus C. Van Horne wrote to Remsen that he had "just received [Remsen's] friendly note of this day, intimating that the banks are reducing their

---

[39]Remsen was precise and meticulous, concerned not just with profit and loss, but also with the propriety of actions. For example, John and Gerard DePeyster, relatives of Remsen's wife, asked for an overnight loan of Manhattan Company funds, which Remsen approved. When the DePeyster business soon failed, Remsen personally reimbursed the Manhattan Company for the lost funds. See the correspondence of Remsen and Charles Wilson Peale concerning the DePeyster estate, October 29, 1816 - November 11, 1820, Remsen Papers, Box 1, NYPL.

accommodation paper of which I've not been unmindful since our last conversations on that subject. My good friend," Van Horne continued, "you seem to be ashamed, but I am not conscious of anything having taken place to weaken that confidence which you have hitherto had in me." As Van Horne understood, the contraction of credit was a normal part of the business ebb and flow.[40]

During this time the Manhattan Company also began a second loan practice which subjected the company to ridicule at a later date. As with other banks, the Manhattan Company committed a considerable portion of its resources to "insider" loans, particularly to directors. Naomi Lamoreaux has discussed this practice in New England banks, noting that banks truly became "engines to supply directors with money." In New England, banks provided financial cement to long-standing ties of kinship and marriage.[41] In New York, bank loans also reinforced political connections and alliances. In the case of the Manhattan Company, the detailed

---

[40]Augustus C. Van Horne to Remsen, June 1, 1822, Remsen Papers, Box 1, Folder 10, NYPL. For the reductions in accommodation loans, see MC Minutes, 2:214 (July 21, 1814); 2:215 (August 15, 1814); 3:141 (September 19, 1818). For other board actions concerning outstanding debts, bad loans, etc., see Ibid., 2:76 (May 10, 1810); 2:83 (June 25, 1810); 2:106 (January 31, 1811); 2:112 (May 23, 1811); 3:75 (December 11, 1817); 3:78 (December 31, 1817); 3:131 (October 12, 1818); 3:138 (November 12, 1818); 3:204 (May 13, 1819); 4:38 (May 22, 1820); 4:242 (January 8, 1824); 5:8 (August 6, 1824). Also MC Journal No. 1, March 24, 1806; Journal No. 5, June 24, 1822. Gibbons, *Banks of New York*, 197-198.

[41]Lamoreaux, "Structure of Early Banks," 175-178.

ledgers which would prove this point no longer exist. It is possible, however, to get a sense of the extent of the practice from some of the correspondence which did survive.

Particularly interesting are the papers of William Edgar, a wealthy merchant and director of the Manhattan Company. There are letters from Henry Remsen discussing discounts made to Edgar, such as the $27,000 note presented on July 16, 1803. There also are numerous letters to Edgar from other individuals seeking Edgar's support in obtaining discounts from the Manhattan Company. For example, Gordon S. Mumford wrote from the House of Representatives in 1808 stating that he had applied for a temporary loan from the Manhattan Company. "Your friendly aid," he wrote to Edgar, "will greatly oblige me." In 1811 Edgar received a number of requests for assistance with discounts, such as the $5,000 request of Jacob Barkers. Logic would indicate that other directors received similar requests for assistance from friends and colleagues; there is no reason to think Edgar was unique in this regard. As a result, directors of the Manhattan Company (and probably other banks as well) controlled a large portion of the capital discounted, both in terms of loans to themselves and because of their influence over loans to others.[42]

---

[42]Remsen to Edgar, July 16, 1803, Edgar Papers, vol. 8, NYPL. Mumford to Edgar, January 19, 1808, vol. 10, ibid. Barkers to Edgar, June 24, 1811, vol. 11, ibid. Edgar's support also was solicited for other company business, such as the election of directors in 1801 and 1802. See J.A. Fairlie to Edgar, December 11,

This practice often was the object of public criticism. In 1811, for example, the Manhattan Company directors felt the need to respond to the "insidious and injurious reports" then in circulation. According to these reports, directors who "receive discounts here, apply their money to usurious purposes, or take advantage of the necessity of others, to extort unreasonable interest or profit on money advanced." The board resolved to "disclaim" such conduct as detrimental to the institution and its directors. Furthermore, even though the board "disbelieved" the reports, they decided that any director involved in "usurious transactions" would be considered an "unworthy member" and not receive additional discounts. As for the people who "raise and propagate such scandalous reports respecting the directors," the board decided that "unless they name the individual Director and substantiate the fact," they would "cease to have the confidence of the Board, and be denied discounts."[43] While these actions may have alleviated the immediate crisis, they did not remove the resentment against directors who had an inside

---

1801, vol. 8, ibid.; Aaron Burr to Edgar, December 7, 1802, vol. 8, ibid. Records also exist for some other key individuals. For Daniel Delany of London, one of the largest shareholders of the company, see Remsen Papers, 1815, Box 1, Folder 10, NYPL. For Robert R. Livingston, see Livingston Papers, NYHS; Remsen Papers, 1806, Box 1, Folder 10, NYPL. For Gouverneur Morris, see Morris Papers, 1808, Columbia University. For John Jacob Astor, see Record Group 1, Box 1, 1802-1803, CMB Archives.

[43]MC Minutes, 2:110-111 (March 11, 1811). Clinton to Remsen, March 16, 1811, Clinton Papers, NYPL.

track to discounts. This issue would resurface during the 1840 investigation of the company.

A few days later, Manhattan Company loan practices were attacked during a debate before the state Council of Revision. As DeWitt Clinton related to Remsen, "Govr. Lewis pronounced a philippic against the M.C." Lewis claimed that the Manhattan Company "courted his business" from the branch of the Bank of the United States and then "called in at once a note of 26,000 D & [made] him pay it up," even having a special meeting for this purpose. As Clinton was about to make "some severe animadversions," Lewis stopped him by saying that since Clinton was absent from this special meeting of the Manhattan Company board, Lewis did not mean to include Clinton in the charge. Since Clinton did not know the facts of the case, all he could do was "enter into a general justification of the *impartiality* of the Directors in all their proceedings as known by me -- the respectability of their characters &c." Even with this limited response, Clinton believed he had "succeeded in removing much of the unfavorable impression that might otherwise have existed." Nevertheless, Clinton asked Remsen to relate to him "the real facts of this case -- How long the note ran without deduction -- the quantity reduced at a time -- and whether it was reduced without notice &c." It seems as though Lewis' charges contained some grains

Henry Remsen, second president of the Manhattan Company, 1808–1825. (*Cour-tesy of the Chase Manhattan Archives.*)

of truth.[44]

To summarize, the main trend of the Remsen years in terms of loans and discounts was the increasing delegation of authority to the officers of the bank. As long as financial times were good, the wisdom of individual loans (except, perhaps, those made to outspoken politicians like Lewis) would not be so crucial. When times turned bad, however, the very existence of the company could depend upon the collectibility of outstanding debts. The great financial pressures after 1837 led to a resurfacing of many of the issues discussed above; the public outcry even forced the bank to make major changes in policies and staffing.

During the Remsen years, the bank was heavily involved with governments at all levels. One would expect no less, based upon the discussions in previous chapters about the founding and charter of the company and the operations of the water works.

Relations with the City of New York centered around two areas. First, since the city was a shareholder in the company, it was involved in the actual operations of the bank as well as the water works. Second, the Manhattan Company, as one of the most powerful banks in the city, was a natural source for possible financing of municipal activities. Throughout the Remsen years, these two aspects

---

[44]Clinton to Remsen, March 16, 1811, Clinton Papers, ibid.

were intimately related.

In terms of the management of the Manhattan Company, the city was guaranteed a voice because the Recorder of the city was an *ex officio* member of the board of directors. The resulting conflicts of interest are obvious, especially in those cases where the city was considering a purchase of the Manhattan Company's water works. Conflicts of interest, however, did not seem to bother nineteenth century business leaders, as shown by the example of DeWitt Clinton discussed in an earlier chapter.[45]

In addition to the Recorder, the city played a role because it was a shareholder in the company. According to the act incorporating the Manhattan Company, the city was permitted to buy 2,000 shares at $50 each; the city quickly did so. Thereafter the city government had to select someone to vote the shares at the annual election of Manhattan Company directors. In general, when DeWitt Clinton was mayor, he voted the city's Manhattan Company shares. In effect, Clinton was voting for himself, since he also served as a Manhattan Company director.[46] The choice of a person to vote the city's

[45]The Recorder remained an ex officio member of the board of directors of the Manhattan Company until 1908, when the office of Recorder was abolished.

[46]The *Minutes of the Common Council* contain the following references to the voting of the Manhattan Company's shares.

shares eventually became moot: after 1811 the city gradually sold its shares in the Manhattan Company. This sale was hastened, no doubt, by the Federalists who controlled the Common Council from 1809 to 1816.[47]

The political connections between the city and the Manhattan Company also are shown by the city's borrowing of funds during Remsen's tenure. In 1799 for example, the city borrowed money to purchase its allotted shares of Manhattan Company stock.[48] Over the next few years the city frequently borrowed from the Manhattan

Year	Person Voting	Citation From Minutes
1799	Richard Varick (Mayor)	2:582 (January 11, 1799)
1801	Philip Brasher	3:62 (November 30, 1801)
1802	Robert Lenox	3:152 (November 29, 1802)
1803	Philip Brasher	3:399 (November 21, 1803)
1804	DeWitt Clinton (Mayor)	3:645 (December 3, 1804)
1806	DeWitt Clinton (Mayor)	4:306 (December 1, 1806)
1807	Robert Bogardus	4:644 (December 1, 1807)
1808	DeWitt Clinton (Mayor)	5:363 (December 5, 1808)
1810	Josiah Hoffman (Recorder)	6:404 (December 1, 1810)
1811	DeWitt Clinton (Mayor)	6:773 (December 2, 1811)
1813	Peter Mesier (Alderman)	7:635 (December 6, 1813)

[47]For the sale of stock, see *Minutes of the Common Council*, 7:716 (March 14, 1814) and 8:124 (January 9, 1815). In 1804 the Common Council defeated a motion to "form a Committee to consider selling New York City's stock in the Manhattan Company." Ibid., 3:449 (January 16, 1804) On this issue see also Nelson M. Blake, *Water for the Cities: A History of the Urban Water Supply Problem in the United States* (Syracuse: Syracuse University Press, 1956), 107.

[48]The *Minutes of the Common Council* indicate that the city borrowed $67,500 for the purpose. See 2:559 (July 15, 1799); 2:566 (August 19, 1799); 2:570 (September 9, 1799); 2:586 (December 12, 1799); 2:610 (February 17, 1800); and 2:641 (June 30, 1800). For the repayment of $25,000 of this total, See MC Journal No. 1, March 14, 1800, March 28, 1800, and April 7, 1800.

Company, with the result that by 1807 the city owed the Manhattan Company $102,715.80 in principal and interest. This was two-thirds of the total municipal debt of $159,656.80.[49]

The city's debt to the Manhattan Company continued to rise. By 1810 the debt totaled over $160,000, prompting Remsen to write to the city government requesting payment on "some of the Bonds" due the company.[50] One group in the Common Council recommended selling the Manhattan Company stock in order to retire the city's debt; they were not able, however, to convince a majority of the council of the wisdom of this action. Instead, the city decided to borrow money from other institutions in order to discharge the debt to the Manhattan Company. Two days later the city borrowed $60,000 from the New York Insurance Company.[51]

The municipal debt remained a sore point throughout 1810. It

---

[49]*Minutes of the Common Council*, 4:330 (January 5, 1807). For the various loans, see MC Minutes, 1:99 (December 21, 1801), 1:196 (July 29, 1805), 1:213 (July 9, 1806); MC Journal No. 1, August 1, 1805, September 5, 1805; *Minutes of the Common Council*, 4:55 (July 29, 1805), 4:80 (September 18, 1805), 4:122 (January 6, 1806), 4:182 (April 21, 1806), 4:242 (July 7, 1806), 4:261 (August 18, 1806), and 4:265 (September 1, 1806).

[50]Ibid., 6:48 (January 29, 1810). For events between 1807 and 1810, see ibid., 4:695 (January 4, 1808), 5:215 (July 25, 1808), 5:471 (March 13, 1809), 5:653-654 (August 28, 1809), 5:657 (September 4, 1809); MC Minutes, 2:10 (July 28, 1808), 2:17 (December 1, 1808), 2:40 (March 16, 1809), and 2:57 (September 4, 1809).

[51]*Minutes of the Common Council*, 6:60 (February 5, 1810), 6:69 (February 7, 1810).

was further complicated by the issue of where the city would deposit its funds. In September the city tried unsuccessfully to obtain a $20,000 loan from a number of banks in order to further reduce the debt owed to the Manhattan Company. One bank, the Mechanics Bank, offered to lend the money provided the city "open[ed] an account with said bank." By a vote of eight to six the Common Council defeated a motion to open an account with and accept a loan from the Mechanics Bank. The Common Council's reason was that "an account opened with [the Mechanics Bank] would change the deposits from the Manhattan Bank, in which last mentioned bank the Corporation [the City of New York] is a large stockholder." In October the city did borrow $50,000 dollars from the Phoenix Insurance Company which it applied against the Manhattan Company loans. Despite this, Remsen found it necessary to write to the city again in November requesting a further payment of the city's debt "in consequence of the applications by the dealers at the bank for discounts." As a result, the Common Council decided to borrow $100,000 from other sources, applying $80,000 to the Manhattan Company debt and using the remaining $20,000 to build a new City Hall.[52]

The State of New York also had multiple relationships with the

---

[52] Ibid., 6:344-345 (September 24, 1810), 6:349 (October 1, 1810), 6:356 (October 5, 1810), 6:394 (November 19, 1810). For an earlier discussion of where to deposit municipal funds, see ibid., 3:701 (March 7, 1805).

Manhattan Company: shareholder, customer, and employer. As will be recalled, the Manhattan Company's revised 1808 charter permitted the state to purchase 1,000 shares of company stock at a total price of $50,000. The state purchased the stock in April 1809.[53]

The state also was a customer of the company, especially for internal improvement funds. In 1808 the Manhattan Company loaned the state $200,000 for unspecified purposes. In 1818 the company agreed to loan the state $1 million at six percent interest for the Erie Canal. The latter case really was an embryonic form of investment banking and syndicate formation: the Manhattan Company agreed to let at least one other bank subscribe $400,000 of the loan amount.[54]

The final relationship involved the state's use of the Manhattan Company as "Transfer Agent." According to the agreement, the Cashier of the Manhattan Company would "perform the duties of issuing certificates, making transfers of and paying dividends on the [New York] State Stock, and all other duties relating to the same, without expense to the State." The Manhattan Company continued as

---

[53]For the purchase, see MC Minutes, 2:43 (April 25, 1809) and MC Journal No. 2, April 29, 1809. A 1927 article concluded that the state had received $1.3 million from this initial investment, an average return of over twenty percent per year for 119 years. "How New York State Has Profited as Stockholder in New York Bank," *Bankers Magazine*, November 1927, found in "General Reference and Misc. History," Record Group 1, Box 1, CMB Archives

[54]MC Minutes, 2:8 (April 25, 1808), 3:94-95 (May 21 - June 1, 1818), and 3:107 (July 13, 1818). See also Redlich, *Molding*, 2:329.

Transfer Agent for the state until well into the twentieth century.[55]

The Manhattan Company clearly used its political position to good advantage with the state and local governments during the Remsen years. Another source of leverage was the fact that both governments were shareholders in the company. This also was a legacy of the political nature of the bank's founding: the political connections influenced the deposit of municipal funds, the state's choice of a transfer agent, and the lending of money to both governments. As with other aspects of the Manhattan Company, it is impossible to separate economic decisions from the political and social environments.

An increasingly important part of the environment during the Remsen years was the emerging banking community. For example, just between 1811 and 1818 the New York State Legislature chartered twenty-three banks.[56] Because of its economic resources and political connections, the Manhattan Company became a leader among banks. This is evident when one looks at cooperative efforts among banks in the city, account relationships with "country" banks, and opposition to the further extension of the banking franchise to new

---

[55]MC Minutes, 3:100 (June 22, 1818).

[56]Seavoy, "Origins" diss., 96.

institutions.

During the Manhattan Company's first years, there were relatively few banks with which it could cooperate. Nevertheless, the company was involved with the Bank of New York, the Merchants Bank, and the New York branch of the Bank of the United States. In 1804 these banks met to discuss the "expediency" of trying to recover money owed by the Newark Banking and Insurance Company. In 1805 there was a general "conference" to discuss the "conduct and business" of the banks. In 1807 the banks met to recommend regulations to prevent overdrafts. And in 1808 the banks appointed representatives to discuss "the present state of commercial credit."[57]

The most significant cooperation among banks, however, took place in times of crisis. In particular the period around the end of the War of 1812, with its economic downturn and suspension of specie payments, forced the banks to cooperate. The Manhattan Company was a full participant in this cooperation. In August 1814 the company appointed representatives to a "General Committee of the Banks" to consider "the state of the Banks & of public credit" and to "adopt such measures for the relief of the merchants as may be deemed advisable." In a highly unusual action, the fiercely-independent

---

[57]MC Minutes, 1:157 (December 27, 1804); 1:161 (January 28, 1805); 1:206 (February 27, 1806); 1:232 (June 18, 1807); and 1:256 (March 3, 1808).

Manhattan Company directors decided to consider any resolutions passed by the General Committee to be "obligatory" on the company.[58]

Two weeks later the General Committee recommended a number of actions which the Manhattan Company board agreed to consider "as binding on this Institution for three months." Among the actions were:

1. The banks were to try to continue payments in specie.

2. If a bank could not pay in specie, "every aid shall be given by the other Institutions, consistent with their own safety."

3. Exchanges between banks would be made every morning "as usual," with a six percent interest on unpaid balances.

4. Debts between banks would be considered "due in specie." A bank's debt to another bank would take precedence over its other debts.

5. The banks would not increase the amounts of their loans and would try to decrease them.

6. Each Tuesday the cashiers would make reports to one another concerning specie on hand and debts due. These reports would be in strict confidence.

7. No bank would enter into a new contract to accept

---

[58]Ibid., 2:216 (August 19, 1814).

country bank notes.[59]

Despite these efforts, the banks still were forced to suspend specie payments. The General Committee met throughout the crisis, with Manhattan Company representatives in attendance. In April 1815 the committee passed two resolutions, one requiring debtor banks to gradually liquidate their obligations to other banks and a second directing all banks to try to resume specie payments as soon as possible. The Manhattan Company tried to comply by reducing its discounts; calling in loans, including those to New York State; and requiring all banks owing it money, including the company's own branches in Utica and Poughkeepsie, to pay the balances and avoid future debts.[60]

By the middle of 1816, however, the Manhattan Company's enthusiasm for cooperation waned. The company served notice that it would withdraw from "the association of the Banks" on July 1, 1817. The Manhattan Company minutes do not give a reason for this action. Before withdrawing, the company decided to settle its debts with other banks; the board approved the sale of $250,000 of United States stock, if necessary to achieve this objective. Following the board's decision, representatives of the other banks visited Remsen asking the Manhattan Company to reconsider. Remsen subsequently recommended

---

[59]Ibid., 2:216-219 (August 29, 1814).

[60]Ibid., 2:232-234 (April 12, 1815).

a reconsideration, but the board defeated the resolution and reaffirmed its decision to withdraw. After this, there is very little evidence of the Manhattan Company's cooperation with other banks. The only other reference in the minutes during the Remsen years was an 1822 meeting to consider moving the banks from the city "on account of the prevailing epidemic."[61]

Another indication of the growing community was the method of exchanging funds among banks. All urban banks faced the problem of collecting notes and drafts drawn on "country" banks of varying fiscal soundness. When this was combined with slow methods of communication, it created a situation fraught with risks for the banks receiving country bank notes. Most banks tried to minimize the risk by establishing "correspondent" relationships with trusted banks in various geographical regions and doing all collecting of funds through them.[62]

The first reference in the Manhattan Company journals to a relationship with another bank is from October, 1799. At that time the Manhattan Company exchanged $18,951 with the Bank of Pennsylvania

---

[61]Ibid., 3:13-14 (June 6-13, 1816); 4:178 (August 22, 1822). For a general discussion of cooperation among banks, see Redlich, *Molding*, 2:288-289.

[62]For general information about interbank relationships, see Redlich, *Molding*, 1:16, 51; Hammond, *Banks and Politics*, 550; Gibbons, *Banks of New York*, 173, 219: and Fenstermaker, *Development*, 42.

for five acceptances, one note, and four post notes.[63]   Eventually the Manhattan Company adopted the increasingly-common practice of exchanging notes with other banks as a way of establishing mutual credit. For example, in 1802 the Manhattan Company and the State Bank in Charleston established a relationship by exchanging $50,000 in notes. The accounts between the banks were to be settled monthly, with the debtor bank paying the creditor bank within thirty days.[64]

The following chart provides a rough measure of the growth of correspondent banking at the Manhattan Company. For each year I have listed the number of correspondent banks and the total number of transactions detailed in the Manhattan Company journals.

---

[63]MC Journal No. 1, October 23, 1799.

[64]MC Minutes, 1:108-109 (September 9, 1802). Another early example was the $20,000 exchange of notes with the Newark Banking and Insurance Company. Ibid., 1:148 (July 26, 1804).

Table 1
Growth of Correspondent Banking
at the Manhattan Company, 1799-1837

Year	No. of Banks	No of Transactions
1799	2	13
1800	2	125
1801	2	186
1802	2	112
1803	3	108
1804	3	123
1805	5	159
1806	4	166
1807	5	203
1808	5	189
1809	9	165
1810	9	233
1811	10	329
1812	12	265
1813	13	273
1814	16	313
1815	12	149
1816	12	139
1817	15	318
1818	16	473
1819	17	350
1820	19	318
1821	21	372
1822	21	384
1823	19	380
1824	21	441
1825	27	502
1826	26	540
1827	29	563
1828	30	593
1829	26	881
1830	24	807
1831	24	778
1832	22	159
1833	20	51
1834	38	306
1835	31	178
1836	27	96
1837	41	134

As one would expect, the banks in this increasingly-large total were of uneven fiscal quality. Many of the "country" banks became debtors to the Manhattan Company, especially during difficult economic times. In 1810 the Manhattan Company board considered charging debtor banks interest for the amount they owed the company. Remsen recommended against charging interest, however, noting that "accounts between Banks often vary, occasioned by trade sometimes taking one direction and at other times another." If the Manhattan Company charged interest, "when the time arrives when the accounts of the banks now in debt change, those Banks may ... demand" interest from the Manhattan Company.[65]

As the economy worsened after 1812, the Manhattan Company took additional actions. First, the company became more selective in establishing account relationships, deciding to deal only with "such other Banks as in their judgment may be deemed proper." In 1815 the company decided it would not receive the notes of unincorporated banks. By 1818 the directors concluded that "it will prove disadvantageous to the Company to allow balances to remain long in any bank." If a bank refused to pay its debt to the company, it would "be necessary to discontinue the collection of drafts ... thro' the instrumentality of such banks." Two months later the board

---

[65]"Motion and report concerning charging interest to debtor banks," October 25, 1810, Manhattan Company Records, NYHS.

instructed the president "to have balances due this Company from Banks out of the City ... liquidated with the least delay." In addition, the board decided not to accept for collection bills or notes "payable south of the City of Baltimore."[66]

The president, however, only had limited success reducing debts. In February 1819 the board learned that "none of the Banks out of the City, which were called upon ... to comply with their engagements, have done so, and that their omission ... had compelled the Company to pay considerable sums in specie, and also to reduce their discounts, which have proved materially injurious to the Company." As a result, the board decided to "change the system, which has so long prevailed, of redeeming the paper of Banks out of the City, beyond the funds which those Banks may have provided *in anticipation* for the purposes."[67] From this time forward, the Manhattan Company tried to avoid being creditor to distant banks. This concern was not an idle one: by 1825, ten of New York State's forty-three banks had failed, most in the years 1819 and 1820.[68]

At the same time that the Manhattan Company was wrestling with

---

[66]MC Minutes, 2:141 (April 9, 1812), 2:252 (August 24, 1815); 3:126-127 (September 24, 1818); and 3:135 (November 2, 1818).

[67]Ibid., 3:168-169 (February 1, 1819).

[68]Seavoy, *Origins*, 94. The first bank in the United States to fail was the Farmers Exchange Bank of Gloester, Rhode Island, in 1809. See Hammond, *Banks and Politics*, 172.

the question of how to deal with debtor banks, it was involved in efforts to limit further competition by blocking the chartering of new banks. As with so many other cases in the Manhattan Company's history, DeWitt Clinton played a central role in the drama.

At the outset it is important to keep in mind that the chartering of banks in New York State in the first half of the nineteenth century involved more than economic considerations. A legislative grant of a banking franchise was more a political than an economic accomplishment. Closely restricting the granting of bank charters gave Republicans another means of rewarding the faithful and punishing opponents. As a contemporary said, since the 1820's "opposition to banks has been a lever in the hands of politicians, with ignorance as its chief fulcrum, to keep parties in office."[69]

A clear example of the political nature of state banking activities is found in the correspondence between DeWitt Clinton and Henry Remsen from 1810 to 1812. During those years, Clinton was

---

[69]Gibbons, *Banks of New York*, 11. See also Sylla, "Early American Banking," 119; Hammond, *Banks and Politics*, 577; and Seavoy, "Origins" diss., 102, 269. Alvin Kass' summary of the subject is a good one: "As far as the chartering of banks is concerned ... the legislative debates were not between some groups that felt that banks were a good thing and others that regarded them as evil ventures, but rather differences centered around the question of whether one ought to enrich oneself by acquiring stock in newly chartered institutions, or whether one's stockholdings in already existing companies would be jeopardized in value by the creation of rival banking operations." *Politics in New York State, 1800-1830* (Syracuse: Syracuse University Press, 1965), 95.

Lieutenant Governor, Mayor of New York City, and a director of the Manhattan Company. Clinton kept Remsen and the directors of the Manhattan Company informed of all legislative activities in the area of banking and did everything he could to prevent harm to the Manhattan Company's interests. At the same time, Clinton had his own interests protected by the Manhattan Company's regular renewal of his notes as they became due.[70]

As discussed above, one interest the Manhattan Company had during these years was reducing the debts owed to it. Clinton played a role in reducing New York State's debt to the company. He conferred with the state comptroller about the repayment of funds and concluded there was "no other way of satisfying the demand of the Manhattan Company" than by having the state borrow sufficient funds from another institution, most likely the Bank of New York. Clinton saw "no objection to this mode and no evil consequences from making the demand" on the state. Clinton's only fear was that the comptroller would be removed for political reasons before the arrangement could be finalized. In typical Clintonian fashion, he

---

[70]For examples of requests for renewals of notes, see Clinton to Remsen, February 4, 1810, April 3, 1810, June 30, 1810, and February 5, 1811, Clinton Papers, NYPL. Concerning Clinton's finances, Remsen wrote the following to his son many years later: "I was told this day, that Governor Clinton's pecuniary affairs were in a most wretched condition, which is much to be regretted, as he has expended a large fortune in benevolent and hospitable acts." Remsen to Henry Rutgers Remsen, February 28, 1828, Folder 3, Remsen Papers, NYPL.

concluded that this removal would "be injurious to us and ... to the public." With Clinton's lobbying, a bill ultimately passed authorizing the comptroller to borrow from one bank to pay another. "Our political news is good in all directions," Clinton wrote in reporting this action. "I shall try and get you the 200,000 Dollars [repayment] from the State before I return [to New York City]."[71]

Clinton's results were more mixed when the issue before the legislature was the chartering of new banks. Some institutions, such as the Mechanics Bank, received charters: the mechanics as a group were so politically powerful that "neither party dare oppose the incorporation."[72] In other cases, proposed banks were defeated in the Senate after receiving approval in the Assembly. In Clinton's words, the Assembly appeared "to be totally indifferent to the public good. Their whole aim is unprincipled electioneering. We must meet our antagonists at every point. Their efforts seem to be heightened by desperation and they stick at nothing."[73]

The debate remained just as impassioned during 1811 -- Clinton more than once referred to the situation in Albany as "Banking

---

[71]The New York State loan is discussed in letters from Clinton to Remsen dated February 4, 1810, February 20, 1810, February 24, 1810, March 5, 1810, March 15, 1810, and March 20, 1810, Clinton Papers, NYPL.

[72]Clinton to Remsen, March 20, 1810, March 15, 1810, ibid.

[73]Clinton to Remsen, April 3, 1810, ibid. The Assembly had passed bills to establish banks at Utica, Catskill, and Newburgh.

Mania." He believed that the subject of increased banking capital "was not properly understood and the danger not rightly estimated." Clinton, therefore, tried to give legislators a "full view of the terrible consequences that might result from the extension of banks." In one case, Clinton opposed the chartering of the City Bank, Long Island Bank, and Western District Bank, with a combined proposed capital of three million dollars. "I have encountered much ill will and expect to encounter more for my conduct on this occasion," wrote Clinton, "but I have acted from the most mature consideration and from the purest motives and with a single view to the best interests of our Country and so acting I feel the approbation of my conscience." By way of contrast, Clinton denigrated the proponents of the City Bank by saying they "call[ed] out the Members [of the legislature] into the lobbies and whisper[ed] like Satan into the ear of Eve." Ironically, these same vipers "have received and still receive abundant favors from our institution -- and I think they ought to be the last men to complain of the want of pecuniary accommodation."[74]

Much to Clinton chagrin, banking mania returned in 1812 in an

---

[74]Clinton to Remsen, February 5, 1811; March 16, 1811; March 20, 1811; March 22, 1811; March 26, 1811; March 28, 1811; March 30, 1811; and April 1, 1811, Clinton Papers, NYPL. Clinton to William Edgar, April 2, 1811, Edgar Papers, Vol. 11, NYPL. See also the tally sheets of legislative votes found in Box 1, Folder 12 of the Remsen Papers, NYPL.

even more virulent form: the agitation for a "Six Million Bank." Clinton feared this bank would be "a great Leviathan that will eventually swallow up the small ones." He promised to "do all I can consistent with my official Station to prevent an augmentation of banks." Remsen communicated Clinton's concerns to the Manhattan Company directors who were of the opinion that "there is more banking capital in this City already than its proper wants require." Nevertheless, the directors decided not to dispatch someone to Albany to lobby against the Leviathan. Rather, they told Clinton they would be "constrained to rely on such exertions as you will be able to make."[75]

The debate over the Six Million Bank, more properly called the Bank of America,[76] took a nasty turn. At one time the legislative galleries were cleared "on an allegation that attempts had been made to bribe two members by offers of money." In Clinton's view, "That corruption has been practised is highly probable but whether it will be discovered is extremely doubtful." While this particular instance of bribery may have been very visible, it was not unique. In Bray Hammond's words, it was the "bribery that disgraced legislative

---

[75]Clinton to Remsen, March 3, 1812, Clinton Papers, NYPL. Remsen to Clinton, March 9, 1812, Box 1, Folder 10, Remsen Papers, NYPL.

[76]This is not the same as the bank chartered in California which eventually became one of the largest in the world.

action on bank charters" which led to the provision in the 1821 state constitution requiring two-thirds approval of each house on bills dealing with incorporation.[77]

I have related at length the cases above in order to show Clinton's frequent and substantive correspondence with Remsen and the Manhattan Company. In Clinton's own words, he did this "in order to make you complete Master of all our banking knowledge."[78] It is hard to believe that Clinton would have gone to this extreme with other banks in the state. Clearly, he kept Remsen and the Manhattan Company informed to such an extent because he viewed them as allies in a political as well as an economic struggle. In nineteenth century New York, the two were intimately related.[79]

---

[77]Clinton to Remsen, March 13, 1812, March 24, 1812, June 1, 1812, Clinton Papers, NYPL. Hammond, *Banks and Politics*, 577-579. For more on the Manhattan Company's efforts to block the chartering of the Bank of America, see MC Minutes, 2:142 (April 13, 1812), 2:147-153 (April 29, 1812), 2:153-154 (May 7, 1812). The Manhattan Company also tried unsuccessfully to get other New York City banks to submit a joint petition to the legislature opposing the Bank of America.

[78]Clinton to Remsen, March 24, 1812, Clinton Papers, NYPL.

[79]For more on Clinton's efforts to block the chartering of other banks, see Dorothie Bobbe, *DeWitt Clinton*, Empire State Historical Publication 11 (Port Washington, New York: Ira J. Friedman, Inc., 1933), 177-78. Clinton and Remsen also were close personal friends. This is shown by two of Clinton's letters to Remsen five months before Remsen married Elizabeth DePeyster. On March 16, 1808 he wrote: "I am rejoiced to hear of your brilliant prospects at the Northern End of the Town. Go on my friend in this praiseworthy course. Settle yourself down in the arms of an affectionate wife -- and depend upon it, after all our toils and

What, then, can we conclude about the Remsen years at the Manhattan Company? Four things come to mind. First, the period after 1799 was a time of innovation in banking, with a groping for solutions to problems. For example, Remsen and his peers were trying to establish policies and procedures in such areas as internal controls at the same time that an expanding population made it increasingly difficult to know one's customers, whether they be individuals or other banks. The structure of banking was evolving in the face of an increasingly complex social and economic environment.

Second, while bank officers assumed greater responsibilities throughout this period, the degree and speed of change was a factor of the qualifications of the bank officers. Remsen, as one of the first professional bankers, was given a great deal of latitude by the Manhattan Company directors. This is shown most clearly in the area of discounts and loans. Therefore in the case of the Manhattan Company, the policies and procedures in certain areas changed at a

---

struggles in making money and in gratifying ambition, but true happiness is not to be found beyond our fine wives." Five days later Clinton wrote, "when you see your Dulcinea tell her that I hope the intended and happy change in her state will I trust be the cause of introducing me to the honor of her acquaintance in the respectable character of the wife of my friend." Clinton Papers, Folder 3, NYPL. Remsen's wife died tragically a few years later: "My dear wife, Elizabeth, died the 25th of August 1826 a little past 3 o'clock p.m. Her youngest child was born on Monday the 14th of August preceding (eleven days before her death). She was in the 39th year of her age." Remsen Papers, Folder 12, ibid.

faster rate than that experienced by the rest of the banking world.

Third, politics and economics were intimately linked during this time, with conflicts of interest a common occurrence. For example, both the state and the city were shareholders as well as customers. Also, the Manhattan Company, as a Republican powerhouse, was regularly informed about political actions that would affect its economic position and responded accordingly. Strategy and structure clearly were influenced by the political events of the day, with DeWitt Clinton serving as a clearinghouse for information and locus of action.

And fourth, in the center of all this activity was Henry Remsen: supervising clerks; granting and calling in loans; establishing correspondent relationships with distant banks; and, perhaps most importantly, dealing with politicians at the city and state levels. It would be easy to say that the growth of the Manhattan Company's banking operations between 1799 and 1825 was "inevitable," based upon its political connections. Such a view, however, would fail to take into account Remsen's influence upon the institution. There are numerous cases in nineteenth century America of other businesses with promising futures.[80] At the Manhattan

---

[80]For example, the Society for Useful Manufactures in New Jersey also had a large capital, perpetual charter, and the support of Alexander Hamilton. Despite these elements in its favor, the company's works were closed down in 1796 after a considerable loss of capital and without any return whatever to the investors. See Joseph

Company, the difference was Henry Remsen's leadership for the first twenty-five years of corporate existence. Perhaps Remsen's importance can best be illustrated by outlining what happened at the Manhattan Company after he left.

The Post-Remsen Years, 1826-1842

Remsen's successors at the Manhattan Company had a firm foundation upon which to build. But while they did not have to face the problems of trying to *establish* an institution, they did have to steer the institution through unchartered waters: changing political approaches to banking, such as the Safety Fund System and the "free banking" statutes; volatile economic conditions during the 1820s and 1830s; and a major public investigation of the company's operations at the end of the period.

The political sphere in which the Manhattan Company and other New York banks operated changed dramatically in the late 1820s. This was due to a unique combination of circumstances involving chartered banks: thirty-one of the forty charters would expire within the next few years. In the past, extending a bank charter would not have been a major difficulty provided one had the proper political connections. A major complicating factor now, however, was New York

---

Stancliffe Davis, *Essays in the Earlier History of American Corporations* (Cambridge: Harvard University Press, 1917; reprint, New York: Russell and Russell, 1965), 2:275-6.

State's 1821 constitution which required two-thirds approval in both houses for granting or modifying charters. Since this constitutional requirement would make it difficult to re-charter banks individually, there was a strong incentive for both politicians and bank officials to find a collective solution to the problem. Also providing an incentive for a new approach was the continuing criticism of the public toward banks. In particular, the expansion of chartered banks in the previous decades led to the issuing of a large number of bank notes of questionable value. Since the public still considered chartered banks to be franchises advancing the common good, there was pressure on politicians to use this window of re-chartering opportunity to benefit the community.[81]

Some individuals recommended advancing the public interest through "free banking," which was first proposed officially in New York State in 1825. The concept was developed in Scotland before 1760 and centered on the premise that banking should be a "free trade" open to all qualified individuals or groups. While I will discuss this concept further below, it is important to note that free banking was not attractive to the Republican hierarchy, known as the Albany Regency,[82] because it would have divorced banking from

---

[81]Redlich, *Molding*, 1:88-89.

[82]"The active management of the successful party was held in the capable hands of that extraordinary group of seasoned politicians known to posterity, as well as to their contemporaries,

politics. Rather than permitting this separation, the Regency first tried to strengthen and improve the existing banking structure.[83]

The Regency's solution to the problem was the Safety Fund System, which is similar to the modern Federal Deposit Insurance Company. The Safety Fund Act of 1829 attempted to remove the stigma from banks by guaranteeing the value of the notes they circulated. This marked the first time that American legislators recognized an obligation to protect the creditors of banks. The fund was raised by

---

as the Albany Regency. This body, formed originally during the post-bellum period when everyone was professing allegiance to the party of Monroe, had consisted at first of William L. Marcy, Samuel A. Talcott, Benjamin F. Butler, Martin Van Buren, Azariah C. Flagg, Edwin Croswell, Silas Wright, and some others. They were all men of keen intellect, political imagination, shrewd practical sense, and untiring energy; men, too, of undoubted integrity, honest in public as well as in private life. They did not, however, disdain the work of practical politics; as a high-minded apologist says, 'They had sense enough to know that, when they were in power, they could be served better in places of trust by their friends than by their enemies ... and they acted accordingly.' They were among the first to practice and perfect many of the political devices that became the commonplaces of the next generation. The legislative caucus -- not for nominating, but for binding a too lax majority -- the official newspaper as an expounder of doctrine they wished to be believed, and, as above stated, the unconcealed use of patronage as a mighty argument for regularity, were peculiarly their work. Yet, in a broader sense, they conceived their dominant position as affording them a unique opportunity to serve the state through mastery." Herbert D.A. Donovan, *The Barnburners: A Study of the Internal Movements in the Political History of New York State and of the Resulting Changes in Political Affiliation, 1830-1852* (New York: New York University Press, 1925; reprint, Philadelphia: Porcupine Press, 1974), 7-8.

[83]For the Scottish roots of free banking, see Redlich, *Molding*, 1:187-196. For the 1825 introduction of the concept into New York State, see Hammond, *Banks and Politics*, 573.

assessing all participating banks (at first, all those whose charters required renewal) an annual tax of one-half of one percent of their capital until they contributed three percent of their capitalization. The fund was to be used to pay the debts of insolvent banks. As Stephen Allen stated, "the careful and provident were to be made answerable for the carelessness, inexperience, or fraudulence of the others." Another key part of the system was the creation of a Bank Commission to inspect the financial practices of participating banks. The was the first permanent state-wide independent regulatory commission in the United States.

Looking at the Safety Fund System as a whole, Bray Hammond concluded that it "was of great practical and political importance. It made the banks of the State of New York a system not only strong and worthy of public trust but congenial to the Albany Regency."[84] Henry Remsen's view of the Safety Fund System was less favorable. "In the upper parts of our State, Banks are asked for small towns where there is not a dollar that can be spared to buy Stock; but the object is to get a Charter, make notes and send them to the Cities for circulation, and send their bank Stock also for sale, and if they

---

[84]For general information on the Safety Fund System, see Redlich, *Molding*, 1:88-91. Hammond, *Banks and Politics*, 352. Seavoy, "Origins" diss., 131-135, 158, 242. "Stephen Allen Memoirs," 116, NYPL.

should explode, the Safety Fund will serve as a plaster."[85]

Interestingly enough, though the politicians who were responsible for the Safety Fund system had won election in 1828 wrapped in the mantle of Jefferson and Jackson, the Safety Fund did not strike a blow for free enterprise. Rather, to use Lee Benson's term, it improved upon the Federalist model of the "positive paternal state." According to this model, the state was the best governor of economic growth and development. The state would grant monopolies, therefore, whenever that seemed the best way to increase national wealth and prosperity. Ultimately, the ideology behind this model "derived from an elitist, paternalistic, antidemocratic concept of the Good Society."[86]

Though the Safety Fund was intended to be a system for *all* New York State Banks, the Manhattan Company was noticeably absent. Since the company had a perpetual charter, it could not be forced to join as a condition of renewal. In order to bring this point home, an arrogant Manhattan Company official, Cashier Robert White, later responded to a Safety Fund delegation sent to ask for the company's financial support in a moment of crisis by offering them instead "a

---

[85]Remsen to Henry Rutgers Remsen, January 16, 1834, Remsen Papers, Folder 6, NYPL.

[86]Benson, *Concept of Jacksonian Democracy*, 86-88, 91-93.

glass of good Manhattan water."[87]

The state responded by challenging the validity of the Manhattan Company's charter. Since in chapter two I discussed at length the case, which the State Supreme Court decided in 1832, I will not repeat the details here. Suffice it to say that this unsuccessful case takes on added significance when seen in its true light, as a political attempt to neutralize the Manhattan Company's charter advantages, thereby forcing it to join the Safety Fund.[88]

Even without the Manhattan Company, the Safety Fund continued throughout the decade. By 1836, however, banknote inflation had overextended New York's credit structure, leaving most Safety Fund banks with low reserves.[89] As credit contracted early in 1837,

---

[87]Beatrice G. Reubens, "Burr, Hamilton and the Manhattan Company," *Political Science Quarterly* 72, no. 4 (December 1957) and 73, no. 1 (March 1958), 49n. My page number refers to the reprint of the two articles found in the CMB Archives.

[88]The People v. the Manhattan Company, 9 Wendell 351. For the relationship to the Safety Fund, see Seavoy, "Origins" diss., 136-137.

[89]Henry Remsen commented in 1828 on the plight of banks. "I think they have discounted paper 12 or 15 months ago, more than they ought to have done, for a certain description of persons, and that this is one other cause for refusing to discount now. The complaint among men of business, wholesale & retail, whether merchants, shopkeepers or others; & manufacturers, merchants, &c. &c. is universal -- there is no money to enable them to buy & sell, or to work & sell, and really when we consider how well they were doing several years ago, the change is to be greatly lamented." Remsen to Henry Rutgers Remsen, February 20, 1838, Remsen Papers, Folder 8, NYPL.

three Buffalo banks failed, causing the Safety Fund to be used for the first time. Beginning with the Panic in May of that year, the nation slid into a five-year depression. The effect on the Safety Fund was devastating. Between 1840 and 1842, eleven Safety Fund banks failed, exhausting the fund. The Safety Fund, therefore, was one of the many victims of the greatest economic crisis of the nineteenth century.[90]

The second major contribution of the period, free banking and general incorporation, was longer lasting. The principle of free banking, as summarized by Fritz Redlich, was that "banking should be a free trade, but that at the same time no bank should be allowed to supply a circulating medium which was not secured outside of the bank and independent of it."[91] After New York rejected free banking in favor of the Safety Fund, the concept appeared in legislation introduced, but not adopted, in Maryland in 1831. But the concept of free banking did not gain wide acceptance until after the economic disruptions of 1837, with Michigan passing the first free banking law in that same year. Within a year of the law's passage, Michigan chartered forty banks under its terms. Within two years, however, more than forty Michigan "free" banks were in receivership. "Thus

---

[90]For the last years of the Safety Fund, see Seavoy, ibid., 158, 242.

[91]Redlich, *Molding*, 1:201. For additional background on free banking, see Donovan, *Barnburners*, 26-31.

America grew great," concluded Bray Hammond bitingly.[92]

Why, then, would New York State enthusiastically embrace free banking in 1838? Because there was a political as well as an economic side to the measure. The most recent state elections had brought the Whigs to power, ousting the long-entrenched Albany Regency. As I already have indicated, one of the major sources of public dissatisfaction with the Regency was its politically-motivated banking policy. Free banking promised to divorce banking from politics: it equalized the opportunity to secure the advantages of incorporation -- and the resulting profits. In Ronald Seavoy's words, it was an economic expression of Jacksonian Democracy.[93]

If this was the case, however, why were the Whigs in New York implementing what at first glance would appear to be a Democratic cause? Once again, the combination of politics and economics made for a very complicated situation in the state. In response to the Safety Fund Act, two anti-monopoly groups emerged to challenge the Albany Regency. The first was the short-lived Equal Rights Party, or "Locofocos." Their solution was to destroy the "positive paternal

---

[92]Hammond, *Banks and Politics*, 601.

[93]This concept is found throughout Seavoy's book and dissertation. See, for example, pages 2-3 of the abstract contained with the dissertation. Redlich said something similar: "Free banking represented so perfectly the underlying spirit of the period that everybody seemed to have been just waiting for the formula." *Molding*, 1:202.

state" which Federalist mercantilism had created and the Regency had nurtured, and to substitute a "negative liberal state" in which all people could pursue their interests unfettered by government. According to the Locofocos, equal rights would be assured only if no charters, monopolies, exclusive privileges or special advantages were granted to any individuals or institutions.

The second anti-monopoly group was the Whigs. In their view, government could not abdicate its responsibilities, as the Locofocos demanded. Rather the state had a *positive* responsibility to act in a way that promoted the general welfare, raised the level of opportunity for all, and aided individuals in developing their full potentials. Such a "positive liberal state" would ensure a level field for all players in the economic game.[94]

The New York free banking law clearly was an expression of this positive liberal state. If the measure had truly followed Locofoco doctrine, it would not have placed any restrictions on the free exercise of banking functions. But this was not the case. The final bill contained two major "positive" features: a regulated general incorporation procedure and a method for guaranteeing the value of

---

[94]This distinction between positive paternal state (Federalists and Albany Regency), negative liberal state (Locofocos), and positive liberal state (Whigs) is taken from Benson, *Concept of Jacksonian Democracy*, 86-109. For more on New York politics, see Donovan, *Barnburners*, 7-12; Amy Bridges, *A City in the Republic: Antebellum New York and the Origins of Machine Politics* (New York: Cambridge University Press, 1984).

the paper currency the banks circulated. While the general incorporation procedure greatly opened the issuing of bank charters, it still kept banking from being totally "free:" incorporators had to meet certain conditions, most importantly in the area of finances. "The result," according to Bray Hammond, "was that it might be found somewhat harder to become a banker than a brick-layer, but not much." The value of paper currency was guaranteed by requiring banks to deposit with the state comptroller 100 percent security for their banknotes. This security had to be in the form of United State or New York State bonds, or mortgages on productive land in the state. Taken as a whole, the free banking act marked an important step in the evolution of laws from individual and special enactments to general statutes of a uniform and comprehensive nature.[95]

New Yorkers quickly flocked to take advantage of the new free banking law. In the first six months, fifty applications were received. These applications are particularly interesting in terms of the Manhattan Company because of the requested duration of the charters. All but four of the first fifty charters were to run for at least 100 years. Fourteen banks wanted charters of 400 or more

---

[95]Hammond, *Banks and Politics*, 572, 593. Seavoy, *Origins*, 154. It is important to note that the free banking statute was not the first general incorporation statute passed by New York for business enterprises. Earlier there had been emergency measures for manufacturing and privateering corporations. The free banking statute, however, marked a *permanent* shift in corporate business policy. Seavoy, "Origins" diss., 194.

years, with two specifying 1,000 years and one specifying 4,050 years. Despite these grandiose plans, more than a quarter of the first eighty banks chartered under the law failed to survive even three years. By the end of 1839, New York had chartered 134 free banks, nearly doubling the number of banks in the state. While most of these banks closed quickly, some made lasting contributions. Most prominent was the Bank of Commerce, a free bank which soon replaced the Manhattan Company as the leading institution in New York City.[96]

The ultimate legacy of free banking, however, was the impetus it gave to the wider use of general incorporation. Throughout the century, banking was the first battleground in the development of state economic policy, the first field on which political generals marshalled their troops. This, too, was the case with general incorporation. After banking, other types of corporations were made subject to general incorporation statutes The 1846 New York State Constitution included a provision authorizing general incorporation statutes for all business corporations. Among the general incorporation statutes passed as a result were: telegraph, manufacturing, mining, mechanical, and chemical corporations (1848); insurance corporations (1849); and railroad corporations (1850). The

---

[96]Hammond, *Banks and Politics*, 596. Redlich, *Molding*, 1:202.

most significant aspect of the railroad statute was that it granted the corporations eminent domain without requiring them to return to the legislature for permission. This broad power led to unrestricted railroad construction and competition. It also was the kind of power seldom granted in charters only fifty years earlier.[97]

It is interesting that the leading scholar of managerial development, Alfred D. Chandler, Jr., did not make the connection between banking and railroads.[98] He saw railroads as being the first modern corporations, formed out of the need to effectively link widespread operations. While this is fundamentally true, there are deeper structural questions which deserve further analysis: How successful and effective would railroads have been if they had been governed by the restrictive charters commonplace fifty years earlier? To what extent was the visible hand of management only operative under modern corporate charters? While these questions obviously require more research, it seems to me that the growth of modern management was as much influenced by the nature of corporate charters as it was by the nature of the enterprise requiring management. The visible hand of management worked best when freed from the restricting glove of a narrow charter. This is why the

---

[97]Seavoy, "Origins" diss., 206. See also ibid., 193-198, 203-207, 278-279.

[98]*The Visible Hand*, passim.

Manhattan Company is so interesting in the history of managerial development. Its charter was more typical of the charters (including railroad charters) issued under general incorporation statutes half a century later. The Manhattan Company, therefore, faced the problem of managing diverse operations years before other corporations.

In addition to the changing political circumstances outlined above, banks in the post-Remsen years also had to adjust to the volatile economic situation in the 1820s and 1830s. In many cases officers and directors departed from the "old ways" instituted by Remsen and his contemporaries. "I apprehend with you," wrote James Taylor to Henry Remsen in 1837, "that great deviations from the old established, and sound modes of business, have taken place of late years; and that a great share of the evils which now afflict us has been caused by mismanagement and cupidity on the part of the Banks themselves." This included "The institution which [Remsen] laboured so long, nobly, and efficiently, to build up; and over which you presided for many years so advantageously for its stockholders & the public."[99]

The best way to illustrate these gradual departures from traditional business practices and their cumulative effect upon the

---

[99]James Taylor to Henry Remsen, May 18, 1837, Remsen Papers, Folder 10, NYPL.

Manhattan Company is to jump to 1840. In that year of continuing economic depression, a public outcry against the Manhattan Company's calling in of loans led the directors to investigate the company's financial situation and operations.

The root of the Manhattan Company's problems was the practice developed during the 1820s of making "Temporary Loans on Stock Securities that might be called in and made available on very short notice." Before 1833 these "call loans" fluctuated between $300,000 and $800,000. In 1833, however, the U.S. Secretary of the Treasury began to place large government deposits in the Manhattan Company. The bank, in turn, used these funds to increase its loans on stock until by 1836 the loans totaled $2.8 million. When the federal government called for its deposits in 1837, the Manhattan Company was forced to call in all its loans. Those issued on the security of stocks, being the most tenuous from the start, were difficult to collect and resulted in large losses to the company.[100] An internal investigating committee recommended that "loans on Stocks be gradually reduced and the line of discounts on good mercantile paper be increased, and that no loans or discounts be made but by the Board of Directors of this company."[101]

---

[100]For a narrative of this situation, see MC Minutes, 6:119-120 (January 13, 1840); 6:122-145 (January 27, 1840).

[101]Ibid., 6:119-120 (January 13, 1840).

At the request of the board, the same committee two weeks later produced a longer document on the financial situation of the company. They reported, for example, a difference of over $76,000 between the General Ledger and the records of individual depositor accounts. This difference reflected poorly on recent management: "This discrepancy we understand has existed for many years and has gradually increased from year to year to the present sum, and the difference cannot be accounted for." The committee also elaborated on its criticism of stock loans. Instead of these questionable loans, the committee recommended that the directors "confine the Business of this Company to ordinary and legitimate banking operations, inviting and encouraging an increase of accounts with mercantile houses of good standing and affording such facilities generally on undoubted business paper as will make it the interest of the mercantile business community to ask such facilities of the Bank to grant them." By doing this the directors would be "promoting the interest of the Stockholders and discharging the duty we owe the community and the authority whence we derive the charter." Both the recommended type of loans and the sense of duty to the community indicate a return to the "old ways" of the Remsen years.

But perhaps the internal investigation is most important for what the report says about the objectives of the Manhattan Company. The following paragraphs, coming at the end of the time period covered in this study, clearly express the forty-year schizophrenia of the Company:

> As Directors we have little else in our minds than a Bank with a
> Capital of $2,050,000 Dollars, While the Charter contemplates a
> Company to supply the City with Pure & Wholesome Water, with the
> privilege of using its surplus only in Banking (although it was
> afterwards extended to the Whole Capital). By the expenses of the
> Water Works & Cost of real estate necessary for its operation, the
> Capital has been reduced to less than $1,600,000 Dolls. and is
> still subject to further expenditures for that object, without any
> income arising from it, from which it will appear that while our
> Loans continue to the amount they now are we have but about
> $500,000 Dollars for Banking purposes.
>
> [As a result] a great responsibility rests on this Board and ...
> great attention and assiduity [are] necessary to restore the
> Capital of this Company to its wanted and legitimate use.[102]

It is interesting to see how the directors separated the company from its
charter and equated what they *wanted* with what was *legitimate*.
After four decades of hearing these arguments, the directors failed to see
the dichotomy.

The internal investigation apparently did not stem the tide of
public criticism. The directors therefore decided to "make a public
expose of the State of Funds of the Said Company." To do this the
directors formed an outside commission to explore the company's "condition
... in every department" and to "report without delay the facts for the
information of the Stockholders." The members of the commission were City
Recorder Robert H. Morris, James Gore King, and James Boorman. The

---

[102]For the full report, see ibid., 6:122-145 (January 27,
1840).

secretary of the commission, the person who analyzed the Manhattan Company's accounts, was Francis W. Edmunds, the President of the Mechanics Bank. The commission's report, published in March 1840, presented a scathing attack upon the present management of the company. I will highlight some of the commission's more significant findings about loan policies and the relative responsibilities of directors, the president, and the cashier. As will be seen, these topics were closely related.[103]

The commission agreed with the internal investigating committee in criticizing the practice of stock loans. Compounding the problem, however, was the Manhattan Company's practice, begun in 1824, of delegating to the officers the authority to make the loans. Under Henry Remsen, this responsibility was carefully executed; under his successors, however, this was not the case. The commissioners were particularly critical of this practice, noting that:

> although *general* Statements were regularly laid before the Board, the *details* of the proceedings of the officers were unknown to the greater portion of the Directors. The commissioners are further requested by the President [Maltby Gelston] to state -- and the fact is admitted by the Cashier [Robert White, the same person who sixteen years earlier had tried to dissociate himself from the supervision of the clerks] -- that the "loans on Stocks were always made and controlled by the Cashier, without the interference of the President."

---

[103]For the establishment of the commission, see ibid., 6:151 (February 14, 1840); 6:154-157 (February 24-26, 1840), and Redlich, *Molding*, 2:48-49. Much of the following discussion is taken from the commission's report to stockholders dated March 14, 1840 and published in the New York *American*, March 18, 1840.

In a letter to the commission, White admitted that while he reported the "aggregate amount" of the loans to the directors, he had not made a "detailed report" to them since 1834. "But," he concluded, "it would of course have been submitted at all times, had they called for it."[104]

The commissioners ultimately concluded that "whatever may be deemed unfavorable in the situation of the Company" arose "from the general inattention of the Directors, and, from ... the lax and injudicious management of its concerns, by the officers on whom the charge devolved." Jonathan Thompson, a director of twenty-six years and soon to be the next president of the company, tried to explain to the commissioners how this could have happened. "It appears," wrote Thompson, "that the mal-administration of the affairs of the Company commenced many years since, and still continues, in consequence of many of the Stockholders (both State and individual) having given their proxies to an officer of the Company [probably Robert White] who assumed the responsibility, and he used them according to his

---

[104]A decade later, a contemporary commenting on general bank practices reported that "it is common for half the members of a bank board to become irregular in their attendance at the meetings for discounting paper, either from engrossment with their own affairs, or because they have confidence in other managers; the tendency of which is to throw the general administration of the bank into the hands of a few persons." Gibbons, *Banks of New York*, 20. Unlike other banks, however, the Manhattan Company changed its practices as a result of the public outcry.

pleasure or discretion."[105]

The editor of the New York *American*, which published the commission's report, agreed with their conclusions. "The loss on the stock and funds of the institution," the editor wrote, "arises wholly from the inattention and neglect of duty of the Trustees or Directors, and from the want of due caution and prudence on the part of the officers." The editor particularly chastised the president: "The whole power of the Bank was, by resolution, delegated to the Cashier and President; and the President seems to think it a palliation -- since the statement is made at his request -- that he did not attend to his share of the responsibility, but left it all to the Cashier." Confidence in the officers was further eroded when, during the commission's investigation, the first teller's cash was found to be $49,000 short. "On being required to explain [First Teller Colin G. Newcomb] precipitately left the Bank and has not since been heard of." As best I can determine, the Manhattan Company never did find the teller or the money.[106]

---

[105]Thompson served as president from 1840 until his death in 1846. He, too, was politically well-connected, having served under Presidents Madison and Monroe as Collector of Taxes and then Collector of Customs for New York. For more information, see "Jonathan Thompson," Record Group 3, Biographical Files, CMB Archives.

[106]In addition to the report of the commissioners, this incident is mentioned in the MC Minutes, 6:158-159 (March 3-7, 1840). As I pointed out when discussing the Brower theft in 1803, banks had and continue to have problems in this area. A later

While the directors failed to pay attention to most of the loans issued by the bank, they certainly did not neglect their own interests. Four directors alone monopolized nearly $600,000 of the bank's discounts and loans, almost one-third of the bank's total. "This, too," the editor of the *American* noted, "during a part of the time when the mercantile community were ground to the dust -- and unable upon any terms to obtain discounts." As I pointed out earlier in this chapter, it was common in the nineteenth century for directors to borrow heavily from their own institutions. The problem here was the extent and timing of the revelation when combined with so many other criticisms of the company.[107]

As a result of the public outcry and investigation, the Manhattan Company significantly changed the way it operated. The

---

example from the Manhattan Company shows that management still had not exercised sufficient control. To quote from the newspaper account of a $160,000 theft in 1885, it was amazing "that the funds of the Manhattan Company's bank were so loosely guarded that it was possible for a paying-teller [the equivalent of the first teller] to abstract [extract?] almost any sum he pleased, even two or three million dollars and escape to Canada before the theft would be discovered. He actually did take $500,000 one afternoon, and then, repentant, returned it the next morning. He might have crippled the bank.... How many other banks are there in New York and in other cities that are at the mercy of their paying-tellers?" *Frank Leslie's Illustrated Newspaper*, August 27, 1887, p. 19.

[107]For more on loans to directors, see Lamoreaux, "The Structure of Early Banks," 171-184. Gibbons noted in the 1850s that the "irregular and careless manner" of discounting bills for directors meant that there was less money available to loan to others. *Banks of New York*, 26-48.

directors voted to return to the original practice of granting loans and discounts only with the approval of a board consisting of at least seven members, thereby decreasing the authority of the president and cashier.[108] The board also decided to end the practice of having directors in name only: from now on directors would be expected to attend meetings regularly. The directors even received a circular advising them of the new policy.[109] The result of these management changes was to return the bank to an operating mode common at the beginning of the century. The board reversed the delegation of wide powers begun under Remsen and reserved most major decisions to itself.

In order to begin afresh, the directors wrote off the following losses which equaled over one-tenth of the company's capitalization:

Tellers' differences	$61,808.23
Overdrawn accounts	36,965.90
Notes receivable	2,037.39
Judgments	77,445.06
Protested bills	38,430.30
Differences in ledger	62,300.68
	278,987.56

Because of these losses, the directors found it "inexpedient to declare a dividend." It took new president Jonathan Thompson five

---

[108]MC Minutes, 6:145-147 (January 27, 1841).

[109]Ibid., 6:150 (February 6, 1840). "Circular to all Directors," February 10, 1840, CMB Archives. For a discussion of other banks, see Gibbons, *Banks of New York*, 20; Redlich, *Molding*, 1:39, 60-63.

years to restore the Manhattan Company to a financial position where it again could pay dividends.[110]

In the wake of this report, it was obvious that staff changes were necessary. Both Cashier Robert White and President Maltby Gelston resigned. The board subsequently requested the resignations of the second and third tellers. An indication of the emotion and tension involved in this situation was an attack by Robert White and his brother Campbell P. White (a Manhattan Company director) upon Jonathan Thompson. White and Thompson had been at odds for some time, as their respective letters to the commission cited above indicate. Perhaps the situation came to a head two days before the attack when Thompson was one of two directors who voted against the following perfunctory resolution: "Resolved that the Board of Directors of this Company take this occasion [White's resignation] to bear testimony to the integrity with which he has discharged his duties." The two assailants clubbed Thompson "with large sticks" as he was about to enter the bank. Thompson was not seriously injured: "[his] head is cut somewhat, and severely bruised -- but he is at his post at the Bank." However the story was reported under the headline "Unprecedented Outrage" in the same edition of the newspaper in which the commission's report was printed, further eroding public

---

[110]For the losses, see MC Journal No. 10, March 4, 1840 and January 5, 1841. For the suspension of dividends, see MC Minutes, 6:221 (January 7, 1841).

confidence.[111]

This was not the end of the Manhattan Company's problems with Robert White. After his resignation the company filed a suit in Chancery Court seeking the return of certain funds White collected and the records detailing these collections. The issue involved the Manhattan Company's business of serving as "Transfer Agent" for the stock of other institutions: the Planters Bank of Tennessee; the Mechanics and Traders Bank of New Orleans; the Commercial Bank of Manchester, Mississippi; the State of New York; and the Canal Commissioners of the State of Ohio. The Manhattan Company claimed that White retained for his own use over $11,000 in fees and over $50,000 in dividends and interest payments for the above institutions. The company pointed out that in 1836 White's annual salary was raised from $4,000 to $6,000 to reflect his increased responsibilities, and that it was the Manhattan Company, not White, which hired the clerks to handle the daily transactions. White

---

[111]For White's resignation, see MC Minutes, 6:161-162 (March 16, 1840). White's letter of resignation can be found in Record Group 1, Box 1, CMB Archives. For Gelston's resignation, see MC Minutes, 6:165 (March 23, 1840). For the second and third tellers, see ibid., 6:167 (March 30, 1840), For the attack on Thompson, see the New York *American*, March 18, 1840, p. 3, col. 2. Three weeks before the attack, White told the board that even though there were reports that in private conversations he had "used offensive language respecting the Board of Directors," he never had done so. MC Minutes, 6:154-156 (February 24, 1840). Campbell P. White resigned as a director later in the year, after settling a rather large indebtedness to the bank. See ibid., 6:205 (October 28, 1840).

countered that his work for the outside institutions was personal rather than part of his official responsibilities as Manhattan Company cashier. Since his actions were "personal," White burned the supporting account books when he resigned. The case dragged on for five years; perhaps Thompson's death in 1846 ultimately cooled the ardor of the Manhattan Company to pursue further its former cashier.[112]

The contrasts between White and Remsen are striking, both in terms of banking professionalism and individual integrity. The importance of key managers in the life of an institution is illustrated by the way the Manhattan Company grew and prospered under Remsen, and foundered and almost failed under White. The charter was the same; the major difference was in the quality of the Manhattan Company's day-to-day leadership. If the positions of these two individuals had been reversed -- if Robert White had been the one

---

[112]The President and Directors of the Manhattan Company v. Robert White, filed April 17, 1841. The case can be found in the Chancery Court Records in the New York State Archives in Albany. Preliminaries to the suit can be found in the MC Minutes, 6:163-164 (March 19, 1840); 6:171-172 (April 27, 1840); 6:177-178 (May 29, 1840); 6:180-181 (June 11, 1840); 6:189 (August 13, 1840); 6:196-197 (September 21, 1840). At the time of the 1840 public investigation of the company, White wrote to the commissioners: "The practice is believed to have been almost universal in this City, for Cashiers to receive compensation for extra services." New York *American*, March 18, 1840, p. 1, col. 4-5. This court case should be of interest to archivists who today still face the problem of informing executives and staff about the difference between "official records" and "personal papers."

charged with establishing the bank on a sound footing in 1799 --
there is reason to doubt that the institution would even have
survived, no less prospered.

Conclusion

The Manhattan Company's initial decisions on structure set the
course for its development over the next half-century. Despite
short-term forays into other areas, the directors quickly adopted
banking as the primary use of the company's "surplus" capital. As
the Manhattan Company developed policies and procedures in the area
of banking, its shear size made it a leader in the banking community.

The key person in developing the Manhattan Company's bank in
the early years was Henry Remsen. The confidence the board had in
Remsen led them to delegate wide responsibilities to him. The most
significant of these responsibilities involved approving discounts to
customers on his own authority. Remsen also used his political
contacts with DeWitt Clinton to protect the company's interests.
Remsen and Clinton spun a web around the city and state governments,
binding them to the Manhattan Company with the multiple relationships
of shareholder, customer, and employer. In addition, Clinton worked
against the chartering of banks thought harmful to the Manhattan
Company.

After Remsen, the situation changed dramatically. On the state
level, banking policy became an even greater source of political

controversy. The Albany Regency tried to maintain its power through the Safety Fund System, only to see the crisis of 1837 undermine the economic arguments behind the system. The developing anti-monopoly sentiment achieved political expression through the free banking act of 1837, a quintessentially Democratic idea implemented by the Whig political opponents of the Regency.

Within the Manhattan Company itself, there also were changes after Remsen. Most important was the significant decline in the level of managerial expertise. Cashier Robert White, a man of questionable judgment, assumed most of the responsibility for discounts. The situation was made more precarious by an increase in the pool of loanable funds caused by large federal deposits in the bank. When the government called for these deposits after 1837, many of the loans proved difficult to collect, resulting in losses to the company.

Internal problems, however, were not the greatest ones facing the Manhattan Company. Widespread displeasure over the Manhattan Company's retrenchment led to a public investigation of the company's practices in 1840. The final report of the investigators castigated the Manhattan Company for its loan practices, including the granting of most loans to directors of the bank. As a result of this report, the Manhattan Company reversed many of its policies, the most significant being the return of control over discounts to the full board of directors.

This 1840 investigation is one of the clearest examples in nineteenth century America of business strategy and structure being changed by social and political pressures. Even as late as 1840, the Manhattan Company's banking operation still was considered to be a public franchise. Widespread concern about the Manhattan Company's loan practices led to a major investigation and public flogging of the company's leaders. Because of the Manhattan Company's political as well as economic position, the public kept a close watch on its activities. Even after forty years, the Manhattan Company remained an object of both envy and scorn. Another example of this is found in the Manhattan Company's short experiment with bank branches detailed in the next chapter.

CHAPTER FIVE

MANAGING THE MANHATTAN COMPANY'S
BANK BRANCHES IN UTICA
AND POUGHKEEPSIE, 1809-1819

> The attack [upon the Manhattan
> Company's branches] will be a party
> one and will be whetted by all the
> rancor of pecuniary and political
> hostility.[1]

In addition to its New York City water and banking operations,

for ten years the Manhattan Company operated bank branches in two

upstate villages, Utica and Poughkeepsie.   This brief branch

experience is important because it further illustrates themes already

presented in this study.   In managing its upstate branches, the

Manhattan Company had to address the same problems it faced with its

other divisions: how much capital to allocate to this enterprise,

how much managerial time and attention to devote to the undertaking,

and how to deal with both the state and local environments.   In

establishing and operating branches, the Manhattan Company once again

had to balance private and public concerns, internal and external

factors, and economic and social considerations.   As with other

aspects of the Manhattan Company's operations at this time, the key

---

[1]DeWitt Clinton to Henry Remsen, February 20, 1810, Clinton
Papers, New York Public Library [hereafter NYPL], New York, New York.

people in achieving the balance were Henry Remsen and DeWitt Clinton.

Background on the Manhattan Company's Branches

It is important to note at the outset that there were differences in the nineteenth century between a "branch" and an "agency." An agency made discounts and purchased bills of exchange with the funds of the principal bank; it did not keep independent accounts with other banks. A branch, on the other hand, performed these functions but also issued bank notes payable at its own building. In addition, branches maintained separate accounting systems. According to these definitions, the Manhattan Company clearly established branches rather than agencies.[2]

The Manhattan Company was not the only bank at the time to have branches. Fifteen southern states had extensive branch banking systems. In the Midwest, it was common to have monopolistic state banks with branches, as in Indiana, Illinois, and Missouri. By way of contrast, New England had a system of small and independent single-unit banks. The major exception was the Vermont State Bank, which had four offices and operated from 1806 to 1812.[3]

---

[2] J. Van Fenstermaker, *The Development of American Commercial Banking, 1782-1837* (Kent, Ohio: Bureau of Economic and Business Research, Kent State University, 1965), 26-27.

[3] For the Southern and New England situations, see Fenstermaker, *Development*, 26-27. For the Midwestern states, see Fritz Redlich, *The Molding of American Banking: Men and Ideas*

While the Mid-Atlantic states tended to follow the New England pattern, there were some notable exceptions. The Bank of Pennsylvania, which was founded in 1793, eventually had offices in Harrisburg, Reading, Easton, Lancaster, and Pittsburgh, in addition to its headquarters in Philadelphia. In 1807, the Farmers Bank of the State of Delaware was founded. In addition to its headquarters in Dover, it had offices in New Castle, Wilmington, and Georgetown. Each of these branches received separate capital and the person in charge of each branch was designated "president." This is similar to the structure the Manhattan Company employed.[4]

The evidence about why the Manhattan Company established branches is thin. It appears the company hoped to take advantage of the fact that there were few banks in the interior of the state. Branches in Utica and Poughkeepsie, therefore, could be profitable both by attracting deposits and by further circulating the notes of the company.[5] It also is highly likely that the Manhattan Company

---

(New York: Hafner Publishing, 1951; reprint, New York: Johnson Reprint Company, 1968), 2:22. For Vermont, see Bray Hammond, *Banks and Politics in America From the Revolution to the Civil War* (Princeton: Princeton University Press, 1957), 166. Alfred D. Chandler, Jr. incorrectly stated that "The largest of the newly specialized merchant banks did not yet find it necessary to set up branches manned by salaried employees." See *The Visible Hand: The Managerial Revolution in American Business* (Cambridge: Belknap Press of Harvard University Press, 1977), 47.

[4] Hammond, *Banks and Politics*, 164-167.

[5] See Manhattan Company [hereafter MC] Minutes, 4:70

established branches in parts of the state where it could achieve some political advantage. Looked at in this way, branches could provide a financial wellspring for hard-pressed Republican allies.[6]

In establishing both of its branches, the Manhattan Company followed a similar pattern. First the company received a petition from a "respectable number of citizens" of the area requesting the establishment of a branch. Undoubtedly, these petitions were far from spontaneous. Second, the board responded to the petitions by concluding that "it would conduce to the interests of the Manhattan Company and to the public good to comply with the said applications." Third, the directors formed a committee to plan for the establishment of the branch. And finally, the directors formally authorized the branch by appointing directors and officers, allocating $10,000 in specie and $90,000 in Manhattan Company notes as each branch's capital, and issuing regulations.[7]

The regulations issued for both branches were very similar.

(December 1, 1817); 2:67 (January 15, 1810). Unless otherwise noted, all MC records are found in the Chase Manhattan [hereafter CMB] Archives, New York, New York.

[6]For the link between politics and banking in New York State, see Lee Benson, *The Concept of Jacksonian Democracy: New York as a Test Case* (Princeton: Princeton University Press, 1961), 86-109.

[7]For an illustration of this process in Poughkeepsie, see MC Minutes, 2:20-26 (January 7-12, 1809). For the issuing of the Poughkeepsie capital, see MC Journal No. 2, April 8, 1809.

Among the most significant were: the Manhattan Company directors would appoint the branch directors, cashier, and clerk; the branch directors would elect one of their number as president; the branch would keep separate books, balance them twice per year, and transfer net profits to the Manhattan Company; branch directors would meet at least once per week to make discounts; the branch cashier would submit weekly reports on the branch's condition; the main office would provide the branch with notes for circulation and the branch would receive customer payments in the notes of the Manhattan Company "as far as they may find it convenient"; the branch directors were permitted to establish any other regulations necessary for "the *interior* management of the office," provided these regulations did not violate law or Manhattan Company regulations; and finally, "the instructions given from time to time by the President and Directors of the Manhattan Company, shall be binding upon the Directors and Officers of the Office of Discount and Deposit."[8] The ability of the branches to implement these regulations, however, was affected by the special circumstances of each locality.

The Poughkeepsie Branch

The Manhattan Company's first branch was located in Poughkeepsie, a thriving village approximately halfway between New

---

[8]MC Minutes, 2:23-26 (January 12, 1809).

York and Albany.[9] In January 1809 the New York City directors appointed five directors for the Poughkeepsie branch: Robert Williams; Nathan Myers; James Tallmadge, Jr.; John L. Frere, Jr.; and Joseph C. Dean. In February the company appointed a cashier for the branch, Samuel Flewwelling, who was the first bookkeeper in New York. In the same month the company purchased a house at the corner of Market and Cannon Streets from General Theodorus Bailey for $4,000 for use as the branch.[10]

As with so many key events in the Manhattan Company's history, DeWitt Clinton was actively involved with the establishment of the Poughkeepsie branch. In January Clinton traveled to Poughkeepsie and reported to William Edgar, one of the leading Manhattan Company directors, that "the federalists and quids are endeavoring by propagating a number of vile reports to excite prejudices" against the planned office. In typical fashion, Clinton recommended that "the best and most effectual mode of Silencing their calumnies is to

---

[9]For general information about Poughkeepsie, see Clyde and Sally Griffen, *Natives and Newcomers: The Ordering of Opportunity in Mid-Nineteenth Century Poughkeepsie* (Cambridge: Harvard University Press, 1978), 1-31.

[10]MC Minutes, 2:21-22 (January 12, 1809); 2:29 (February 2, 1809); 2:39 (February 20, 1809). MC Journal No. 2, February 21, 1809.   Edmund Platt, *Eagle's History of Poughkeepsie*, "Branches: Poughkeepsie and Utica," Record Group 1, Box 2, CMB Archives. In March 1810, Bailey wrote to Remsen requesting a $30 payment for two "Franklin Stoves" he left in the house and which he considered to be "fixtures." Bailey to Remsen, March 16, 1810, MC Records, New-York Historical Society [hereafter NYHS], New York, New York.

expedite the institution as much as possible." Clinton also mentioned a "silly piece" in the newspaper attacking the branch, and offered to "write and send to you for publication a short piece vindicatory of the measure."[11]

In March, Clinton wrote Remsen that he had reason to think "much misrepresentation and many disingenuous practices have been used to excite prejudices generally against the Directors of the Poughkeepsie office." Clinton then detailed what he knew about the five directors, calling one a "very decent man," and another a "respectable unexceptionable character." Clinton concluded that it might be "for the best" to increase the number of directors. He recommended two men "of property and respectability," Derick A. Brinkerhoff of Fishkill and Martin Hoffman of Poughkeepsie, who subsequently were elected. Clinton closed by "entreating" Remsen to "steer clear of federalism and quiddism" in selecting other directors.[12]

---

[11]Clinton to Edgar, January 18, 1809, Edgar Papers, Volume 10, NYPL. For more on Clinton's role in the Manhattan Company's branches, see Dorothie Bobbe, *DeWitt Clinton*, Empire State Historical Publication 11 (Port Washington, New York: Ira J. Friedman, 1933), 133, 140-2.

[12]Clinton to Remsen, March 1, 1809, Clinton Papers, Folder 3, NYPL. The extent of the friendship between Clinton and Remsen is shown by a letter from four days later in which Clinton wrote: "My compliments to Mrs. Remsen and tell her if you dare to take good care of the *young President*." Ibid., March 5, 1809. In addition to Brinkerhoff and Hoffman, three other directors were added in April to make the branch "more popular and beneficial." The other directors

The branch officially opened on April 17, 1809, five days after Henry Remsen personally swore in the new directors. The Poughkeepsie directors elected James Tallmadge, Jr. to serve as president of the branch. The Poughkeepsie branch also started its own minute book, which still survives in the Chase Manhattan Archives. The first few pages of this book reproduce minutes of the New York directors relevant to the establishment of the branch.

It did not take long for political infighting and personal animosity to rear their ugly heads at the Poughkeepsie branch. In January 1810 one of the Poughkeepsie directors, Robert Williams, wrote to William Edgar in New York complaining about the operations of the branch, especially the conduct of its president, James Tallmadge. The New York directors decided to inform Tallmadge of the complaints and also to ask the Poughkeepsie cashier to make a confidential report on the operations of the branch.[13]

Remsen's letter to Poughkeepsie cashier Flewwelling requesting the report is a remarkable document, both for what it asked and for what it did not ask. Because of the insights the letter offers into how the branch operated during its first year and how it met or

---

were General David Van Ness of Rhinebeck, Cyrenus Crosby of Amenia, and Samuel Thorn of Washington. MC Minutes, 2:41-42 (April 14, 1809). Poughkeepsie Minutes, 13-14 (May 24, 1809). Each of these directors purchased five shares of Manhattan Company stock. See MC Journal No. 2, July 25, 1809 and August 14, 1809.

[13]MC Minutes, 2:64-66 (January 3, 1810).

frustrated local needs, it is worth listing Remsen's eleven specific areas of concern. Remsen's questions to Flewwelling were:

1. Did the directors or others use the discounts they received for "usurious purposes," presumably re-lending the money?

2. Did the board refuse discounts to potential customers who would have been "beneficial to the office," lending instead to individuals with less pecuniary potential?

3. Did the directors receive discounts "to so large an amount" that the paper of other individuals had to be refused?

4. Were the large discounts to one particular director, J.S. Freare, justified by his "ability as a Director, punctuality of attendance, or monies kept by him in the Office?"

5. Have the directors opened personal and business accounts with the branch, as one would expect? Did the size of these accounts justify the extent of the discounts to the directors?

6. In terms of discounted bills not repaid at maturity, have the directors "put [them] in suit *prematurely*, not for the purpose of securing their payment, but of giving to the Notary and Attorney lucrative jobs." Has this led to valid complaints by customers?

7. Have the directors "by their acts and proceedings rendered the Office obnoxious and unpopular except the obnoxiousness and unpopularity (if any exist) originating merely from party or political motives?"

8. Is there any "project on foot" in Poughkeepsie or elsewhere in Dutchess County to charter another bank? If there is such a plan, has it been "occasioned, strengthened or furthered by the oppressive, partial and unjust conduct of the Direction of the Poughkeepsie Office" in the cases outlined above?

9. Do the directors "attend regularly to the discharge of their duties" except when they are sick or absent from the village?

10. Would it be best to make a change in the directors of the branch? In this regard, Remsen crossed out two important points before sending the letter. One asked if it would be best to substitute "men of the *same politics*." The second deleted paragraph asked "Whether a change in the Direction, by the substitution of men of *different politics* in lieu of one or more of the present Directors, seeing that the Agency of the Columbia Bank at Poughkeepsie [a rival establishment] is entirely composed of federal characters, could now be of advantage in softening down and neutralizing such

opposition to the Poughkeepsie office, as has arisen from party or political motives."

11.   Has the "character of the Office for fairness and integrity" been compromised or its "true interests sacrificed for improper [the word "party" was struck out] purposes." Also struck out was a sentence stating that "it may be proper" for a bank to show a preference for its customers "especially where there are *two rival* Institutions, Rivals in business as well as in political sentiment."[14]

The deleted sections noted above would indicate that Remsen's first draft of the Flewwelling letter included a much heavier emphasis on party and politics than did the final draft. Whether Remsen or the board of directors softened these comments is impossible to say.

Flewwelling replied to Remsen several days later. He denied knowing about any discounts used for usurious purposes. In terms of using discounts to attract deposits, he pointed out that although the farmers of the area were "rich (as Farmers)" their wealth was in land, not cash. He stated his belief that discounts to directors did not lead to the rejection of the paper of other individuals. "They

---

[14]Remsen to Flewwelling, January 9, 1810, MC Records, NYHS. As will be recalled, similar concerns were raised about the New York City office, particularly the loans to directors. See chapter four.

[the directors] have some little claim from their services, and some of them keep accounts with the office, whereas nine-tenths of those who obtain discounts keep none." As to Freare, the branch gave him a large discount because his business was being solicited by the rival Bank of Columbia. On the question of filing suits for protested notes, he strongly stated that putting notes in suit "merely for the purpose of being profitable to the Attorney is an act that I never could knowingly consent to."

After answering the procedural questions, Flewwelling then turned to the broader political ones. "It is well known," he began, "that the establishment of this office was opposed by a part of the community, and undoubtedly in this Village by the richer part, this opposition I believe has rather encreased, from the monied support given them by the Bank of Columbia, in establishing an office here." Despite this, Flewwelling did not believe that local board actions had made the Manhattan Company branch unpopular, "for in discounting of notes the only question has been -- Is the paper unexceptionable." Flewwelling knew of no plans under way in the region to seek a bank charter, though there had been rumors six months earlier. "They say if a Bank is useful to the County and profitable to the Stockholders, why not allow the inhabitants of the County to be subscribers of such stock." According to Flewwelling, these plans did not arise from the conduct of the directors, but "from the private and interested motives" of the people involved.

Flewwelling then turned to the question of new directors. The main problem was the limited number of candidates. "If you divide the men fitting to be trusted with the direction of money into two parties in a place so small as this, it is not easy to obtain for each exactly such as could be wished." The Bank of Columbia "undoubtedly as respects business made the best selection," but these men of different politics would not consent to serve on the Manhattan Company board even if the company wished to change directors. In addition, since the Bank of Columbia had "more money" at its disposal than the Manhattan Company branch, potential directors of a different political persuasion "would not relinquish the greater for the less."

The one person Flewwelling did recommend replacing was Robert Williams, the person who originally complained to the New York directors. According to Flewwelling, it was "well known" that Williams planned to have the Manhattan Company branch "promote his interests in some shape or other." When this did not come to pass, "a bitterness and rancour took place between him and Mr. Tallmadge.... If I can judge from circumstances within my knowledge, I should say [Williams] would be willing to destroy by *any means* that power which he conceives he has been instrumental in placing in the hands of men whom he hates." Because of this, Williams was of "no use" as a director, since his presence "always produces distrust and destroys that freedom of communication so essentially requisite."[15]

Though Williams soon left the board, the controversy did not end. Williams apparently disparaged the branch directors to anyone who would listen. This included DeWitt Clinton, whom Williams met in Albany. Williams informed Clinton that "the proceedings of [the] Board were so adverse to the interests of the establishment, that he was compelled as a man of integrity to resign." In particular, Williams repeated the charge that the board made discounts for "usurious purposes." Clinton told the Poughkeepsie directors he did not "place the least confidence" in Williams' charges because he believed Williams was "a man utterly destitute of veracity."[16]

By early March, Williams' attacks had become so widespread that the Poughkeepsie directors felt it necessary to explain the conflict to the New York directors. As noted above, the root of the problem was Williams' disappointment at not being elected branch president. The Poughkeepsie directors said they voted against Williams because of "public disapprobation" against his being elected president. In order not to "materially injure the prospects of the institution," the directors rejected Williams' "anxious application." Prior to the vote, Williams threatened one director *"That if he was not chosen*

---

[15]Flewwelling to Remsen January [17?] 1810, MC Records, NYHS.

[16]Clinton to Poughkeepsie Directors, February 26, 1810, Poughkeepsie Minutes.

President -- there should be the damned'st schisms in the board."
To others he said *"that as he succeeded in obtaining the presidency*
he would either be a friend or a foe to the institution." The
directors believed Williams was completing "his threatened revenge"
by the recent "slanders" against the branch.[17]

A couple of weeks later, the dispute went public in a very
visible way. Since Williams was a state senator, he used the forum
of a legislative debate "to criminate the proceedings of the Branch
at Poughkeepsie." Clinton reported to Remsen that he had responded
to Williams' charges and proved him "guilty of falsehood, duplicity,
and villainy." Clinton believed he had "completely put down the
calumnies that were brought forward against us" by "Judas
Williams."[18]

The subject of the Senate debate during which Williams leveled
his charges was a bill directed against the Manhattan Company's
branches. According to Clinton, "the establishment of [the] branches
has excited the jealousy of other Banks and the peculiar malisuity of

---

[17]Poughkeepsie Directors (Tallmadge, Myers, Freare, Dean, and Hoffman) to President and Directors of the Manhattan Company, March 7, 1810, Poughkeepsie Minutes, 17-25. Clinton's letter also was sent to New York City.

[18]Clinton to Remsen, March 28, 1810, April 3, 1810, Clinton Papers, NYPL. See also Clinton to Poughkeepsie directors, March 30, [1810?], Clinton Letterbooks, 17:77, Columbia University; James Tallmadge, Jr. to Remsen, April 7, 1810, MC Records, NYHS; MC Minutes, 2:72 (April 12, 1810).

federalism." The proposed bill would have restrained the Manhattan Company from establishing branches. In addition, since the bill would be retroactive, the Manhattan Company would have had to close its existing branches. Clinton prepared for the legislative fight by requesting copies of the Poughkeepsie and Utica petitions. Clinton expected that "the attack will be a party one and will be whetted by all the rancor of pecuniary and political hostility."[19] The restraining bill, which Clinton called "an abominable violation of our charter," did pass the Assembly. The Senate defeated the bill, however, by a vote of eighteen to five. "The majority was very large," according to Clinton, "and [the] minority was composed of federalists only." In typical fashion, Clinton concluded "Our opponents with virulence approaching the diabolical were completely silenced in argument."[20]

The above incident is important because it shows how, in the context of nineteenth century banking, a personal dispute between two directors could become a weapon in a political attack against the Manhattan Company. Clinton clearly saw the link between economics and politics in the Williams case, and used all his resources to

---

[19]Clinton to Remsen, February 12, 1810, February 20, 1810, Clinton Papers, Folder 3, NYPL.

[20]Clinton to Remsen, March 28, 1810, March 29, 1810, ibid. For additional information, see Clinton to Remsen, March 5, 1810, March 15, 1810, ibid.; MC Minutes, 2:68 (February 26, 1810).

block the two-pronged assault.

Even after the Manhattan Company's Poughkeepsie branch survived this major crisis, there was a continuing link between economics and politics. While many examples could illustrate this, I will focus on one: the ongoing debate over the amount of capital allocated to the Poughkeepsie branch. As I pointed out in the chapters on the water works and the New York City bank, allocating capital was one of the major decisions the company's directors faced -- though the Manhattan Company's capital was large, it was not unlimited. Decisions were necessary, therefore, on how best to use the capital to advance the economic and political interests of the company. The complicating factor with the branches was the existence of prominent, local directors whose views of economics and politics often differed from those of their New York City counterparts.

In November 1810, the Poughkeepsie directors wrote to New York requesting "an augmentation of the Capital of this branch" by at least $100,000. The Poughkeepsie directors argued that the capital of the branch was "too small" and the operations "too limited" to produce advantages "either to the public or to the main Bank." They stated their belief that a larger capital would lead to increased discounts and would attract new customers at the expense of the Columbia Bank agency located in the same city. The existing limited capital forced the Poughkeepsie directors to refuse some discounts, thereby leading the public to believe "the stories industriously propagated by those hostile to this office, that there is a monopoly of Bank Stock and of Bank favours, which must be counteracted by the establishment of a Dutchess County Bank." According to the Poughkeepsie directors, the idea of a new bank was "becoming prevalent and popular." They believed the local inhabitants would apply to the state legislature for a charter "unless an increase of the capital of this branch should promise a more general accommodation, and furnish a Banking Capital more proportionate to the wealth of the County." The last argument, in particular, appears designed to take advantage of the New York directors' political concerns over rival institutions.[21]

The New York directors appointed a committee to consider the branch's request for increased capital. The committee pointed out that since branch deposits were "inconsiderable," the branch only made a profit on "the paper money or Bank bills they keep in circulation." The committee noted the desirability of discounting for short periods of time, no longer than sixty days, because this allowed the bank's capital to revolve like a "great circulating wheel," thereby increasing profits. With this proviso in mind, the New York directors ultimately authorized sending another $50,000 in

[21]Poughkeepsie Directors to the President and Directors of the Manhattan Company, November 3, 1810, Poughkeepsie Minutes, 28-33.

Manhattan Company bank notes to each branch.[22] This increase in capital, however, did not satisfy the Poughkeepsie directors for long. One year later they again requested additional funds to meet the "frequent opportunities presented for exchanging [Manhattan Company] notes for notes of other Banks." The Manhattan Company board responded to this request by sending another $76,000 in notes to each branch.[23]

The question of branch capital took a different turn during the economic recession following the War of 1812. As will be recalled, the main bank called in all debts owed to it, including the debts of the branches. In mid-1814, the New York directors ordered the branches to reduce their discounts twenty percent within sixty days, in order to pay their debts to the main bank. If this did not prove sufficient, the branches were ordered "to make further reductions in their discounts, until their respective debts be paid."[24]

This 1814 action marked a change in emphasis for the branches. Rather than continued expansion, the branches entered a period of retrenchment which ultimately led to their closing. In 1816 the Poughkeepsie branch was directed to reduce its discounts by $5,000 within sixty days, and $5,000 more each succeeding sixty days, until

---

[22]MC Minutes, 2:93-101 (December 13, 1810).

[23]Ibid., 2:143-144 (April 20, 1812).

[24]Ibid., 2:215 (July 28, 1814).

further notice. The Utica branch, in turn, was given targets twice as high. The New York City directors intended to use the resulting funds to settle debts owed to other banks "and to prepare for a return to specie payments."[25] Though the Poughkeepsie directors established regulations designed to reduce discounts,[26] their efforts were not successful. Once the New York directors realized this failure, they sent the New York cashier to Poughkeepsie to take possession of "all the Manhattan notes, as well those of the Company [New York City] as those of said office [Poughkeepsie], and bring them back with him to New York."[27]

For all intents and purposes, the Poughkeepsie directors thereby were prevented from making discounts. In early 1817 the Poughkeepsie directors complained to New York that the absence of discounts caused them to lose many valued customers to rival institutions. Furthermore, even some of the directors "left our office" for greener pastures. Two of the directors, in fact, established their own separate "private banks." In general, the termination of discounts resulted in "a singular and unsettled state of public affairs" and led people to ask "Whether this office will commence business and if so, about what time and what dependence can

---

[25]Ibid., 3:8-9 (March 14, 1816).

[26]See Poughkeepsie Minutes, 51 (June 12, 1816).

[27]MC Minutes, 3:15 (June 18, 1816).

be placed upon it by those who should become its customers." Since it was the uncertainty which was so damaging to the office, the directors advocated "a declaration of our intentions to recommence business by a prudential yet limited discounting."[28]

By the summer of 1817, the Poughkeepsie office was permitted to extend credit under very limited circumstances. The New York City directors authorized the branch to renew discounted notes as they fell due, provided the notes were reduced when renewed and large debts were secured by mortgage. Any notes not adequately secured were to be "put in suit."[29]

Despite this limited resumption of discounts, the handwriting was on the wall for both Poughkeepsie and Utica. In October, the New York City directors designated the president and one board member as a committee to visit the branches. One month later this committee reported to the directors on the condition of the branches. According to the committee, Utica was in good fiscal health, with little reason to expect losses. Poughkeepsie, on the other hand, was in a "less favorable situation;" the committee anticipated losses on some of the debts owed to the branch. On December 1, 1817, the New York City directors acted on the committee report. They concluded that "the multiplication of Banks in the interior of the State, and

---

[28]Poughkeepsie Minutes, 52-55 (January 27, 1817).

[29]MC Minutes, 3:59 (July 7, 1817).

the depreciation of the paper of said Banks" had "destroyed the usefulness" of the branches. They voted, therefore, to close the branches, giving Utica one year to collect outstanding debts and Poughkeepsie only nine months.[30]

Over the next year and a half the Poughkeepsie branch wound up its affairs: over $230,000 in Poughkeepsie notes was counted and burned; as many of the outstanding debts as possible were settled or placed in suit; the banking house was rented to Frederick Harrison for use as a "genteel boarding house;" and the "books and papers" of the office were sent to New York City. The Poughkeepsie branch, which had survived a major political test early in its existence, ultimately fell victim to changing economic circumstances.[31]

The Utica Branch

The Manhattan Company's experience in Utica was similar in many ways to that of Poughkeepsie: politics, especially in the

---

[30]Ibid., 3:68-72 (December 1, 1817).

[31]For the bank notes, see ibid., 3:76 (December 24, 1817) and 3:96 (June 11, 1818). For the debts, see ibid., 3:87-88 (April 6, 1818); 3:107-109 (July 20-23, 1818); 3:212 (June 14, 1819); 3:232-233 (August 12, 1819). For the disposition of the banking house, see ibid., 3:252-254 (October 21-25, 1819); 4:21 (March 9, 1820). For the books and papers, see ibid., 3:254 (October 25, 1819). Some branch bank notes never were "presented for redemption" in New York City. In 1836 the directors "supposed [the notes] to have been lost or destroyed" and credited profit and loss for $4,285 in Poughkeepsie notes and $7,284.50 in Utica notes. See MC Journal 10, June 30, 1836.

person of DeWitt Clinton, played a key role in the founding of the branch; the office survived a major political challenge early in its existence; and there was a constant tension between the branch and the main office over the amount of capital allocated to Utica.

As with Poughkeepsie, the Manhattan Company directors received a petition from Utica requesting the establishment of a branch. The directors then authorized a branch, passed the same basic rules and regulations as those for Poughkeepsie, and allocated $100,000 in capital.[32]

Two weeks later, Clinton already was exploring possible banking houses in Utica. He expected quickly to have some resolution "on this subject as on that of Directors."[33] Within a matter of days Clinton reported to Remsen that he had located a brick house costing $3,000 which would require an equal amount for improvements such as a vault. Clinton closed the letter by "entreating" Remsen "to consider Mr. Mitchell's application for a Clerkship in a favorable light. In gratifying him, you will gratify a great number of your friends."[34]

In July 1809, the New York directors appointed the following twelve directors for the Utica office: Francis A. Bloodgood, James

---

[32]MC Minutes, 2:30-39 (February 9-13, 1809). For the capital, see MC Journal 2, September 30, 1809.

[33]Clinton to Remsen, March 1, 1809, Clinton Papers, Folder 3, NYPL.

[34]Clinton to Remsen, March 9, 1809, ibid.

S. Kip, Solomon Wolcott, Marcus Hitchcock, John Bellinger, Apollos Cooper, Thomas Walker, Nathan Williams, Nathan Smith, William Floyd, Henry Huntington, and Ephraim Hart. Elected president was Nathan Williams, a prominent attorney and politician. Williams was born in 1773 in Williamston, Massachusetts. Among his accomplishments were: District Attorney, Chenango County, 1802; District Attorney, Sixth District, 1801-1813; District Attorney, Oneida County, 1818-1821; U.S. House of Representatives, 1805-1807; New York State Assembly, 1816, 1818-1819; Delegate to the New York State Constitutional Convention, 1821; and Circuit Judge, 1823-1833. Williams died on September 25, 1835.[35]

Appointed cashier of the branch was Montgomery Hunt, the second teller of the Manhattan Company's main bank in New York City. Hunt was born in Westchester County and graduated from Columbia College in 1792. He eventually became one of the leading financial and political figures in Utica. For example, he was a presidential elector in 1816, casting his vote for James Monroe. Hunt also was a high-ranking Mason and Master of the Utica Lodge. He died in 1837 in St. Croix, where he had gone to try to improve his health. Hunt's importance, however, extended even beyond his death: his son, Ward

---

[35]For the election of directors, see MC Minutes, 2:54 (July 31, 1809); Utica *Saturday Globe*, August 28, 1897, p. 5. For Williams' biography, see M.M. Bagg, *The Pioneers of Utica* (Utica: Curtiss and Childs, 1877), 60-62.

Hunt, became a justice of the U.S. Supreme Court; his grandson, Montgomery Sicard, became a Rear Admiral in the U.S. Navy.[36]

A third person prominent in the Manhattan Company's Utica branch and in banking in New York State was Henry B. Gibson, the original clerk of the branch. Born in 1783 in Reading, Pennsylvania, Gibson worked in the Utica office of County Clerk Francis Bloodgood, a future Manhattan Company branch director. Gibson accompanied Hunt and other Manhattan Company officials to the rival Bank of Utica in 1812, a situation I will discuss below. In 1813 Gibson and Hunt had a disagreement which led to Gibson's resignation. Gibson spent the next seven years as a merchant in New York City, followed by thirty-six years as cashier of the Ontario Bank at Canandaigua. A contemporary called him "the most uniformly successful country banker the state has produced." He also was president of the Auburn and Rochester Railroad, and a director of the New York Central Railroad. At the time of Gibson's death in 1863, his fortune was estimated to be greater than $1 million.[37]

Under the leadership of these people, the Utica branch opened

---

[36]For Hunt's appointment, see MC Minutes, 2:58 (September 7-14, 1809). For Hunt's biography, see Bagg, *Pioneers*, 318; Utica *Saturday Globe*, August 28, 1897, p. 5.

[37]For Gibson's election, see MC Minutes, 2:54 (July 31, 1809). For Gibson's biography, see Bagg, *Pioneers*, 274-275.

for business on October 13, 1809.[38]   The early reports from the branch were very favorable.   To the eyes of an experienced politician like Henry Remsen, however, Montgomery Hunt was quite naive.   "The Cashier ... flatters himself," Remsen wrote to William Edgar, "that the opposition to [the branch] by certain violent politicians, will die away, in consequence of the impartial and accommodating conduct he is determined to evince to all."[39]

Naturally, the political opposition to the Utica branch did not die away.   In March 1810, Clinton informed Remsen that there was a petition before the Senate to charter a bank in Utica.   A bill with a capital of $350,000 ultimately did pass the Assembly, but was defeated in the Senate in early April.   According to Clinton, the supporters of this and similar bills were "totally indifferent to the public good," their "whole aim" being "unprincipled electioneering." Clinton then exhorted Remsen that "We must meet our antagonists at every point.   Their efforts seem to be heightened by desperation and they stick at nothing."[40]

The political opposition also got very personal.   "I am sorry

---

[38]MC Minutes, 2:59 (October 16, 1809).   The Manhattan Company ultimately spent $4,868.37 on property for a banking house. See MC Journal 2, October 30, 1809.

[39]Remsen to Edgar, October 30, 1809, Edgar Papers, Vol. 10, NYPL.

[40]Clinton to Remsen, March 15, 1810, April 3, 1810, Clinton Papers, NYPL.

to inform you," Clinton wrote to Remsen, "that unfavorable reports have reached me respecting our Cashier at Utica. It is said that he has been caressed exceedingly by two federalists and that he enters into their views and that he is assuming and consequential in his intercourse with the Directors." While Clinton expected that a complaint might be lodged against Hunt, he said he "had heard nothing that assails his fidelity in a pecuniary way."[41]

Indeed a complaint *was* lodged against Hunt several months later for his manner of dealing with the president and directors of the Utica branch. While the New York directors took no formal action against Hunt, they had Remsen write an "official" letter to Hunt expressing the "regret they felt on the occasion." Hunt's lengthy reply explained the "misunderstandings and differences of opinion" in Utica. According to Hunt, "some of [the] members" of the Utica board wanted "business conducted in a loose, informal manner, convenient to the indulgence of favoritism." This particularly was the case with discounts, where some directors preferred to circulate potential notes one at a time, rather than discussing them at formal meetings. Though Hunt's objection to this practice had been "rather animated," causing the complaint, all was now quiet at the branch. "This the effect of my submission to certain things and not a conviction of

---

[41]Clinton to Remsen, March 5, 1810, ibid.

their propriety."[42]

Not all the problems with the Utica branch, however, were internal or private. As with Poughkeepsie, the Utica branch experienced a major public crisis. The year was 1812 and the situation involved the establishment of a rival bank in Utica.

As discussed in the last chapter, 1812 was a time of great agitation across the state for the chartering of banks. In particular, the Manhattan Company's New York directors were concerned about the establishment of the "Six Million Bank" in Manhattan. One way the directors tried to enlist upstate allies against the Six Million Bank was by supporting the chartering of another bank in Utica. In January the New York directors informed their Utica counterparts that they would receive up to $100,000 in the notes of another Utica bank, provided no other bank was established in New York City. Two months later Remsen told Clinton that this "arrangement" would "satisfy the people of Utica and to the Westward, who had the power to prevent the incorporation of any additional Bank for this City."[43]

Despite this understanding, the Utica president was "violent for the 6 Million Bank," according to Clinton, when the matter came

---

[42]Remsen to Hunt, September 13, 1810, MC Records, NYHS. Hunt to Remsen, September 30, 1810, ibid.

[43]MC Minutes, 2:138-139 (January 6, 1812). Remsen to Clinton, March 9, 1812, Remsen Papers, Box 1, Folder 10, NYPL.

before the legislature. Clinton was certain the Utica bank would pass, and furthermore believed there was an "arrangement" among supporters of the Utica and Six Million Banks whereby "the latter will gain great strength." Apparently the arrangement was successful, since both banks received charters.[44]

A bigger surprise, however, awaited the Manhattan Company. When the Bank of Utica was chartered on June 1, 1812, the legislation "named for its Directors the gentlemen who are Directors of the [Manhattan] Company's Office ... in said village." The New York directors, therefore, sent a committee composed of Remsen and one director to Utica to assess the situation.[45] The committee reported that all but two of the Manhattan Company's directors decided to join the new bank. In addition, both the branch cashier and clerk resigned to join the rival institution.[46]

The Bank of Utica ultimately was very successful. It opened for business on December 8th with an authorized capital of $1 million (the actual capital, however, rarely exceeded $600,000). Interestingly enough, the Bank of Utica also had experience with branches, running an office in Canandaigua from 1816 to 1850 and turning down similar requests from Geneva and Buffalo. In 1865 the Bank of Utica

---

[44]Clinton to Remsen, March 11, 1812, Clinton Papers, NYPL.

[45]MC Minutes, 2:157-159 (June 25, 1812).

[46]Ibid., 2:161-164 (July 6-August 3, 1812).

received a national charter, changing its name to the First National Bank.[47]

This was not the last experience the Manhattan Company's Utica branch had with a rival institution. In October 1813, the president and three of the directors of the Manhattan Company's branch wrote to the New York directors stating their intention "to apply to the Legislature at their ensuing session for a Charter for a new bank at Utica." They wanted to know if, in the face of a new bank, the Manhattan Company directors would "think it worth their while to continue their present establishment at Utica." The Manhattan Company directors responded that they did not "think it necessary" to close the branch on that account. Nothing came of the 1813 attempt to charter an additional bank; perhaps the Manhattan Company's response played a part in this result.[48]

In 1815, however, a third bank *was* established at Utica, a branch of the Ontario Bank headquartered in Canandaigua. James Kissam, the Manhattan Company's Utica cashier at the time, resigned to become cashier of the Ontario Branch Bank. In addition, Robert

---

[47]For general information on the Bank of Utica, see Bagg, *Pioneers*, 315-317; John J. Walsh, *Vignettes of Old Utica* (Utica: Utica Public Library, 1982), 47. The records of the Bank of Utica survive in the Oneida Historical Society in Utica. Included in the General Ledger is an account with the Manhattan Company's Utica branch which runs from December 9, 1812 to May 31, 1814.

[48]MC Minutes, 2:188-189 (November 11, 1813).

Troup of Geneva wrote to the New York directors claiming that the president of the Manhattan Company's Utica branch and several of his friends "had connected themselves with the Ontario Branch Bank at Utica." Troup and other citizens of Geneva followed this information with a request that the Manhattan Company's Utica branch be moved to Geneva. The New York directors decided not to move the branch for two reasons: the move would result in much inconvenience, and some expense and loss; and second, before any move could take place, the debts of the branch would have to be collected in order to have sufficient capital to operate in Geneva. In the end, the Manhattan Company branch did not move and existed side-by-side with the Ontario Branch Bank. In 1855 the Ontario Branch severed its connection with the Canandaigua bank and became the Ontario Bank. It was forced to close in 1857.[49]

Despite these crises with rival institutions and the resulting changes in directors and officers, the Manhattan Company's Utica branch consistently was more profitable than its Poughkeepsie counterpart. This is illustrated by table two, which compares the net profits of both branches. Across the ten years of the Manhattan Company's experience with branches, the Utica office was almost twice as profitable as the Poughkeepsie one. Though the reason for this

---

[49]For general information on the Ontario Branch Bank see Walsh, *Vignettes*, 48-49; Bagg, *Pioneers*, 337. For the Troup letter, see MC Minutes, 2:247 (July 10, 1815).

increased profitability is not clearly explained in the extant records, we can surmise, based upon the information on the closing of the branches presented in the previous section, that Utica's discounts were sounder, resulting in fewer losses on uncollected debts.

Table 2
Net Profits at the
Poughkeepsie and Utica Branches, 1809-1819

Time Period		Net Profits		
From	To	Poughkeepsie	Utica	Pough/ Utica %
?	06/01/1809	217.12	--	N/A
06/01/1809	11/30/1809	1,091.02	--	N/A
12/01/1809	05/31/1810	1,849.08	2,612.67*	70.77
06/01/1810	11/30/1810	3,198.16	5,334.42	59.95
12/01/1810	05/31/1811	2,626.28	4,513.84	58.18
06/01/1811	11/30/1811	2,451.53	5,271.99	46.50
12/01/1811	05/31/1812	3,244.29	5,647.44	57.45
06/01/1812	11/30/1812	4,187.32	6,734.41	62.18
12/01/1812	05/31/1813	6,046.83	7,540.96	80.19
06/01/1813	11/30/1813	7,908.88	10,577.48	74.77
12/01/1813	05/31/1814	7,616.24	13,393.23	56.87
06/01/1814	11/30/1814	5,213.40	12,909.19	40.39
12/01/1814	05/31/1815	3,212.33	8,126.20	39.53
06/01/1815	11/30/1815	4,431.73	9,263.72	47.83
12/01/1815	05/31/1816	1,123.03	N/A	N/A
06/01/1816	11/30/1816	2,409.60	6,019.44	40.03
12/01/1816	05/31/1817	2,490.51	4,780.42	52.10
06/01/1817	11/30/1817	1,364.93	3,285.73	41.54
12/01/1817	05/31/1818	1,552.45	3,073.60	50.51
06/01/1818	11/30/1818	1,500.02	1,904.11	78.78
12/01/1818	05/31/1819	939.92	N/A	N/A
	TOTALS	64,674.67	110,988.85	58.27%

*Covers 10/31/1809 - 5/31/1810

As with the Poughkeepsie branch, there was a constant tension between Utica and New York over the amount of capital allocated to the branch. Only one month after the branch opened, the Utica directors requested an additional $100,000 in capital. While the New York directors decided not to increase the capital, they did vote to exchange an additional $50,000 in Manhattan Company notes for notes of other banks. According to the New York directors, this would help by "increasing the circulation of our notes and ... replacing the amount in specie and foreign notes here."[50] Beginning in 1810, the capital of the branch was "increased at different times by supplies of new notes, and decreased by returns of mutilated notes." By 1815 the capital of the Utica branch totaled $373,176.37.[51]

Even this increased capital, however, did not survive the retrenchment of the next few years. As discussed in the previous section, both branches were required to reduce discounts in order to settle accounts with the main bank. Also, after the decision to close the Utica branch in 1817, representatives of the Manhattan Company tried to collect outstanding debts from branch customers. This continued until 1820.[52] Once the branch closed, the banking

---

[50]MC Minutes, 2:66-67 (January 15, 1810).

[51]Ibid., 2:252-256 (September 27, 1815).

[52]For the retrenchment and closing of the branch, see ibid., 3:23 (July 30, 1816); 3:68-72 (December 1, 1817). For the settlement of debts, see ibid., 3:93 (May 14, 1818); 3:118-119

house was used as a private residence. Its most prominent occupant was Colonel John E. Hinman who lived in the house from 1827 to 1867. Hinman was Utica sheriff from 1821 to 1831 and mayor from 1850 to 1853.[53]

After the closing of the branches, the Manhattan Company received a number of requests to reopen old branches or establish new ones. In 1824, a request came from Utica to reopen the branch. Other requests came from Rochester in 1822 and 1826, and Geneva in 1825.[54] The Manhattan Company did not comply with any of these requests. After Utica and Poughkeepsie, the Manhattan Company did not have another branch for 100 years. On February 11, 1918 a merger with the Bank of the Metropolis gave the Manhattan Company a second office in Union Square. The next branches came on January 6, 1920 when the Manhattan Company's merger with the Bank of Long Island brought in thirteen additional branches.[55]

(August 20, 1818); 3:130 (October 5, 1818); 3:133-134 (October 26, 1818); 3:187-188 (March 15, 1819); 4:17 (February 24, 1820). The New York State Archives in Albany has the Supreme Court Records for Utica during this time period. The records contain a series called "Transcripts of Dockets of Judgment" which details the Manhattan Company's suits for the recovery of debts in Utica.

[53]Walsh, *Vignettes*, 47.

[54]MC Minutes, 4:161-162 (April 22-25, 1822); 4:181 (September 19, 1822); 4:260 (May 13, 1824); 5:56 (November 10, 1825); and 5:66 (February 23, 1826).

[55]See "Branches -- List," Record Group 1, Box 2, CMB Archives.

Conclusions

In most treatments of nineteenth century branch banking, economics is seen as the prime motivator in establishing branches. This is true to a certain extent, and the Manhattan Company most definitely was aware of the economic implications of its decisions. For example, the Manhattan Company's directors clearly stated on several occasions that they established branches in order to circulate their bank notes as widely as possible. And in closing the branches, the directors remarked that the proliferation of country banks, combined with depreciated bank notes, made branches less desirable than they had been a few years earlier.

This detailed look at the Manhattan Company's branches, however, makes clear that more than economics was involved. Politics was evident in the selection of directors and in Remsen's long, confidential letter to the Poughkeepsie cashier requesting clarification on the branch's operations. Each branch also experienced a major political challenge early in its existence: Poughkeepsie in the form of a public attack by a disgruntled director and would-be president, and Utica by the defection of almost the entire local leadership to a rival banking institution.

Since more than economics was involved, the Manhattan Company's New York directors gave the branches a great deal of time and attention. Unlike the Water Works, which the officers and directors frequently ignored except when called to task by the public, Remsen and the New York directors were intimately involved in the daily economic and political concerns of the branches. This is shown by the frequent and detailed correspondence among Remsen, Clinton, and the other directors. The minutes also reflect a considerable involvement in the affairs of the branches. Briefly stated, the Utica and Poughkeepsie branches were almost as carefully monitored and rigorously controlled as the main bank in New York City. The next chapter will test the validity of these conclusions about the relative positions of the Water Works and the branches by looking at the career patterns of individuals associated with each division.

CHAPTER SIX

CORPORATE FORM AND CAREER
PATTERNS: THE PEOPLE OF
THE MANHATTAN COMPANY

> In these new business bureaucracies,
> as in other administrative hierarchies
> requiring specialized skills, selection
> and promotion became increasingly based
> on training, experience, and performance
> rather than on family relationship or
> money. With the coming of modern
> business enterprise, the businessman,
> for the first time, could conceive of a
> lifetime career involving a climb up the
> hierarchical ladder. In such enter-
> prises, managerial training became
> increasingly longer and more
> formalized.[1]

The previous three chapters of this study have explored the way

the Manhattan Company managed its different divisions: the water

works, the main bank in New York City, and the upstate bank

branches. The chapters documented differing degrees of managerial

attention to and financial support of the several divisions. The

central conclusion was that key decisions about strategy and

structure often were affected directly by such external factors as

political pressure, public criticism, and the threat of competition.

---

[1]Alfred D. Chandler, Jr., *The Visible Hand: The Managerial Revolution in American Business* (Cambridge: Belknap Press of Harvard University Press, 1977), 8-9.

A secondary conclusion was that the main bank and the branches received the bulk of financial and managerial resources. While the water works was a very large and publicly visible entity, the Manhattan Company's officers and directors often considered it a distraction from banking, their preferred use of "surplus" capital. As a result, the water works largely was left to its own devices, except in times of public outcry or possible threats to the Manhattan Company's lucrative charter.

This chapter will test these conclusions from another angle by examining the career patterns of individuals associated with each division of the Manhattan Company. I will look at the extent to which the strategy and structure of the company were reflected in career paths of individuals. Among the expectations of career patterns one would have, based upon the above conclusions, are the following: If the water works indeed *was* independent, there should be little movement of individuals between the water works and the bank. If the bank branches *were* considered central to achieving the Manhattan Company's objectives, service with a branch should not have hurt one's career and might even have led to further advancement within the company. And finally, if the branches *were* so central, there should be a noticeable change in career patterns once the branches closed.

It is important to realize at the start, however, that this analysis of career patterns is *not* a mobility study along the lines pioneered by Stephan Thernstrom.[2]   Such a project, while

interesting and important, would require another volume and several

years of work.   Rather, this chapter is designed to test whether the

managerial priorities so clearly expressed in the Manhattan Company's

minutes, correspondence, and other records are reflected in the

career experience of employees.   This is a much narrower scope with

more modest objectives than a mobility study.[3]

---

[2]Stephan Thernstrom, *Poverty and Progress: Social Mobility in a Nineteenth Century City* (Cambridge, 1964).   Other examples of this genre are: Allan Dawley, *Class and Community: The Industrial Revolution in Lynn* (Cambridge: Harvard University Press, 1976); Michael B. Katz, *The People of Hamilton, Canada West: Family and Class in a Mid-Nineteenth Century City* (Cambridge: Harvard University Press, 1975); Clyde and Sally Griffin, *Natives and Newcomers: The Ordering of Opportunity in Mid-Nineteenth Century Poughkeepsie* (Cambridge: Harvard University Press, 1978); and Thernstrom, *The Other Bostonians: Poverty and Progress in the American Metropolis, 1880-1970* (Cambridge: Harvard University Press, 1973).

[3]Several authors has looked at various aspects of the career patterns of bankers.   An early work was Fritz Redlich, *The Molding of American Banking: Men and Ideas*, 2 vols. (New York: Hafner Publishing, 1947, 1951; reprint, New York: Johnson Reprint Company, 1969). Among recent works are Naomi R. Lamoreaux, "Banks, Kinship, and Economic Development: The New England Case," *Journal of Economic History* 46 (September 1986):   647-667; Lamoreaux, "The Structure of Early Banks in Southeastern New England: Some Social and Economic Implications," *Business and Economic History*, 2nd ser. 13 (1984):   171-184; Larry Schweikart, "Antebellum Southern Bankers: Origins and Mobility," *Business and Economic History*, 2nd ser. 14 (1985):   79-103; Schweikart, "Private Bankers in the Antebellum South," *Southern Studies* 25 (Summer 1986):   125-134; and Schweikart, *Banking in the American South From the Age of Jackson to Reconstruction* (Baton Rouge: Louisiana State University Press, 1987).   I previously published much of this chapter in the following article: Gregory S. Hunter, "The Development of Bankers: Career Patterns and Corporate Form at the Manhattan Company,

Water Works

By and large, the officers and directors of the Manhattan Company did not wish to devote much time, energy, or money to the water works. As a result of this policy, the water works was almost totally independent in day-to-day affairs. Under normal circumstances, the superintendent (or contractor) seldom consulted with the officers of the bank. He maintained the physical plant, added new customers, collected the water revenue, and resolved problems and complaints. It took a major crisis, like the 1821 discovery of fraud and mismanagement on the part of the recently deceased contractor, before controls were tightened.

The independence of the water works is reflected in the data presented in Table 3. From 1799 to 1842 there were only three positions of any importance at the water works: clerk, collector of the water revenue, and superintendent (called contractor from 1811-1821). It should not be surprising that the directors of the Manhattan Company tended to hire engineers for the top position at the water works: it was necessary for the superintendent to have a detailed knowledge of pumps, water pressure, and other related matters. Perhaps this technical gulf between the superintendent and the directors also contributed to the independence of the division.

1799-1842," *Business and Economic History*, 2nd ser. 14 (1985): 59-77.

The other positions at the water works usually were filled by friends of the directors. Once the directors voted to fill a position, they virtually forgot that it existed until it again became vacant. While there was a "water committee" of the board, it did little except in time of crisis. Day in and day out the water works was out of sight and out of mind.

Table 3
Positions and Personnel
at the Water Works, 1799-1842

Clerk	Collector of Water Revenue	Superintendent
Samuel Hoyt 1800-1801		Joseph Browne 1799-1803
Caleb Leach ("Agent") 1800-1803		Caleb Leach 1803-1806
	Edward McLaughlin 1805-1807	John Fellows 1806-1811
	James D. Bissett 1807 (Porter in Bank, 1800-1807)	
		F. Huguet "Contractor" 1811-1821
	Peter Aymar 1822	
John L. Gardiner 1821-1822	John L. Gardiner 1822-1824	John Lozier 1821-1842
Anthony L. Bleecker 1822-1824; ?-1833 (Check Clerk in Bank, 1824)	Anthony L. Bleecker 1824	
Thomas M. Shapter 1824 (Asst. Clerk & Check Clerk in Bank, 1824-1825)		
Rainetaux (?) 1824-1833		
	James Lozur (?) 1836-?	Jacob Lozier 1842

NOTES:
From 1800-1805 the clerk also served as collector
From 1811-1821 a "contractor" ran the water works

Indicative of this is the fact that from 1799 to 1842 only three people moved between the bank and the water works, all in low-level positions. James D. Bissett, who was made collector of the water revenue in 1807, had spent the previous seven years as porter in the bank (the equivalent of a modern day messenger). Anthony L. Bleecker, both clerk and collector in the 1820s, served for a brief time as a clerk in the bank. And Thomas M. Shapter moved from clerk of the water works in 1824 to the bank, where he served over the next two years as assistant clerk and check clerk. Clearly, the water works was not the fast track for advancement in the Manhattan Company.

But was there room for advancement *within* the water works? This certainly was possible. Caleb Leach moved from the position of "agent" (an amorphous classification somewhere between clerk and collector) to become the second superintendent of the water works. In the 1820s John L. Gardiner spent two years as clerk and then two years as collector before his death in 1824, and Bleecker filled in for a short time as collector.

What, then, can we conclude about career patterns at the water works? Three things seem reasonable. First, the water works and its employees were isolated from the mainstream of the Manhattan Company's activities. While they had a great deal of freedom, they also were seldom considered for promotions at the bank. Second, in filling the top position at the water works the directors tended to hire experienced engineers from outside the company. There is only one instance of someone from the inside being promoted to superintendent. And third, it was possible to advance from clerk to collector. Since the water works was a separate operation with separate books, most of its detailed records are lost. But even with the scattered information I have, there are two instances of such advancement taking place.

In sum, the career patterns at the water works accurately reinforce the impression gained from the minutes and other records that this division was largely independent from the company's other operations.

The Upstate Branches

From 1809 to 1819 the Manhattan Company engaged in an experiment in branch banking by establishing offices in two important upstate villages, Utica and Poughkeepsie. As discussed in chapter five, the Manhattan Company's directors believed branches could be profitable both by attracting deposits and by further circulating the notes of the company. As it turns out, the branches also were "profitable" for individual Manhattan Company staff members. The branches became a powerful career accelerator for many at the parent bank. Even those who did not transfer to Utica or Poughkeepsie, however, benefited from the state of flux, as promotional possibilities dominoed through the ranks. Throughout these ten years the centrality of the branches is shown by the career patterns of Manhattan Company employees.

Table 4
Cashiers at the
Poughkeepsie Branch

Name	Previous Positions	Subsequent Career
Samuel Flewwelling 1809-1810	Bookkeeper 1801-1804 Bookkeeper & Runner 1804 Book. & Asst. Teller 1804-1805 First Bookkeeper 1805-1809	Cashier, NYC 1810-1816
John S. Hunn 1810	First Bookkeeper 1799 Second Teller 1799-1805 (NYC Street Commissioner, 1805-?)	Resigned due to financial difficulties, 1810
Daniel Coolidge 1810-1815	Second Discount Clerk 1806-1808 Bookkeeper 1806-1808 Fourth Bookkeeper 1808-1809 Third Bookkeeper 1809-1810 First Bookkeeper 1810	Unknown
James Nazro 1815-1816	Assistant Clerk 1809 Second Discount Clerk 1809 Disc. Clerk & 4th Book. 1809 First Discount Clerk 1809-1810 First Bookkeeper 1810-1815	Unknown
William W. Nexsen 1816-?	Second Discount Clerk 1809-1809	Unknown

Table 5
Cashiers at the
Utica Branch

Name	Previous Positions	Subsequent Career
Montgomery Hunt 1809-1812	Asst. Discount Clerk 1800 Fourth Bookkeeper 1800-1801 First Bookkeeper 1801-1805 Second Teller 1805	Cashier, Bank of Utica, 1812-1834 Died in St. Croix, 1837
James Kissam 1812-1815	Assistant Clerk 1807-1808 Second Discount Clerk 1808 First Discount Clerk 1808-1809 Disc. Clerk & 3rd Teller 1809 Third Teller 1809-1810 Second Teller 1810-1812	Cashier, Utica Branch of the Ontario Bank, 1815-?

NOTE: The records do not indicate who succeeded Kissam as Utica cashier.

Tables 4 and 5 summarize the career patterns of the seven people who served as cashier at either Utica or Poughkeepsie. Three conclusions are apparent. First, while local people were hired as clerks for the branches, all of the cashiers were promoted from the New York City bank. It is logical that the New York City directors entrusted the branches to people they knew, rather than relying on unproven individuals from the local area. In all banks at this time, the cashier's position was much too important to subject it to chance.

The second conclusion about the branches is that the people who became cashiers were not the highest level clerks in the parent bank in New York City. While three individuals had risen as high as second teller, three others were no higher than first bookkeeper and one was only second discount clerk. Service in the branches, therefore, was a way for mid-level clerks to break the promotional logjam in New York City.

The third conclusion is that it was possible to parlay experience in a branch into a much better position at the main bank in New York City or in another banking institution. Once an individual had proven himself worthy of the responsibility of cashier, the expansion of banking in the state offered a number of options for further personal and career growth.

The best way of illustrating these conclusions is by looking at three specific individuals. Samuel Flewwelling was hired in 1801 as bookkeeper in New York City. After being promoted to assistant teller in 1804, Flewwelling spent the next four years as first bookkeeper. At this point Flewwelling's career in New York City probably would have stalled behind Andrew Seaman, who served as second teller from 1808-1809 and first teller from 1809-1817. The branches, however, offered Flewwelling another option. He became the founding cashier at the Poughkeepsie branch, serving from 1809-1810. The experience gained at Poughkeepsie in turn helped him in New York City. When the cashier's position in the main bank became vacant in 1810, Flewwelling received the appointment and served for seven years. It is interesting that Flewwelling was appointed over Seaman, who still was first teller at the main bank and who normally would have advanced to cashier. Seaman eventually did become cashier, but only after Flewwelling left the Manhattan Company in 1817. Clearly in this case, branch experience changed the normal course of promotion in New York City. Also, the ease with which Flewwelling moved between divisions indicates the close relationship between the branches and the main bank.

The second case, that of James Kissam, is almost as dramatic. Kissam was hired in 1807 as assistant clerk in New York City. In the next three years he received four promotions: second discount clerk, first discount clerk, third teller, and second teller. He then spent two years as second teller, stalled (as was Flewwelling) behind First Teller Andrew Seaman. In 1812, Kissam was appointed cashier at the

Utica branch, an office he held for the next three years. Unlike Flewwelling, however, Kissam did not return to the main bank in New York City. (He was stalled behind Seaman as first teller and Flewwelling as cashier.) Kissam instead became cashier of the branch of the Ontario Bank located in Utica.

The final person I will look at is James Nazro. Like Kissam, Nazro experienced rapid promotions. From 1809-1810 he served in the following five positions: assistant clerk; second discount clerk; discount clerk and fourth bookkeeper; first discount clerk; and first bookkeeper. During that time his salary jumped from $600 to $900, a fifty percent increase. Nazro then served as Poughkeepsie cashier from 1815-1816; his subsequent career in unknown.

Nazro is important, however, because he illustrates the chain-reaction effect the branches had upon mid-level clerks. When Nazro was appointed first bookkeeper in 1810, he was the fourth person in a year to hold that position. Two of his predecessors (Flewwelling and Daniel Coolidge) moved to the branches, as did Nazro himself. It was this type of person -- a solid professional in mid-career -- who went to the branches. The lower level clerks, in turn, benefitted by more rapid advancement through the ranks in New York City.

Career patterns at the branches differed significantly from those at the water works. While the water works and its personnel were isolated from the mainstream of the Manhattan Company's operations, the branches were an integral part of the company's central banking function. This is shown by the "percolator effect" the branches had among low- and mid-level clerks at the New York bank: serving in a branch not only advanced one's career, it opened up possibilities for those lower on the ladder.

The path between the main bank and the branches, however, was largely one-way, with only Flewwelling returning to the New York City bank. I suspect this is because people who had served as cashier at one of the branches, and had experienced the freedom and power this position entailed, did not wish to return to New York City in a subordinate role. Service in the branches had enabled them to jump from mid-level clerks to senior management. Only one position in the main bank -- that of cashier -- could now entice them. As shown particularly by the cases of Montgomery Hunt and James Kissam, the proliferation of banks across the state at this time often offered better prospects outside of the Manhattan Company.

The Main Bank in New York City

In order to really appreciate the centrality of the branches to the Manhattan Company's operations as well as their importance as career accelerators, it is necessary to look at what happened at the main bank after the closing of the branches. Logically, one would expect a slowing of the rapid turnover and promotions. This, indeed, was the case.

Table 6 is a listing of all the individuals who held one of four key positions at the main bank between 1799 and 1842: first bookkeeper, second teller, first teller, and cashier. My choice of positions to trace was based on a number of factors. As the previous section indicated, first bookkeeper and second teller were the primary spawning grounds for branch cashiers. I included first teller and cashier because they were the ultimate promotional possibilities in New York City. I excluded president, however, because of the nature of the position at this time: most presidents were chosen for their ability to instill confidence in and attract business from customers, rather than for their professional expertise and long experience as bankers. Henry Remsen was the notable exception.

Table 6
Career Patterns at the New York City Bank
Four Key Positions, 1799-1842

Year	1st Bookkeeper	2nd Teller	1st Teller	Cashier
1799	John S. Hunn John Rathbone	Ralph Thurman <u>John S. Hunn</u>	Whitehead Fish	Henry Remsen
1800	"	"	"	"
1801	"	"	"	"
	<u>Montgomery Hunt</u>			
1802	"	"	"	"
1803	"	"	"	"
1804	"	"	"	"
1805	"	"	"	"
	<u>Sam. Flewwelling</u>	<u>Montgomery Hunt</u> T. Stoutenburgh		
1806	"	"	"	"
1807	"	"	"	"
1808	"	"	"	"
		Andrew Seaman	T. Stoutenburgh	Whitehead Fish
1809	"	"	"	"
	Gabriel Theriott	James Bleecker	Andrew Seaman	"
1810	"	"	"	"
	<u>Daniel Coolidge</u> <u>James Nazro</u>	<u>James Kissam</u>	"	<u>S. Flewwelling</u>
1811	"	"	"	"
1812	"	"	"	"
		James Gelston		
1813	"	"	"	"
1814	"	"	"	"
1815	"	"	"	"
	A. Rainteaux			
1816	"	"	"	"
1817	"	"	"	"
		Brown King	James Gelston	Andrew Seaman
1818	"	"	"	"
1819	"	"	"	"
		James A. Funk		Robert White
1820	"	"	"	"

NOTE: Underlined names were involved with the upstate branches

Table 6 (Continued)

Year	1st Bookkeeper	2nd Teller	1st Teller	Cashier
1821	A. Rainetaux	James A. Funk Wm. Shepherd	James Gelston James A. Funk	Robert White
1822	"	"	"	"
1823	"	"	"	"
1824	"	"	"	"
1825	"	"	"	"
1826	"	"	"	"
1827	"	"	"	"
1828	"	"	"	"
1829	"	"	"	"
		Rich. Sterling	Wm. Shepherd	
1830	"	"	"	"
1831	"	"	"	"
1832	"	"	"	"
	Andrew Garr		Edward Tailer	
1833	"	"	"	"
1834	"	"	"	"
1835	"	"	"	"
	Adam Tiebout	Stephen Richard Colin Newcomb	Rich. Sterling Stephen Richard	
1836	?	"	"	"
		Robert Roberts	Colin Newcomb	
1837	?	"	"	"
1838	?	"	"	"
1839	?	"	"	"
1840	?	"	"	"
			James Morrison	Wm. Vermilye
1841	?	?	"	"
1842	?	Alex. Allaire	"	"
			John G. O'Brien Adam Tiebout	James Morrison

NOTE: It is impossible to determine incumbents for some positions beginning in the late 1830s. At that time the Manhattan Company stopped listing quarterly salaries in the minutes, probably because the company established a separate payroll ledger (which unfortunately does not survive).

Although the name of the first bookkeeper for the late 1830s is unknown, Tiebout probably stayed in the position. The reason for this assumption is Tiebout's appointment as first teller in 1842. To be considered for this appointment, it is logical that during the intervening years he remained with the company in a responsible position.

At first glance, Table 6 appears to show a slowing of advancement after the branches, at least in two of the four positions: Anthony Rainetaux served seventeen years as first bookkeeper and Robert White served twenty-one years as cashier. In an effort to be more precise, however, I have developed Table 7. In this table I have broken my time period into four roughly equal sections: pre-branches (1799-1808), branches (1809-1819), and two groupings for post-branches (1820-1830 and 1831-1842). Within each section I have computed the average number of years a person served in each position. I am using this as my rough measure of turnover.

Table 7
Main Bank in New York City:
Average Length of Service in Four Key Positions
Before, During, and After Branches

	1st Book.		2nd Teller		1st Teller		Cashier	
	# of Indiv	Years/ Indiv	# of Indiv	Years/ Indiv	# of Indiv	Years/ Indiv	# of Indiv	Years/ Indiv
Pre-Branches 1799-1808 (10 years)	4	2.5	5	2.0	2	5.0	2	5.0
Branches 1809-1819 (11 years)	5	2.2	6	1.8	3	3.7	4	2.8
Post-Branches 1820-1830 (11 years)	1	11.0	3	3.7	3	3.7	1	11.0
Post-Branches 1831-1842 (12 years)	3	4.0	5	2.4	8	1.5	3	4.0

NOTE: Due to overlapping terms, the same person may be counted in more than one bracket.

The results in Table 7 are dramatic. There was more rapid turnover in each position while the Manhattan Company had branches than in the decade immediately preceding the branches' establishment. Also, from 1820 to 1830 there was a sharp reversal of this trend in three of the four positions (the fourth position kept the same rate). The average length of service for first bookkeeper jumped from 2.2 to 11.0 years; for second teller from 1.8 to 3.7 years; and for cashier from 2.8 to 11.0 years. Without the branches as a release valve, people tended to stay in their positions for a longer period of time.

The twelve years from 1831 to 1842 saw an easing of this trend toward longevity. But in only one position, that of first teller, was there more rapid turnover than during the decade of the branches. In assessing turnover during this time period, however, it is important to keep two related factors in mind. The first was the Panic of 1837 and its resulting economic and social dislocations. The second was the fact that in 1840 the Manhattan Company faced its most serious challenge and its greatest fiscal crisis. As will be recalled, a general housecleaning in the wake of a public investigation of the company led to changes in the positions of president, cashier, first teller, second teller, and third teller. Under these circumstances, it is surprising that the post-1830 period did not show even greater turnover.

Granted Table 7 shows a correlation rather than a causal

relation and granted that it is not a sophisticated statistical instrument. Nevertheless, using even a rough measure such as "average length of service" makes clear that promotion and advancement at the Manhattan Company's main bank in New York City were greatly affected by the existence of the upstate branches. Even the years after 1835 did not witness the same rapid turnover in key positions as the company experienced from 1809 to 1819. Unlike the water works, the branches clearly were an integral part of the Manhattan Company's operations.

Conclusions

This chapter has been a first attempt at assessing how the Manhattan Company's corporate structure was reflected in the turnover and advancement of employees. Much remains to be done, especially locating information about the careers of former Manhattan Company employees who moved to other institutions.[4] But even with the

---

[4] Assuming that the Manhattan Company's bookkeeping was typical of other banks, the main way of locating this information would be by reading the extant minutes of all other banks in the hope of finding payroll lists. The problem is that most of the nineteenth century banks no longer exist: there was a continuing series of mergers which resulted in the major New York City banks we find today. While the Chase Manhattan Archives has a good collection of minute books from merged banks, the same may not hold true for other New York City banks. As can be seen, the tracking of low-level bankers between institutions is a formidable task beyond the scope of this study. As a first step toward beginning such a project, however, I have produced an appendix to this volume which lists in detail all individuals associated with the Manhattan company as

preliminary treatment presented here, three conclusions appear valid.

First, the two major divisions of the company, water supply and banking, were virtually independent of one another. In terms of daily operations, they were two separate companies. This is clear at the management level: the officers and directors seldom concerned themselves with the water works except in times of crisis. This separation also is apparent from the career patterns of Manhattan Company employees: there was no significant movement between the two divisions. While there are instances of advancement *within* the water works, Manhattan Company officials seldom looked to the water works when filling positions in the bank.

Second, the Manhattan Company's brief experiment with branches had a profound impact upon the entire banking operation. In ten short years, seven low- and mid-level clerks in New York City moved to the responsible position of cashier in a branch. This set off a chain reaction of rapid advancement for clerks even lower on the promotional ladder. Similarly the officers and directors in New York City were actively involved with the branches. The Manhattan Company's minutes and Henry Remsen's correspondence are full of references to the branches. This active involvement reinforces the centrality of the branches to the Manhattan Company's operations. Clearly, the parent bank did not treat the branches like orphans;

---

reflected in the minutes. My hope is that additional researchers will compile similar lists for other nineteenth century banks.

rather, they were highly favored children.

My final conclusion relates to corporate form and career patterns in the first half of the nineteenth century. The Manhattan Company had a form uncommon for its time: a multi-unit corporation flowing from a distinctly modern charter. It also had career development unusual for its time, due to the presence of two separate New York City divisions and two upstate bank branches. These two aspects -- corporate form and career patterns -- were intimately connected at the Manhattan Company and probably at other institutions as well. To look at only one aspect would be to see only one side of the coin. Future studies must consider both sides in order to achieve a balanced view of corporate and professional development in nineteenth century America.

CONCLUSION

In this study I have looked at the development of the Manhattan Company from 1799 to 1842. My analysis has had two focal points. The first was the modern charter of the company and its effect upon operations. At the time of the Manhattan Company's founding, most charters for businesses were very narrow in scope, detailing precisely what a company could and could not do. Most charters also were for limited durations and the amount of capital usually was kept small. These general patterns were even more apparent with corporations chartered for banking or other financial purposes. Legislatures tended to carefully structure banks because the ability of banks to issue their own notes amounted to a public franchise for the circulation of currency. Also behind the tight legislative control of banks was the political motivation of granting banking powers to one's supporters and denying them to one's opponents. Access to financial resources therefore was a political as well as an economic lever.

In this context, the Manhattan Company's charter clearly was atypical. The stated laudable purpose of supplying New York City with water led otherwise astute Federalist politicians, including Alexander Hamilton, to ignore a Trojan Horse near the end of the charter. The so-called "surplus capital clause" opened the way for the Manhattan Company to engage in banking and other activities with virtually no legislative control or oversight. In engaging in these activities, the company would benefit from a perpetual charter and a $2 million capitalization. As such it would be both an economic and political force in the state and the nation.

The second focus of this study was the interweaving of internal and external affairs throughout the Manhattan Company's history. The Manhattan Company was on the cusp of a change in the public's perception of corporations. In 1799, all business corporations were considered public franchises, similar to modern utilities. Businesses were permitted to operate because they provided a necessary service to the public within their geographical areas. With the Manhattan Company, the franchise nature of its water works was obvious: the public had a reasonable expectation that the company would meet a demonstrated civic need. Banking, however, also was viewed as a franchise to be bestowed by the legislature. Therefore the availability of capital and the terms of credit were of great interest to merchants and other individuals. The tension between the public nature of banking and the private desires and objectives of the directors came to the fore on several occasions, both in New York City and with the upstate branches. Achieving a balance between these internal and external factors was one of the major managerial challenges facing the leaders of the Manhattan Company.

The Water Works

Though the Manhattan Company was chartered to supply New York City with water, there is no doubt that the directors came to view the water works as a distraction from their central interest in banking. At the very beginning, the directors decided on a low-cost approach to supplying the city with water, opting for a well on Manhattan Island rather than tapping upstate rivers and streams. Furthermore, once the water works was established, the officers and directors of the company largely left this division alone except in times of public criticism or crisis. In particular, the directors became attentive to the water works whenever there was a possibility that the company could be accused of not meeting its charter obligations and might therefore be forced out of existence. At such times, the company both committed extra funds to the water works and attempted to sway public opinion about the nature and extent of the company's operations.

This is not to say, however, that the Manhattan Company did *nothing* in the area of water supply or completely neglected its obligations in this regard. If the Manhattan Company was completely unresponsive, it would not have mattered how much the public complained or how great was the threat posed by other water companies: the directors would have proceeded apace without worrying about the consequences. But this was not the case from 1799 to 1842. While we can argue about the *adequacy* of the measures the directors undertook, they clearly *did* take steps to supply New York City with water. Never did they completely turn their backs on the public and dismiss the company's water supply obligations.

In evaluating the water works, it also is important to compare New York City with other nineteenth century American cities. When looked at in this way, it is clear that every city faced problems in improving its supply of water. Many cities experienced the same tension between the desire to make water supply a municipal function and the necessity of capitalizing such a large project without exhausting the public treasury. As a result of this tension, several cities tried private companies for the supply of water. In one case, that of Baltimore, the city even went from a *public* water works to a *private* company.

New York also was not alone in its struggle over the best source for a supply of water. Bostonians had a similar difference of opinion about whether water should come from local or distant sources. Boston ultimately committed itself to a more distant source at about the same time as New York City. The difficulty of supplying water from a distant source was further illustrated by the New York Croton Project's complexity and millions of dollars in cost overruns.

This comparison with other cities is not intended to completely exonerate the Manhattan Company's leaders. Rather, it is designed to show that other cities faced similar problems with water supply even when it was divorced from banking. While the Manhattan Company undoubtedly could have done more, it is unfair to say that it did nothing at all or that its solutions were atypical for the times. Perhaps it ultimately is a question of expectations: because of the Manhattan Company's large capitalization, prominent supporters, and initial rhetoric, both the public of the time and historians of today expected a nobler effort than they encountered. In this sense, it is not so much that the Manhattan Company could have done *more* for water supply, but that it did not do *everything* for the cause.

Banking in New York City

Throughout this time period, banking clearly was the Manhattan Company's main interest. This is shown by the amount of managerial time and attention devoted to this activity as well as by the career patterns of people associated with the company. For example, the Manhattan Company's key leaders, Henry Remsen and DeWitt Clinton, were involved in all aspects of the banking operation. Their voluminous correspondence sheds a great deal of light upon the nature of the Manhattan Company's operations.

This correspondence particularly shows the links between internal and external factors. Because of the franchise nature of nineteenth century banking, the Manhattan Company's leaders always had to be aware of the public consequences of their private decisions. Whether it involved loan policies or the allocation of capital among divisions, the company's leaders had to be prepared to face public scrutiny of their actions. In extreme cases, such as the 1840 investigation of the company, a public outcry could lead to a complete reversal of policies and a thorough housecleaning of staff.

Economics and politics were similarly connected. While other scholars such as Bray Hammond and Ronald Seavoy have documented this connection in the granting of bank charters, this study has shown that the links continued even after a company was in operation. The link between politics and corporations in New York went beyond the Albany Regency and the state legislature. For example, the 1830 suit against the Manhattan Company stemmed as much from a political desire to regain control over the company as it did from an economic desire to force the company to join the Safety Fund. At no time in its history was the Manhattan Company far from the politics of the day.

Henry Remsen was particularly skillful at balancing the diverse demands upon him. Under his leadership, the Manhattan Company prospered both economically and politically; in fact, it became both a financial and a political leader. The situation deteriorated under Remsen's less astute successors, particularly Robert White. White's injudicious use of the economic powers delegated to him by the board of directors led to a public outcry against the company's loan policies and the 1840 investigation of its operations. It took years for the company's next outstanding leader, James M. Morrison, to restore the company to its previous positions of economic health and social prominence.

The Upstate Branches

The Manhattan Company's experience with upstate branches serves to reinforce these conclusions about the interconnection of politics and economics in the ongoing operations of the company. Clinton and Remsen regularly corresponded about all aspects of branch affairs. Whether the matter at hand was the appointment of local directors, the parrying of political threats in the individual villages, or the answering of public attacks in the state legislature, Clinton and Remsen considered politics as well as economics.

Each branch, in fact, faced a major political challenge early in its existence. In Poughkeepsie, a disgruntled aspirant to the presidency led to a division among the directors and a public airing of the feud at the state level. In Utica, almost the entire branch leadership resigned to join a recently-chartered rival banking establishment. Furthermore, in the case of both branches, the New York City leadership was conscious of local political splits, being as concerned about "federalists and quids" as they were about discounts and loans.

In addition to the political awareness and involvement noted above, the centrality of the branches to the Manhattan Company's mission is further illustrated by the career paths of the individuals associated with the branches. Service at a branch helped advance the careers of several Manhattan Company employees; it also created promotional opportunities for those who remained in New York City. This was not the case with the water works, where both career patterns and managerial involvement point to an independent division within the Manhattan Company.

Though the Manhattan Company was involved with branches for only ten years, this short period of time should not cause one to minimize the significance of the branches. Many of the trends exhibited elsewhere in the Manhattan Company -- the political under-current of the attacks upon the Manhattan Company's economic policies, the migration of local disagreements to a statewide forum, and the association of political well-being with economic advancement -- were apparent in the branches.

Implications of this Study

This detailed analysis of one major nineteenth century corporation has several implications for the wider field of business history. First and foremost is the conceptual framework linking Chandler's strategy and structure with Hammond's political and social environments. While additional work still needs to be done on other corporations and industries, it appears as though this linkage may go far in explaining some of the vagaries of corporate development.

An example from the railroad industry reveals the possibilities. It would be important to study the degree to which railroad development was accelerated by general incorporation statutes. What was the experience of New York's railroads before the 1850 general incorporation statute for that industry? Were strategy and structure circumscribed by restrictive charters? What changes occurred after 1850? Does general incorporation help explain these changes?

Or, to return to banking, it would be interesting to study additional "improvement banks" -- banks linked with such internal improvements as canals, turnpikes, and railroads. Was the experience of these multi-unit enterprises similar to that of the Manhattan Company? To what extent did social and political factors affect the strategy and structure of *these* institutions? In short, how unique was the Manhattan Company's experience?

A second major implication of this study involves the use of detailed employee records for other purposes besides mobility research. While the leaders of an institution may *say* one thing, it is important to find ways of verifying their statements against some objective measure. In this study I used payroll lists to test the degree to which each Manhattan Company division was independent. Tracing the changing career patterns of employees may offer a window into the inner workings of other nineteenth century institutions. Where did management commit personnel resources? What does the changing nature of these commitments tell us about modifications in strategy and structure? Was management saying one thing and doing another?

Again, an example may reveal some of the possibilities. It would be interesting to look at the careers of employees in the early telephone and oil industries to see how their experiences reflected changing managerial priorities. How did career patterns change during periods of horizontal or vertical integration? What effects did local environments have on career development? Such a study would combine social and business history in a way not previously done.

Ultimately what I am suggesting is a circular approach to the study of management. I am trying to avoid seeing managerial strategy and structure, societal pressures and concerns, and employee career patterns as three separate lines. In the traditional linear approach, the three paths may grow closer at times, but they never really intersect. In my approach, each of these elements would be a separate circle: overlapping one another and offering insights into the other two categories. In this way managerial strategy, societal influences, and individual careers all would be given equal emphasis by business historians trying to explain the development of institutions and industries. It is an approach offering great possibilities.

In a letter quoted at the beginning of this volume, DeWitt Clinton spoke of leaving a lesson to posterity. The legacy Clinton hoped to leave was that the political cause of "republicanism" was intimately connected with the prosperity of sympathetic economic institutions. The officers and directors of the Manhattan Company clearly shared Clinton's belief that politics and economics were closely connected. They made this principle one of the bases for their management of the institution. While the Manhattan Company's leaders learned their lessons well, it has taken until now for historians to begin to understand and appreciate this fact.

APPENDIX:

INDIVIDUALS ASSOCIATED WITH

THE MANHATTAN COMPANY

The following is a listing of all individuals associated with the Manhattan Company from 1799 to 1842. The list includes officers, staff members, and directors; it is taken primarily from the minutes of the company found in the Chase Manhattan Archives. Salaries are on an annual basis, unless otherwise noted.

In terms of directors, the list details all committees on which a person served. In this way it is possible to determine which directors were most active and which directors dealt with particular issues. Since directors were elected in December of each year, I decided it was not necessary to provide the exact annual election date. This helped to reduce the size of the listing, especially when dealing with long term directors of the company.

In terms of staff members, I hope this list will be the first step in a larger project to document career patterns across nineteenth century banks. Once researchers compile similar lists from the records of other banks, it will be possible to trace the movement of low- and mid-level bankers in New York City and elsewhere.

Name	Activities
Adams, William B.	Assistant clerk, $500, 5/12/1817.
Aliber, S.M.	Resigned as clerk, 3/9/1834.

Allaire, Alexander, Jr.   Assistant clerk, $200, 4/9/1834; $300, 9/30/1834; $500, 3/31/1836; bookkeeper, $800, 9/30/86; 2nd teller, $1,000, 12/31/1842.

Allaire, Edward C.   Assistant clerk, $400, 9/30/1825; runner, $400, 12/27/1825; last listed as runner, $800, 3/31/1836.

Arden, James   Director, 11/14/1803, 1804-1809; committee to burn bank notes, 1803-1805; comm. to consider transferring water works to New York City, 1804; comm. to view land prior to purchase, 1805; vice president, $1,500, 12/10/1805; water comm., 1806, 1807; comm. to examine unpaid discounts, 1806; comm. to examine plans to build new banking house, 1806; comm. to make loans on voyages, 1807; resigned as vice president, 6/1807; comm. to investigate water complaints, 1809; comm. to consider MC situation re: discounts and loans, 1810.

Astor, William B.   Director, 3/24/1840; comm. of examination, 1840; resigned 7/10/1840.

Aymar, Peter   Resigned as collector of water revenue, 8/8/1822.

Baldwin, Herman   Assistant clerk, $600, 7/3/1810; bookkeeper, $800, 7/23/1810; resigned 8/27/1812.

Baldwin, Russell   Assistant clerk, $300, 12/1/1812.

Barr, John J.   Assistant bookkeeper, $900, 9/15/1836.

Bayard, William, Jr.   Director, 1819-1823, 1825; water comm., 1819.

Beekman, Stephen D.   Director, 1828-1832, 1834-1835, 1838-1839; resigned 7/10/1840.

Bellinger, John   Director, Utica, 7/31/1809.

Berry, John   Assistant clerk, $600, 9/5/1804; bookkeeper, $800, 12/31/1804; 2nd bookkeeper, $800, 3/31/1808.

Bissett, James D.   Porter, $300, 12/31/1800; $350, 12/31/1802; $400, 12/31/1804; collector of water revenues, 5/18/1807.

Bleecker, Anthony L.	Clerk in water office, 11/18/1822; check clerk, 4/19/1824; clerk in water office, 4/26/1824; collector of water revenue, 9/16/1824; assistant clerk, $300, 12/31/1830; listed in water office, 1/7/1833.
Bleecker, James W.	Assistant clerk, $600, 6/1/1806; runner, $700, 12/14/1806; $800, 12/31/1807; assistant 2nd teller, $800, 2/25/1808; 3rd teller, $800, 6/30/1809; 2nd teller, $1,000, 9/8/1809.
Bleecker, Leonard A.	Assistant clerk, $600, 6/24/1809.
Bleecker, William	Notary, 8/13/1799; notice of his death, 8/16/1818.
Bloodgood, Francis A.	Director, Utica, 7/31/1809.
Bloom, George	Attorney, Poughkeepsie, 5/24/1809.
Bloom, Jonathan	Director, Poughkeepsie, 12/5/1811, 5/13/1813.
Blunt, George W.	Director, 1841, 1842; quarterly comm., 12/1841, 7/1842, 12/1842.
Bogert, John G.	Solicitor, 5/5/1803; notary, 8/13/1818; notice of his death, 12/18/1828.
Bowne, John R.	Assistant clerk, $600, 8/15/1804; left 4/19/1805; assistant clerk, $500, 2/29/1808; $600, 9/30/1808; runner, $800, 12/31/1810; left 10/23/1813; runner, $800, 5/10/1814; left 10/8/1814.
Bowne, Walter	Director, 1801-1816; comm. to examine cash, 1801; comm. on employment of surplus capital, 1801; water comm., 1802-1804, 1806-1807, 1815; comm. to assess street damage, 1804; comm. to consider transferring water works to New York City, 1804; comm. to view land prior to purchase, 1805; comm. to burn bank notes, 1805, 1807; comm. to examine unpaid discounts, 1806; comm. to plan for a new banking house, 1806; comm. to make loans on voyages, 1807; comm. to confer with other banks re: overdrafts, 1807; comm. to explore necessity of having a vice president, 1807; comm. to confer with the Common Council re: hydrants, 1807;

comm. to go to Utica to consider possible directors, 1809; comm. to investigate water complaints, 1809; comm. to consider increasing capital of Utica office, 1810; comm. to investigate protested discounts, 1811; comm. to consider country bank accounts, 1812; comm. to consider situation of Utica office, 1812; comm. to purchase stock, 1812; comm. on reduction of debt, 1814; comm. on immediate concerns, 1814; resigns as director, 2/3/1817.

Brennan, George S. Assistant clerk, $250, 5/8/1834; $300, 9/30/1834; $500, 3/31/1836; bookkeeper, $800, 9/30/1836.

Brinckerhoft, Derick A. Director, Poughkeepsie, 4/14/1809; comm. to repair banking house, 1811.

Broome, John Director, 1799-1800, 11/15/1804, 1805-1809; comm. to devise by-laws and regulations, 1799; comm. of accounts, 1799; comm. on annuities and insurance, 1799; comm. to burn bank notes, 1804-1805, 1807; comm. to view land prior to purchase, 1805; comm. to consider branch at Utica, 1808; comm. to go to Utica to buy office, 1809; death reported, 8/31/1810.

Broome, William T. Attorney and solicitor, 8/27/1799.

Brower, Benjamin Assistant clerk, $500 7/7/1800; bookkeeper, $800, 12/31/1801; absconded with $10,000.

Brown, James Director, 9/16/1832, 1834-1835; finance comm., 1835.

Brown, John Assistant clerk, $300, 4/27/1835.

Brown, Silas Director, 1841-1842; quarterly comm., 12/1842.

Browne, Henry Assistant clerk, $500, 7/24/1805; 2nd discount clerk, $700, 6/5/1806; runner, $800, 2/25/1808; assistant teller, $800, 12/31/1810.

Browne, Joseph Superintendent of water works, $1,500, 6/17/1799; committee on repaving of streets, 1801; extra allowance of $1,000 voted 12/28/1801; became New York City street commissioner, 1803.

Bruce, Robert Assistant clerk, $600, 9/1/1815; left 6/30/1817.

Bull, Henry	Bookkeeper, $800, 2/20/1809; 4th bookkeeper, $800, 6/30/1809; 2nd discount clerk, $700, 9/30/1809.
Burr, Aaron	Director, 1799-1801; committee to examine cash, 1799-1800; water comm., 1800; comm. on revised charter, 1800; comm. to prevent counterfeiting, 1800.
Burritt, Ranson	Clerk and bookkeeper, Poughkeepsie, $400, 4/3/1816.
Byrne, James	Porter, $300, 8/30/1832; $400, 3/31/1836; $500, 9/30/1836.
Church, John B.	Director, 1799-1803; comm. to consider disposition of MC's money, 1799; comm. on annuities and insurance, 1799; comm. on new plates and printing paper, 1800; comm. to prevent counterfeiting, 1800; comm. to "superintend the business of this company," 1800; comm. to purchase steam engine, 1802; water comm., 1802; comm. to burn bank notes, 1803.
Clarke, Thomas B.	Assistant clerk, $600, 12/2/1815; left 2/10/1816.
Clason, Isaac	Director, 1801-1814; comm. to consider transfer of water works to New York City, 1804; comm. to confer with other banks, 1805; water comm., 1807; comm. to make loans on voyages, 1807; comm. to explore necessity of having a vice president, 1807; mention of his death, 3/6/1815.
Clinton, DeWitt	Director, 1803-1812; comm. to consider amendments to charter, 1804; comm. to confer with other banks, 1805; comm. to consider branch in Utica, 1808; comm. to consider measures conducive to the interests of the company, 1810.
Coles, John B.	Director, 1799-1803; comm. to investigate best way of obtaining water, 1799; water comm., 1799-1803; comm. to "superintend the business of this company," 1800; comm. to audit accounts, 1801; comm. to assess street damage, 1804.
Coolidge, Daniel	2nd discount clerk, $700, 1/9/1805; bookkeeper, $800, 6/5/1806; 4th bookkeeper, $800, 3/31/1808; 3rd bookkeeper, $800, 6/30/1809; 1st bookkeeper, $900, 6/1/1810; Poughkeepsie cashier, 6/22/1810; resigned 12/12/1815.

Cooper, Apollos   Director, Utica, 7/31/1809.

Coster, Henry A.   Director, 1799-1800; comm. to inspect cash, 1800.

Coster, John G.   Director, 1810-1832, 1834-1839; water comm., 1810, 1813-1814, 1825-1826, 1828; elected president 12/13/1825; president 1825-1829; comm. to investigate protested discounts, 1811; comm. to consider state of the water works, 1811; comm. to purchase stock, 1812; comm. on the reduction of debt, 1814; comm. to consider state of finances, 1814; comm. to meet with other banks re: finances, 1814; comm. on immediate concerns, 1814; comm. to purchase $100,000 in specie, 1817; comm. to meet with other banks re: overdrafts, 1817; comm. on banking business, 1817; comm. re: lot on Pine Street, 1818; standing comm., 1818-1826, 1830, 1832, 1834, 1836-1839; comm. to meet with other banks re: epidemic, 1822; comm. to counteract charges that MC is not supplying the city with water, 1823; finance committee, 1829-1829, 1825; resigned as director, 9/13/1840.

Crommelin, Daniel   Extra clerk (temporary), 6/29/1805; assistant clerk, $500, 9/30/1805; $600, 6/6/1806; runner, $700, 10/9/1806; assistant clerk, $600, 1807.

Crosby, Cyrenus   Director, Poughkeepsie, 4/14/1809.

Crosby, William B.   Director, 8/3/1826, 1827-1832, 1834-1835, 1837-1840; standing comm., 1826, 1830-1832, 1834, 1837-1840; water comm., 1827; finance comm., 1827-1829, 1835; law comm., 1831; comm. to review salaries, 1840; monthly examining comm., 1840-1841; resigned as director 11/29/1841.

Crowell, Arthur F.R.   Check clerk, $300, 6/29/1836; assistant clerk, $400, 9/30/1836; transmission clerk, 12/31/1842.

Cunningham, Hugh   Director, Utica, 7/10/1812.

Cuylar, James   Assistant clerk, $500, 12/31/1801; $600, 12/31/1802; left 8/15/1804.

Davenport, Charles W.   Bookkeeper, $800, 12/31/1801; left 8/18/1804.

Davis, Mathew L.   Runner, $800, 8/13/1799.

Danna, James	Director, Utica, 8/31/1812.
Dean, Joseph C.	Director, Poughkeepsie, 1/12/1809.
Delafield, William	Assistant clerk, $600, 6/14/1815; discount clerk, $800, 8/21/1815; left 6/30/1825.
Devereux, John C.	Director, Utica, 7/10/1812; resigned 11/19/1813; director, Utica, 6/9/1814.
Devereux, Luke	Director, Utica, 11/19/1813; resigned 6/2/1814.
Dickinson, John L.	Assistant clerk, $600, 3/30/1811; runner pro tem, $800, 10/23/1813; assistant clerk, $600, 5/10/1814; runner, $800, 10/8/1814; runner, $700, 5/1/1820; left 11/21/1825.
Doolittle, Jesse W.	Director, Utica, 10/6/1814.
Drake, Jacob	Director, 5/5/1817.
Duncan, Thomas	Paid to tend the water works engine, 1811.
Edgar, William, Jr.	Director, 1799-1822; comm. to consider disposition of MC funds, 1799; comm. of accounts, 1799; comm. on insurance rates, 1799; comm. to examine cash, 1799, 1801; comm. on plates and printing paper, 1800; water comm., 1800, 1818; comm. on expediency of changing banking room, 1800; comm. on employment of surplus capital, 1801-1802; comm. to purchase steam engine, 1802; comm. to consider transferring water works to New York City, 1804; comm. to confer with other banks, 1805; comm. to examine plans to build new banking house, 1806; comm. to make loans on voyages, 1807; comm. to confer with NYC re: transfer of water works, 1807; comm. to consider branch at Poughkeepsie, 1808; comm. to go to Utica to consider possible directors, 1809; comm. to consider measures conducive to the interests of the company, 1810; comm. on country bank accounts, 1812; comm. to purchase stock, 1812; standing comm., 1819-1821; notice of his death, 10/2/1823.
Evertsen, George B.	Director, Poughkeepsie, 5/13/1813.
Fairlie, James	Director, 1803-1822; water comm., 1803, 1818;

comm. to assess street damage, 1804; comm. to consider amendments to charter, 1804; comm. to recover the paper of the New Ark banking Co., 1804; comm. to plan for new banking house, 1806; comm. to burn bank notes, 1807; comm. to confer with other banks re: overdrafts, 1807; comm. to explore necessity of having a vice president, 1807; comm. to confer with the Common Council re: hydrants, 1807; comm. to confer with the Common Council re: transfer of water works, 1807; sent to Albany to petition for a revision of the MC charter, 1808; comm. to consider branch in Utica, 1808; comm. re: lot on Pine Street, 1818; resigns as director, 12/1/1823.

Farmar, Thomas

Director, 10/7/1805, 1806-1807, 1810-1817; comm. to examine cash, 1805; comm. to burn bank notes, 1805; comm. to examine unpaid discounts, 1806; water comm., 1807, 1810-1816; comm. to consider state of the water works, 1811; comm. to go to Utica, 1812; comm. to purchase stock, 1812; resigned as director, 8/31/1818.

Fellows, John

Superintendent of water works, 7/9/1806; office abolished 11/11/1811.

Ferguson, John

Director, 1829-1831; law comm., 1831; notice of his death, 9/10/1832.

Few, William

Director, 12/14/1807, 1808-1812, 1826; comm. to confer with Common Council re: transfer of water works, 1807; comm. to meet with other banks re: commercial credit, 1808; comm. to confer with owner of coal mine, 1808; comm. to consider increasing commission of collector of water works, 1808; comm. to consider compensation for injury, 1808; comm. to consider branch at Poughkeepsie, 1808; comm. to go to Utica to consider possible directors, 1809; comm. to investigate water complaints, 1809; comm. to go to Utica to buy office, 1809; comm. to consider increasing capital of Utica office, 1810; comm. to consider MC situation re: discounts and loans, 1810; comm. to examine bad debts, 1810; comm. to consider measures conducive to the interests of the co., 1810; water comm., 1810-1811; comm. to consider state of the water works, 1811; comm. to consider situation at Utica office, 1812; comm. to purchase stock, 1812.

Fish, Whitehead	1st teller, $1,250, 6/17/1799; $1,600, 3/31/1800; cashier, $2,000, 2/18/1808; resigned 4/9/1810 to become New York City treasurer.
Flewwelling, Samuel	Bookkeeper, $800, 12/31/1801; bookkeeper and runner, $800, 6/30/1804; bookkeeper and assistant teller, $800, 12/31/1804; 1st bookkeeper, $900, 1/25/1805; Poughkeepsie cashier, $1,250, 2/2/1809; Cashier, New York, $2,000, 5/7/1810; comm. to meet with Mechanics Bank re: proposed Bank of America, 1812; comm. to consider situation in Utica, 1812; comm. on immediate concerns, 1814; resigned as cashier, 12/26/1816; sued Manhattan Company, 1818.
Floyd, Augustus	Notary, 12/19/1828; resigned 4/9/1835.
Floyd, William	Director, Utica, 7/31/1809.
Forbes, Alexander	Notary, Poughkeepsie, 4/3/1816.
Forbes, John B.	Clerk and bookkeeper, Poughkeepsie, $400, 8/16/1810; $500, 2/4/1813; resigned 11/29/1815.
Freare, John S., Jr.	Director, Poughkeepsie, 1/12/1809; comm. to examine cash, 1809; comm. to repair banking house, 1811.
Funk, James A.	Assistant clerk, $600, 7/3/1815; assistant 2nd teller, $800, 7/30/1815; 3rd teller, $800, 9/30/1817; 2nd teller, $1,000, 3/1/1819; 1st teller, $1,250, 7/1/1821; $1,500, 9/30/1826; notice of his death, 4/6/1829.
Gantz, George W.	Assistant clerk, $400, 7/22/1824; resigned 12/13/1824.
Gardiner, John L.	Clerk in water works, 4/12/1821; collector of water revenue, 11/14/1822; notice of his death, 9/13/1824.
Gardiner, Robert S.	Interest clerk, $800, 7/15/1818; stock clerk, $800, 12/31/1821; left 3/31/1822.
Garr, Andrew	Assistant clerk, $300, 4/29/1828; bookkeeper, $800, 6/30/1829; 1st bookkeeper, $1,000, 7/2/1832; resigned 4/22/1835.

Gautier, Andrew, Jr.

Assistant clerk, $500, 2/1/1804; discount clerk and runner, $700, 9/30/1804; runner, $700, 12/31/1804; left 7/31/1805.

Gelston, David

Director, 2/28/1811, 1811-1815, 1823; comm. to remonstrate against incorporation of new water company, 1824; comm. to prevent incorporation of New York Water Company, 1824; comm. to represent the MC in Albany, 1824.

Gelston, James

Assistant clerk pro tem, $600, 12/23/1807; assistant clerk, $500, 3/1/1808; assistant clerk, $600, 9/30/1808; discount clerk, $800, 7/1/1810; 2nd teller, $1,000, 8/16/1812; 1st teller, $1,500, 1/6/1817; resigned 3/12/1821.

Gelston, Maltby

Director, 1816-1818, 1825-1832, 1834-1839; comm. to visit branches, 1817; standing comm., 1825, 1830-1832, 1834, 1836-1839; elected president, $2,500, 12/8/1829; finance comm., 1829, 1835; water comm., 1829-1832, 1834-1835, 1837-1839; law comm., 1831; salary $3,500, 10/3/1836; real estate and building comm., 1838-1839; resigned as president and director, 3/23/1840.

Gibson, Henry B.

Clerk, Utica, 7/31/1809.

Gill, John

Clerk, $500, 5/26/1842.

Goedecken, C.H.

Discount clerk, $700, 12/31/1801.

Gould, Jesse

Bookkeeper, $800, 8/4/1815.

Gray, Neil

Bookkeeper, $800, 7/24/1815; assistant 2nd teller, $800, 3/1/1819; resigned 8/15/1825.

Halsted, William M.

Director, 11/12/1840, 1840-1842; comm. of examination, 1840; water comm., 1840-1842; quarterly comm., 1841.

Hammersby, Thomas

Director, 1825-1832; notice of his death, 10/2/1834.

Handy, John H.

Director, Utica, 12/7/1815.

Hannah, John

Assistant clerk, $300, 6/2/1836; $400, 9/30/1836; $600, 7/1/1839.

Harburger, John S.

Assistant transfer clerk, $800, 12/13/1842.

Harrison, Richard	Comm. to revise charter, 1800.
Hart, Ephraim	Director, Utica, 7/31/1809; left 5/13/1813.
Havens, Henry	Director, 9/8/1840, 1840-1841; comm. of examination, 1840-1841; quarterly comm., 1842.
Heelas, George W.	Assistant clerk, $400, 3/9/1834; $600, 6/30/1834; transfer clerk, $800, 7/13/1835; $1,000, 12/31/1835; $1,500, 7/11/1842.
Hickox, A.	Director, Utica, 8/3/1812; replaced 8/31/1812.
Hitchcock, Marcus	Director, Utica, 7/31/1809.
Hoffman, Martin	Director, Poughkeepsie, 4/14/1809; comm. to investigate bad debts (NYC), 1810.
Hoyt, Edwin	Director, 1840-1842; comm. of examination, 1841; standing comm., 1841-1842; comm. to transfer money from 1st teller, 1842.
Hoyt, John C.	Director, Utica, 7/10/1812.
Hoyt, Samuel	Clerk, water works, $500, 9/30/1800; $600, 12/31/1801.
Huguet, F.	Contractor of water works, 11/11/1811; voted an allowance of $1,000/year, 1/25/1813; notice of his death, 3/12/1821.
Hunn, John S.	1st bookkeeper, $900, 8/13/1799; 2nd teller, $1,000, 12/10/1799; resigned to become NYC street commissioner, 1/14/1805; cashier, Poughkeepsie, 4/27/1810; resigned due to financial problems, 6/22/1810.
Hunt, Montgomery	Assistant discount clerk, $500, 3/31/1800; 4th bookkeeper, $600, 7/7/1800; 1st bookkeeper, $900, 12/31/1801; 2nd teller, $1,000, 1/21/1805; left 6/25/1805; cashier, Utica, $1,500, 9/7/1809; resigned 8/3/1812.
Huntington, Henry	Director, Utica, 7/31/1809.
Hyer, Garrit	Director, 9/21/1818, 1818-1823, 1825; water comm., 1819-1820, 1822-1823; comm. to examine cash, 1824; notice of his death, 7/20/1826.

Ireson, William	Assistant clerk, $500, 11/18/1799; discount clerk, $800, 3/31/1800.
Jeffrey, William	Assistant clerk, $400, 3/31/1837.
Jermain, A.	Clerk, Utica, 6/2/1814.
Johnson, Bryan	Director, Utica, 8/3/1812.
Johnson, John	Director, Poughkeepsie, 5/13/1813.
Jones, Edward R.	Director, 1819-1823, 1825; water comm., 1819-1820, 1822-1823; resigned as director, 12/15/1825.
Jones, Isaac	Director, 1819-1824; standing comm., 1819-1824.
Jones, John	Assistant clerk, $600, 12/31/1801; 1st discount clerk, $800, 12/31/1803; 1st discount clerk and bookkeeper, $800, 6/30/1804; bookkeeper, $800, 9/30/1804.
Kennedy, David S.	Director, 1823, 1825-1832, 1834-1835, 1838-1840; finance comm., 1827-1828; law comm., 1831; comm. of examination, 1840; standing comm., 1840; resigned as director, 11/22/1841.
King, Brown	Assistant clerk, $600, 6/21/1815; bookkeeper, $800, 9/30/1815; 2nd teller, $1,000, 1/6/1817; resigned 1/21/1819.
King, William G.	Bookkeeper, $800, 12/13/1842.
Kip, James S.	Director, Utica, 7/31/1809.
Kissam, James	Assistant clerk, $600, 4/2/1807; 2nd discount clerk, $700, 2/25/1808; 1st discount clerk, $800, 10/14/1808; discount clerk and 3rd teller, $800, 9/30/1809; 3rd teller, $800, 12/31/1809; 2nd teller, $1,000, 12/31/1810; Utica cashier, $1,250, 8/6/1812; resigned 6/15/1815.
Kissam, William A.	Assistant clerk, $300, 6/2/1836; $400, 9/30/1836; resigned 11/5/1836.
Laight, William	Original director, 1799; resigned, 5/16/1799.
Lawrence, Abraham R.	Director, 1813; water comm., 1813; comm. to

consider state of finances, 1814; comm. to meet with other banks re: finances, 1814.

Lawrence, John L.	Director, 1841-1842.
Lawrence, William	Director, 1817-1825; comm. on banking business, 1817; comm. to go to Utica re: debts, 1818; standing comm., 1818-1819, 1821-1824; comm. to go to Poughkeepsie to close office, 1819; water comm., 1820; comm. to counteract charges that the MC forfeited its charter due to not supplying NYC with water, 1823.
Lawton, Charles	Assistant clerk, $600, 8/22/1812.
Leach, Caleb	Agent of water works, $1,000, 12/29/1800; superintendent, 8/1/1803; resigned 7/3/1806.
Ledyard, Daniel	Assistant clerk, $500,, 10/7/1815; bookkeeper, $800, 3/6/1817; 3rd teller, $800, 8/15/1825; $1,000, 12/31/1833.
Lewis, George	Director, 1804-1816; water comm., 1804, 1806; comm. to examine cash, 1805; comm. to make loans on voyages, 1807; comm. to confer with Common Council re: transfer of water works, 1807; comm. to meet with other banks re: commercial credit, 1807; comm. to consider branch at Poughkeepsie, 1808; comm. to investigate water complaints, 1809; comm. to consider increasing capital of Utica office, 1810; comm. to consider measures conducive to the interests of the co., 1810; comm. to investigate protested discounts, 1811; comm. to consider situation of Utica office, 1812; comm. to meet with other banks re: finances, 1814; comm. on immediate concerns, 1814; comm. to sell 6% stock, 1816; resigned as director, 12/31/1816.
Lewis, Juan F.	Discount clerk, $800, 8/20/1799; assistant teller, $800, 3/31/1800.
Livingston, Brockholst	Director, 1799-1802; comm. to consider disposition of MC's money, 1799; comm. to devise by-laws and regulations, 1799; comm. on annuities and insurance, 1799; comm. to revise charter, 1800; comm. on expediency of changing banking room, 1800; comm. on employing surplus capital, 1802; resigned as director 11/10/1803.

Livingston, John R.	Director, 1801-1802; comm. to examine cash, 1801; comm. on employment of surplus capital, 1801; water comm., 1802.
Livingston, John R. Jr.	Elected notary, 4/27/1835; resigned 4/6/1840.
Livingston, Maturin	Director, 1803; water comm., 1803-1804; comm. to assess street damage, 1804; appointed Recorder of NYC (ex officio director of MC), 11/1804; comm. to burn bank notes, 1804; comm. to consider amendments to charter, 1804; comm. to confer with other banks, 1805.
Lord, David, Jr.	Mentioned as counsel of MC, 5/29/1840.
Lozier, Jacob	Superintendent, water works, 7/21/1842.
Lozier, James	Collector of water revenue, 6/2/1836.
Lozier, John	Superintendent, water works, 4/12/1821; resigned 7/21/1842.
Ludlow, Daniel	President, $2,500, 11/11/1799; $2,000, 12/10/1805; director, 1799-1807; water comm., 1800, 1802, 1806, 1807; comm. to superintend the business of the co., 1800; comm. to purchase steam engine, 1802; comm. on recovering the paper of the New Ark Banking Co., 1804; comm. to confer with other banks, 1805; comm. to examine unpaid discounts, 1806; comm. to make loans on voyages, 1807; comm. to confer with other banks re: overdrafts, 1807; resigned as president and director, 2/11/1808.
Lynch, James	Director, Utica, 9/10/1812.
Mandeville, Matthew	Porter, $600; discharged 7/3/1819.
Mappa, John	Director, Utica, 8/3/1812.
Masters, Thomas	Director, 9/8/1840, 1840-1842; water comm., 1841-1842; comm. to transfer funds from 1st teller, 1842; quarterly comm., 1842.
Maynard, W.	Director, Utica, 8/31/1812.
McAllister, Samuel	Bookkeeper, $600, 12/1/1825; $800, 3/31/1826; left 3/31/1834; bookkeeper, $800, 9/30/1835; $900, 3/31/1836.

McBride, James	Director, 1817-1832, 1834-1842; comm. on banking business, 1817; comm. re: lot on Pine Street, 1818; standing comm., 1820, 1825-1826, 1830-1832, 1834, 1836-1842; water comm., 1822-1825; comm. to examine cash, 1824; finance comm., 1827-1829, 1835; comm. to examine state of the bank, 1840; comm. to review salaries, 1840; comm. on examination, 1840; quarterly comm., 1841.
McLaughlin, Edward	Collector of water revenue, 5% commission, 5/9/1805; commission raised to 10%, 11/14/1805; resigned 5/1807.
McNeill, Frederick A.	Assistant clerk, $300, 5/19/1828; $500, 9/15/1830; discount clerk, $500, 12/31/1830; left 3/31/1832.
McQueen, Robert	MC purchased a steam engine from him, 1803; one year contract to work the engine and raise water, 1808; contract still in force, 1811; MC purchased another engine from him, 1812.
Meyer, John	Assistant clerk and bookkeeper, $700, 1/8/1805; bookkeeper, $800, 9/30/1805; left 5/30/1806.
Miller, Morris S.	Director, Utica, 7/10/1812.
Mitchell, Edward	4th bookkeeper, $800, 9/7/1809.
Morehead, John	Director, 9/10/1838, 1838-1839; comm. on examination, 1840; resigned as director, 11/30/1840.
Morrison, James Martin	1st teller, $1,700, 3/16/1840; cashier, $2,000, 2/3/1842; standing comm., 1842; water comm., 1842; quarterly comm., 1842.
Myers, Nathan	Director, Poughkeepsie, 1/12/1809; comm. to repair banking house, 1811.
Nazro, James	Assistant clerk, $600, 1/11/1809; 2nd discount clerk, $700, 5/15/1809; discount clerk and 4th bookkeeper, $800, 9/30/1809; 1st discount clerk, $800, 12/31/1809; 1st bookkeeper, $900, 7/1/1810; Cashier, Poughkeepsie, 7/20/1815.
Neil, F.W.	Clerk; notice of his death, 5/10/1832.

Neilson, Anthony B.   Assistant clerk, $500, 4/21/1822; resigned 4/19/1824.

Nelson, John, Jr.   Elected notary, 3/26/1840.

Nevins, Jacob R.   Director, 1842.

Newcomb, Charles   Assistant clerk, $300, 4/27/1835; $500, 3/31/1836; Bookkeeper, $800, 9/30/1836.

Newcomb, Colin G.   Assistant clerk, $300, 12/31/1830; assistant teller and corresponding clerk, $600, 7/2/1832; corresponding clerk, $800, 9/30/1834; transfer clerk, $1,000, 6/30/1835; 2nd teller, $1,200, 9/30/1835; 1st teller, $1,500, 9/30/1836; showed a $49,000 difference in his cash and left the bank, 1840.

Newcomb, James M.   Check clerk, $300, 6/29/1836; assistant clerk, $400, 9/30/1836; bookkeeper, $800, 9/30/1837.

Nexsen, Elias, Jr.   Clerk, Poughkeepsie, 4/10/1809; resigned 7/30/1810.

Nexsen, John   Assistant clerk, $600, 5/22/1815; discount clerk, $800, 8/18/1815.

Nexsen, William W.   2nd discount clerk, $700, 10/24/1808; resigned 5/15/1809; cashier, Poughkeepsie, 1/22/1816.

Nicoll, Edward A.   Assistant clerk, $600, 8/18/1815; bookkeeper, $800, 1/6/1817; left 3/6/1817.

North, Thomas   Director, Poughkeepsie, 8/31/1810.

O'Brien, John G.   Assistant clerk, $300, 9/30/1835; $500, 3/31/1836; corresponding clerk, $800, 9/30/1836; $1,000, 7/1/1839; 1st teller, $1,700, 2/7/1842; resigned 7/21/1842.

O'Rourke, Farrell   Porter $300, 11/19/1835; $400, 1/6/1840.

Osgood, Samuel   Director, 1799-1802; comm. to investigate the best way of supplying water, 1799; comm. on insurance rates, 1799; water comm., 1799-1800; comm. on plates and printing paper, 1800; comm. to inspect cash, 1800; comm. to destroy bank notes, 1801; comm. on repaving streets, 1801.

Paulding, William	Director, 1826-1827, 1829-1832, 1834-1835, 1838-1839; water comm., 1826; comm. on examination, 1840; resigned as director, 11/30/1840.
Penfold, Edmond	Director, 11/12/1840, 1840-1842; comm. on examination, 1840-1841; water comm., 1840-1842; comm. to transfer funds from the 1st teller, 1842.
Phelan, John	Discount clerk, $800, 9/5/1804; 1st discount clerk, $800, 12/31/1804; resigned 10/13/1808.
Phelps	Director, 1824.
Phoenix, Daniel	Director, 1802-1810; comm. on employing surplus capital, 1802; comm. to burn bank notes, 1803-1805, 1807; comm. to examine cash, 1805; comm. to examine unpaid discounts, 1806; comm. to consider increasing capital of Utica office, 1810; resigned as director, 3/4/1811.
Platt, Ebenezer, Jr.	Assistant clerk (temporary), $300, 9/1/1813; assistant clerk, $500, 10/23/1813; left 6/13/1815.
Popham, John	Assistant clerk, $400, 4/9/1813; $500, 10/23/1813; left 5/22/1815.
Prevost, John B.	Secretary of board, $1,500, 4/17/1799; Director, 9/2/1801 (Recorder of City of New York); comm. to destroy bank notes, 1801, 1803; no longer listed as secretary, 12/31/1801.
Purdy, Cornelius	Bookkeeper, $800, 7/9/1812; resigned 5/13/1815.
Rainetaux, Anthony C.	Bookkeeper, $800, 4/27/1810; 1st bookkeeper, $900, 7/21/1815; clerk in water office, 9/23/1824; 1st bookkeeper, $1,150, 9/30/1829; clerk in water office, 1830-1833.
Rathbone, John, Jr.	2nd bookkeeper, $800, 8/13/1799; 1st bookkeeper, $900, 12/10/1799.
Raub, John Herman	Porter and attendant, $250, 12/31/1799; porter, $300, 6/30/1800; $350, 12/31/1801; $400, 12/31/1804; no longer listed as porter, 9/30/1807.

Raymond, Alfred   Clerk and bookkeeper, Poughkeepsie, $500, 11/29/1815.

Remsen, Henry   Cashier, $2,500, 6/3/1799; president, $2,500, 2/17/1808; Director, 2/17/1808, 1808-1824; comm. to meet with other banks re: commercial credit, 1808; comm. to confer with owner of coal mine, 1808; comm. to consider raising the commission of the collector of water works, 1808; comm. to consider compensation for injury, 1808; comm. to consider branch at Poughkeepsie, 1808; comm. to investigate water complaints, 1809; comm. to consider increasing Utica capital, 1810; comm. to consider discounts and loans, 1810; comm. to investigate bad debts, 1810; comm. to consider measures conducive to the interests of the co., 1810; water comm., 1810-1820, 1822, 1824; comm. to investigate protested discounts, 1811; comm. to consider state of the water works, 1811; comm. to meet with the Mechanics Bank re: proposed Bank of America, 1812; comm. to consider situation of Utica office, 1812; comm. to go to Utica, 1812; comm. on reduction of debt, 1814; comm. to consider state of finances, 1814; comm. to meet with other banks re: finances, 1814; comm. on immediate concerns, 1814; comm. to sell 6% stock, 1816; comm. to purchase $100,000 in specie, 1817; comm. to examine protested bills, 1817; comm. to meet with other banks re: overdrafts, 1817; comm. to visit branches, 1817; comm. on banking business, 1817; comm. to go to Utica re: debts, 1818; standing comm., 1818-1822, 1824; comm. to go to Poughkeepsie to close office, 1819; comm. to meet with other banks re: epidemic, 1822; comm. to prevent incorporation of New York Water Works Co., 1824; comm. to examine cash, 1824.

Richard, Henry   Clerk, $300, 9/15/1836.

Richard, J.H.   Assistant clerk, $400, 8/26/1836.

Richard, Stephen C.   Assistant clerk, $400, 12/30/1825; $500, 12/30/1826; $600, 3/31/1828; $800, 4/28/1828; correspondence clerk, $800, 6/30/1831; transfer and corresponding clerk, $1,000, 7/2/1832; 2nd teller, $1,200, 6/30/1835; 1st teller, $1,500, 7/13/1835; resigned 6/13/1836.

Roberts, Robert, Jr.	Assistant clerk, $300, 3/31/1829; $400, 9/15/1830; bookkeeper, $800, 7/2/1832; $900, 3/31/1836; 2nd teller, $1,200, 9/30/1836; resignation requested by directors, 3/30/1840.
Roosevelt, Nicholas	MC purchased steam engine from him, 1799; rescinded 6/17/1799.
Russell, William H.	Director, 1840; comm. on examination, 1841; resigned as director, 11/22/1841.
Rutgers, Gaine	Paid $150 for three months service as runner, 3/11/1824.
Rutgers, Henry	Director, 1804-1823, 1825-1828; water comm., 1804, 1806; comm. to consider transferring water works to NYC, 1804; comm. to examine cash, 1805; comm. to examine unpaid discounts, 1806; comm. to plan for new banking house, 1806; comm. to burn bank notes, 1807; comm. to confer with Common Council re: hydrants, 1807; resigned as director, 2/26/1811; elected director, 3/7/1811; comm. to consider state of finances, 1814; comm. to counteract charges that the MC forfeited its charter for not supplying NYC with water, 1823; comm. to remonstrate against incorporation of a new water company, 1824; comm. to prevent incorporation of New York water Works Co., 1824; comm. to examine cash, 1824.
St. John, Samuel	Assistant clerk, $400, 7/10/1810; $600, 3/31/1811; discount clerk, $800, 8/22/1812.
Sanger, Richard	Director, Utica, 8/3/1812.
Seaman, Andrew	Assistant clerk, $600, 8/21/1804; discount clerk, $700, 12/31/1804; discount clerk and bookkeeper, $800, 3/31/1805; bookkeeper, $800, 6/30/1805; assistant teller, $800, 9/30/1805; 2nd teller, $1,000, 2/23/1808; 1st teller, $1,500, 9/7/1809; cashier, $2,500, 12/30/1816; comm. to examine protested bills, 1817; comm. on banking business, 1817; left as cashier, 9/22/1819; notice of his death, 11/25/1819.
Shapter, Thomas M.	Clerk in water office, 4/19/1824; assistant clerk in bank, $400, 4/26/1824; resigned as check clerk, 2/3/1825.

Shearman, Ebenezer B.	Director, Utica, 8/3/1812.
Shepherd, William J.	Assistant clerk, $600, 7/27/1815; bookkeeper, $800, 9/1/1815; 2nd teller, $1,000, 7/1/1821; $1,100, 9/30/1826; 1st teller, $1,500, 4/6/1829; out due to illness, 3/12/1832; salary discontinued but given a gratuity of $400, 10/29/1832.
Sill, Theodore	Director, Utica, 5/13/1813; resigned, 11/29/1813.
Skates, Benjamin	Porter, $350, 9/30/1800.
Skinner, Thomas	Director, Utica, 10/11/1810.
Slosson, William	Attorney for MC, 10/6/1814.
Smith, John	Director, 1813-1815; notice of his death, 10/24/1816.
Smith, Melancthon	3rd bookkeeper, $600, 1/13/1800.
Smith, Nathan	Director, Utica, 7/31/1809.
Smith, Pascal	Director, 1799-1804; comm. to devise by-laws and regulations, 1799; comm. of accounts, 1799, 1801; comm. on insurance rates, 1799; comm. on repaving street, 1801; water comm., 1802; deceased 10/1805.
Smith, Waters	Assistant clerk, $500, 11/11/1799; 2nd bookkeeper, $800, 12/10/1799.
Staats[?]	Porter, $350, 9/15/1800.
Stagg, John L.	Assistant clerk, $500, 12/31/1810; assistant 2nd teller, $800, 8/28/1812; left 7/29/1815.
Stansbury, Arthur J.	Discount clerk, $700, 12/31/1803; left 9/3/1804.
Starr, Ephraim	Extra clerk (temporary), 6/29/1805; assistant clerk, $500, 7/19/1805.
Sterling, Richard	Assistant clerk, $600, 3/31/1822; left 4/21/1822; check clerk, $400, 12/13/1824; discount clerk, $800, 6/30/1825; bookkeeper, $800, 9/8/1825; 2nd teller, $1,100, 4/6/1829; $1,200, 6/30/1834; 1st teller, $1,500, 6/30/1835.

Stevens, John	Director, 1799-1800; comm. to investigate best way of supplying water, 1799; water comm., 1799-1800; comm. to destroy bank notes, 1801; erected steam engine, 1801; made improvements to steam engine, 1805.
Stoutenburgh, Augustus	Assistant clerk, $300, 6/11/1832; $400, 9/30/1834; $500, 3/31/1836; assistant teller, $800, 9/30/1836; resignation requested by directors, 3/30/1840.
Stoutenburgh, Thomas	Assistant clerk, $600, 12/31/1801; bookkeeper, $800, 12/31/1803; bookkeeper and 3rd teller, $800, 3/31/1805; assistant teller, $800, 6/30/1805; 2nd teller, $1,000, 9/30/1805; 1st teller, $1,500, 2/23/1808; dismissed 9/7/1809.
Suffern, Thomas	Director, 8/3/1826, 1826-1832, 1834-1839; water comm., 1827-1832, 1834-1839; real estate and building comm., 1838-1839; comm. to examine the state of the bank, 1840; comm. to perform duties of cashier, 1840; comm. of examination, 1840; monthly examining comm., 1840.
Sutter, John	Porter, 1804; $500 salary, 5/18/1807; $600, 9/30/1809; resigned 4/2/1829 after 25 years as porter; given a gratuity of $500.
Tailor, Edward N.	Assistant clerk, $500, 3/31/1817; $600, 3/31/1819; $700, 9/30/1820; interest clerk, $800, 3/31/1822; $1,000, 6/30/1826; transfer clerk, $1,100, 6/30/1829; 1st teller, $1,500, 7/2/1832; $2,000, 10/27/1834; resigned 5/4/1835.
Tailor, Royal F.	Assistant bookkeeper, $800, 12/6/1832; resigned 9/1/1837.
Tallmadge, James, Jr.	Director, Poughkeepsie, 1/12/1809; President, Poughkeepsie, 5/24/1809; Counsel, Poughkeepsie, 2/23/1815; comm. to examine cash, 5/24/1809; comm. to repair banking house, 1811.
Targee, John	Director, 5/5/1817; comm. to represent MC in Albany, 1824.
Taylor, George E.	Assistant clerk, $400, 12/30/1825; $500, 3/31/1828; discount clerk, $800, 4/28/1828; left 9/15/1830.

Taylor, James

Assistant clerk, $600, 12/31/1810; bookkeeper, $800, 3/31/1812; left 7/17/1815.

Theriott, Gabriel S.

Assistant clerk, $600, 12/12/1804; bookkeeper, $800, 3/31/1805; 3rd bookkeeper, $800, 3/31/1808; 1st bookkeeper, $900, 2/4/1809; resigned 5/15/1810.

Thompson, Jonathan

Director, 1814-1832, 1834-1842; comm. to examine protested bills, 1817; comm. to meet with other banks re: overdrafts, 1817; water comm., 1817-1820, 1824-1832, 1834-1841; comm. to examine brokers and accounts, 1818; standing comm., 181, 1825-1826; 1840-1841; comm. to counteract charges that the MC forfeited its charter by not supplying NYC with water, 1823; comm. to remonstrate against incorporation of a new water co., 1823; comm. to prevent incorporation of New York Water Works Co., 1824; comm. to examine cash, 1824; real estate and building comm., 1838-1839; comm. to review salaries, 1840; comm. to perform duties of cashier, 1840; quarterly comm., 1841; elected president, 3/24/1840.

Thorn, Samuel

Director, Poughkeepsie, 4/14/1809; resigned 11/28/1811.

Thurman, Ralph

2nd teller, $1,000, 8/20/1799; resigned 12/1799.

Tiebout, Adam T.

Assistant clerk, $400, 2/11/1825; Bookkeeper, $800, 9/30/1825; $1,000, 6/30/1835; 1st bookkeeper, $1,000, 9/30/1835; $1,200, 3/31/1836; 1st teller, $1,500, 12/31/1842.

Todd, William

Director, 1824-1832, 1834-1842; water comm., 1824-1832, 1834-1840; comm. to examine the state of the bank, 1840; comm. to perform duties of cashier, 1840; comm. of examination, 1840; quarterly comm., 1841; standing comm., 1841-1842.

Townsend, Walter

Assistant clerk, $600, 5/31/1804; discount clerk, $700, 8/21/1804.

Tuttle, George H.

Assistant clerk, $500, 9/30/1835; $600, 3/31/1836; left 6/30/1836.

Tweddale, G.W.

Assistant clerk, $300, 5/12/1832; $500, 7/1/1833; $600, 3/10/1834; bookkeeper, $900, 3/31/1836.

Van Buren, John D.	Director, 11/15/1841, 1841-1842; quarterly comm., 1841-1842.
Van Ness, David	Director, Poughkeepsie, 4/14/1809.
Van Renssalaer, James	Director, Utica, 11/29/1813.
Vermilye, William M.	Cashier, $4,500, 3/19/1840; standing comm., 1840; water comm., 1840; resigned 11/25/1841.
Walcott, Solomon	Director, Utica, 7/31/1809.
Walker, Benjamin	Director, Utica, 7/10/1812.
Walker, Samuel	Assistant clerk, $600, 9/4/1812; left 6/3/1814; bookkeeper, $800, 5/14/1815; left 7/22/1815.
Walker, Thomas	Director, Utica, 7/31/1809; mentioned as Utica president, 5/18/1815.
Watson, John C.	Assistant clerk, $600, 10/16/1804; runner, $700, 8/1/1805; assistant clerk, $600, 10/9/1806.
Watts, John	Director, 1799-1802; comm. to examine cash, 1799; comm. on annuities, 1799; water comm., 1800; comm. to destroy bank notes, 1801.
White, Campbell P.	Director, 10/2/1834, 1834-1835, 1838-1839; real estate and building comm., 1837-1839; resigned 10/28/1840.
White, Robert	Director, 3/13/1815, 1815-1818; cashier, $2,500, 11/29/1819; $4,000, 3/31/1826; $6,000, 10/3/1836; comm. to sell 6% stock, 1816; comm. to purchase $100,000 in specie, 1817; water comm., 1817, 1820, 1822, 1824-1832, 1834-1839; comm. to examine broker accounts, 1818; standing comm., 1818-1822, 1824-1826, 1830-1832, 1834, 1836-1839; comm. to prevent incorporation of New York Water Works Co., 1824; comm. to represent MC in Albany, 1824; finance comm., 1827-1829, 1835; real estate and building comm., 1838-1839; resigned as cashier, 3/16/1840.
Whitehead, William	Assistant clerk, $500, 12/10/1799; 2nd discount clerk, $600, 7/7/1800; runner, $800, 12/31/1801; left 5/31/1804.

Whittlesey, Edward   Check clerk, 9/8/1825; assistant clerk, $500, 9/30/1825.

Williams, Nathan   Director, Utica, 7/31/1809; resigned 8/5/1811; director, Utica, 7/10/1812; minutes state he is director and attorney, 6/1/1815.

Williams, Richard S.   Director, 1840; resigned 11/8/1841.

Williams, Robert   Director, Poughkeepsie, 1/12/1809.

Wright, Augustus   Director, 11/11/1816, 1816-1818; comm. to examine protested bills, 1817; water comm., 1817.

Wylley, James   Messenger of board, 4/17/1799; porter, $400, 10/24/1799.

Yates, Richard   Assistant clerk, $400, 6/30/1825; discount clerk, $800, 9/8/1825; left 4/21/1828.

SOURCES CONSULTED

Primary Sources

Chase Manhattan Archives, New York, New York. Record Group
Number 1, Records of the Manhattan Company.
  Minutes, 1799-1842 (6 volumes).
  Journals, 1799-1842 (10 volumes).
  Ledgers, 1799-1842 (5 volumes).
  Poughkeepsie Branch Minutes, 1809-1818 (1 volume).
  Water Works Records.
      Ledger, 1799-1821 (1 volume).
      Journal, 1817-1821 (1 volume).
      Revenue Books, 1820-1844 (6 volumes).

New York Public Library, New York, New York.
  Henry Remsen, Jr. Papers.
  DeWitt Clinton Papers.
  William Edgar Papers.
  Isaac Bronson Papers.
  Wynant Van Zandt, Jr. Papers.
  Stephen Allen Memoirs
  John Delafield Letterbooks
  William Alexander Papers
  William Constable Papers
  Robert Henderson Daybook
  Robert Troup Papers

New-York Historical Society, New York, New York.
  Manhattan Company Records
  LeBoeuf Collection
  McBean Collection
  Richard Dodge Papers
  Remsen Family Papers
  Campbell P. White Papers
  Elisha Boudinot Papers
  Robert R. Livingston Papers (microfilm)
  Aaron Burr Papers (microfilm)
  Stephen Allen Papers.
  Lynch & Stoughton Letterbooks
  James Duane Papers
  Alexander McDougall Papers
  Frederick Rhinelander Letterbooks
  Jeremiah Wadsworth Papers
  Society of the Cincinnati Records

319

State of New York, Department of Archives and Records Administration, Albany, New York.
Supreme Court Records, Transcripts of Dockets of Judgment, Utica, 1809-1819 (Series J0135).
Court of Chancery Records
Index to Enrolled Decrees, 1815-1847 (Series J0064).
Chancery Papers (Series J0070).
Court of Errors Records, Index (Series J0158).
Department of Audit and Control, Commissioners of the Canal Fund, Index to Minutes, 1817-1854 (Series B0316).

Utica Public Library, Utica, New York.
Utica *Saturday Globe*, 1897-1901.
Clippings File

Oneida Historical Society, Utica, New York.
Bank of Utica Records, 1812-1814.
Utica *Patriot*, 1808-1816.
Utica *Patriot and Patrol*, 1816-1821.
Utica *Columbian Gazette*, 1809-1819.
Utica *Patrol*, 1815-1816.
Utica *Club*, 1815
Utica City Directories, 1817, 1828.

Columbia University, Rare Book and Manuscript Library, New York, New York.
DeWitt Clinton Papers, volumes 13, 16, 17, and 21.
Fish Family Papers.
Gouverneur Morris Papers.

Minutes of the Common Council of the City of New York, 1675-1776. New York: Dodd Mean and Company, 1905.

Minutes of the Common Council of the City of New York, 1784-1831. New York: City of New York, 1930.

Report of the Commissioners Appointed to Investigate the Condition of the Manhattan Company: Together With the Minutes of Their Proceedings and Various Statements Relative Thereto, March 14, 1840. New York: James P. Wright, 1840.

Syrett, Harold C., ed. *The Papers of Alexander Hamilton.* New York: Columbia University Press, 1975.

Secondary Sources

Adams, Donald R., Jr. *Finance and Enterprise in Early America: A Study of Stephen Girard's Bank.* Philadelphia: University of Pennsylvania Press, 1978.

Albion, Robert Greenhalgh. *Rise of New York Port, 1815-1860.* New York: Charles Scribner's Sons, 1939; reprint, Hamden, Conn.: Archon Books, 1961.

Anderson, Letty. "Hard Choices: Supplying Water to New England Towns." *Journal of Interdisciplinary History* 15 (Autumn 1984): 211-34.

Appleby, Joyce. *Capitalism and the New Social Order: The Republican Vision of the 1790s.* New York: New York University Press, 1984.

Background for Tomorrow: An Historical Sketch of the Bank of the Manhattan Company. New York: Bank of the Manhattan Company, 1950.

Baldwin, Simeon E. "American Business Corporations Before 1789." *American Historical Review* 8 (April 1903): 449-65.

Beckhart, B.H. "Outline of Banking History From the First Bank of the United States Through the Panic of 1907." American Academy of Political and Social Science *Annals* 99 (January 1922): 1-16.

Bender, Thomas. *New York Intellect: A History of Intellectual Life in New York City from 1750 to the Beginnings of Our Own Time.* New York: Alfred A. Knopf, 1987.

Benson, Lee. *The Concept of Jacksonian Democracy: New York as a Test Case.* Princeton: Princeton University Press, 1961.

Blackford, Mansel G., and K. Austin Kerr. *Business Enterprise in American History.* New York: Houghton Mifflin, 1986.

Blake, Nelson M. *Water for the Cities: A History of the Urban Water Supply Problem in the United States.* Syracuse: Syracuse University Press, 1956.

Blandi, Joseph G. *Maryland Business Corporations, 1783-1852.* Baltimore: Johns Hopkins University Press, 1934.

Bobbe, Dorothie. *DeWitt Clinton.* Empire State Historical Publication 11. Port Washington, New York: Ira J. Friedman, Inc., 1933.

Bragg, M.M. *Memorial History of Utica, New York*. Syracuse: D. Mason and Company, 1892.

_____. *The Pioneers of Utica*. Utica: Curtiss and Childs, 1877.

Brearly Service Organization. *Manuscript History of the Manhattan Company*. New York: Manhattan Company, 1930.

Bridges, Amy. *A City in the Republic: Antebellum New York and the Origins of Machine Politics*. New York: Cambridge University Press, 1984.

Bruchey, Stuart. *The Roots of American Economic Growth, 1607-1861: An Essay in Social Causation*. New York: Harper and Row, 1965.

Buttenwieser, Ann L. *Manhattan Water-Bound: Planning and Developing Manhattan's Waterfront From the Seventeenth Century to the Present*. New York: New York University Press, 1987.

Cadman, John W., Jr. *The Corporation in New Jersey: Business and Politics, 1791-1875*. Cambridge: Harvard University Press, 1949.

Cameron, Rondo. *Banking in the Early Stages of Industrialization*. New York: Oxford University Press, 1967.

Carosso, Vincent P. *Investment Banking in America: A History*. Cambridge: Harvard University Press, 1970.

Chaddock, Robert E. *The Safety Fund Banking System in New York, 1829-66*. Washington, D.C.: Government Printing Office, 1910.

Chandler, Alfred D., Jr. *The Visible Hand: The Managerial Revolution in American Business*. Cambridge: Belknap Press of Harvard University Press, 1977.

_____. "The Emergence of Managerial Capitalism." *Business History Review* 56 (Winter 1984): 473-503.

_____. "The Beginnings of the Modern Industrial Corporation." *Proceedings of the American Philosophical Society* 130 (December 1986): 382-9.

Checkland, S.G. *Scottish Banking: A History, 1675-1973*. Glasgow: Collins, 1975.

Clapham, Sir John. *The Bank of England: A History*. Cambridge: The University Press, 1944.

Clark, W.A. *The History of Banking Institutions Organized in South Carolina Prior to 1860*. Columbia, South Carolina: The State Company, 1922.

Cleveland, Harold Van B., and Thomas F. Huertas. *Citibank, 1812-1970*. Cambridge: Harvard University Press, 1986.

Cochran, Thomas C. *New York in the Confederation: An Economic Study*. Philadelphia: University of Pennsylvania Press, 1932.

_____. "The Business Revolution." *American Historical Review* 79 (1974): 1449-66.

_____. *Two Hundred Years of American Business*. New York: Basic Books, 1977.

_____. *Frontiers of Change: Early Industrialization in America*. New York: Oxford University Press, 1981.

_____. *Challenges to American Values: Society, Business, and Religion*. New York: Oxford University Press, 1985.

Cottrell, P.L., and B.L. Anderson. *Money and Banking in England: The Development of the Banking System, 1694-1914*. Newton Abbot: David and Charles, 1974.

Countryman, Edward. *A People in Revolution: The American Revolution and Political Society in New York, 1760-1790*. Baltimore: Johns Hopkins University Press, 1981.

Crick, W.F., and J.E. Wadsworth. *A Hundred Years of Joint Stock Banking*. London: Hodder and Stoughton, 1936.

Davis, Andrew McFarland. "Provincial Banks, Land and Silver." *Publications of the Colonial Society of Massachusetts* 3 (1900).

Davis, Joseph Stancliffe. *Essays in the Earlier History of American Corporations*. Cambridge: Harvard University Press, 1917; reprint, New York: Russell and Russell, 1965.

Dethloff, Henry C., and C. Joseph Pusateri. *American Business History: Case Studies*. Albuquerque: University of New Mexico Press, 1987.

Dewey, Davis R. *State Banking Before the Civil War*. Washington, D.C.: Government Printing Office, 1911.

DiBacco, Thomas V. *Made in the U.S.A.: The History of American Business*. New York: Harper and Row, 1987.

Dodd, Edwin M. *American Business Corporations Until 1860*. Cambridge: Harvard University Press, 1954.

Doerflinger, Thomas M. *A Vigorous Spirit of Enterprise: Merchants and Economic Development in Revolutionary Philadelphia*. Chapel Hill: University of North Carolina Press, 1986.

Domett, Henry W. *A History of the Bank of New York, 1784-1884*, 3rd ed. New York: Riverside Press, 1884; reprint, New York: Greenwood Press, 1969.

Donovan, Herbert D.A. *The Barnburners: A Study of the Internal Movements in the Political History of New York State and of the Resulting Changes in Political Affiliation, 1830-1852*. New York: New York University Press, 1925; reprint, Philadelphia: Porcupine Press, 1974.

Dorfman, Joseph. *The Economic Mind of American Civilization, 1606-1865*. New York: Viking, 1946.

Douglass, Elisha P. *The Coming of Age of American Business: Three Centuries of Enterprise, 1600-1900*. Chapel Hill: University of North Carolina Press, 1971.

Early Days of the Bank of New York. New York: Bank of New York, 1901.

Early New York and the Bank of the Manhattan Company. New York: Bank of the Manhattan Company, 1920.

East, Robert A. *Business Enterprise in the American Revolutionary Era*. New York: Columbia University Press, 1938.

_____. "The Business Entrepreneur in a Changing Colonial Economy, 1763-1795." *Journal of Economic History* 6 (1946): 16-27.

Edwards, George Wilson. *New York as an Eighteenth Century Municipality, 1731-1776*. Studies in History, Economics and Public Law, No. 178. New York: Columbia University, 1917; reprint, New York: AMS Press, 1968.

Elazar, Daniel J. "Banking and Federalism in the Early American Republic." *Huntington Library Quarterly* 28 (May 1965): 301-20.

Eliason, Adolph. *The Rise of Commercial Banking Institutions in the United States.* Minneapolis: University of Minnesota, 1901.

Evans, George H. *Business Incorporations in the United States, 1800-1943.* New York: National Bureau of Economic Research, 1948.

Feiner, Susan. "The Financial Structures and Banking Institutions of the Antebellum South." Ph.D. diss., University of Massachusetts, 1981.

Fenstermaker, J. Van. "The Statistics of American Commercial Banking." *Journal of Economic History* 25 (1965): 400-13.

_____. *The Development of American Commercial Banking, 1782-1837.* Kent: Bureau of Economic and Business Research, Kent State University, 1965.

Fox, Dixon Ryan. *The Decline of Aristocracy in the Politics of New York, 1801-1840.* Studies in History, Economics and Public Law, No. 198. New York: Columbia University Press, 1919; reprint, New York: AMS Press, 1976.

Freedman, Charles E. *Joint-Stock Enterprise in France, 1807-1867.* Chapel Hill: University of North Carolina Press, 1977.

Friedman, Lawrence M. *A History of American Law.* New York: Simon and Schuster, 1973.

Gibbons, J.S. *The Banks of New York, Their Dealers, the Clearing House, and the Panic of 1857.* New York: D. Appleton, 1859; reprint, New York: Greenwood Press, 1968.

Goldman, Joanne. "The New York City Sewer System, 1800-1866: The Evolution of a Technological and Managerial Infrastructure." Unpublished paper delivered at the 1988 Annual Meeting of the Organization of American Historians.

Gras, N.S.B. *The Massachusetts First National Bank of Boston, 1784-1934.* Cambridge: Harvard University Press, 1937.

Greene, Evarts Boutell. *The Revolutionary Generation, 1763-1790.* New York: Macmillan, 1943.

Griffin, Clyde and Sally. *Natives and Newcomers: The Ordering of Opportunity in Mid-Nineteenth Century Poughkeepsie.* Cambridge: Harvard University Press, 1978.

326

Hacker, Louis M. *Alexander Hamilton in the American Tradition.* New York: McGraw-Hill, 1957.

Hammond, Bray. "Long and Short Term Credit in Early American Banking." *Quarterly Journal of Economics* 49 (1934-35): 79-103.

_____. "Free Banks and Corporations: The New York Free Banking Act of 1838." *Journal of Political Economy* 44 (1936): 197-205.

_____. *Banks and Politics in America From the Revolution to the Civil War.* Princeton: Princeton University Press, 1957.

Hammond, Jabez D. *The History of Political Parties in the State of New York.* Syracuse: Hall, Mills, 1852.

Handlin, Oscar, and Mary Flug Handlin. "Origins of the American Business Corporation." *Journal of Economic History* 5 (1945): 1-23.

_____. *Commonwealth -- A Study of the Role of Government in the American Economy: Massachusetts, 1774-1861.* Rev. ed. Cambridge: Harvard University Press, 1969.

Hartog, Hendrik. *Public Property and Private Power: The Corporation of the City of New York in American Law, 1730-1870.* Chapel Hill: University of North Carolina Press, 1983.

Hartz, Louis. *Economic Policy and Democratic Thought: Pennsylvania, 1776-1860.* Cambridge: Harvard University Press, 1948.

Hedges, Joseph Edward. *Commercial Banking and the Stock Market Before 1863.* Johns Hopkins University Studies in Historical and Political Science, series 56, no. 1. Baltimore: Johns Hopkins University Press, 1938.

History of the Chemical Bank, 1823-1913. New York: Chemical Bank, 1913; reprint, New York: Arno Press, 1980.

Horowitz, Morton J. *The Transformation of American Law, 1780-1860.* Cambridge: Harvard University Press, 1977.

Horsefield, J.K. "The Duties of a Banker: The Eighteenth Century View." *Economica*, new series 8 (1941): 37-51.

Hunter, Gregory S. "The Development of Bankers: Career Patterns and Corporate Form at the Manhattan Company, 1799-1842." *Business and Economic History*, 2nd ser. 14 (1985): 59-77.

Hunter, Louis C. *Steam Power: A History of Industrial Power in the United States, 1780-1930*. Charlottesville: University Press of Virginia, 1985.

James, F. Cyril. "The Bank of North America and the Financial History of Philadelphia." *Pennsylvania Magazine of History and Biography* 64 (1940): 56-87.

Jeffreys, James B. *Business Organization in Great Britain*. New York: Arno Press, 1977.

Jensen, Merrill. *The New Nation: A History of the United States During the Confederation, 1781-1789*. New York: Alfred A. Knopf, 1950.

Kass, Alvin. *Politics in New York State, 1800-1830*. Syracuse: Syracuse University Press, 1965.

Klebaner, Benjamin J. *Commercial Banking in the United States: A History*. Hinsdale, Illinois: Dryden Press, 1974.

_____. "State Chartered American Commercial Banks, 1781-1801." *Business History Review* 53 (Winter 1979): 529-38.

Knox, John Jay. *A History of Banking in the United States*. New York: B. Rhodes and Co., 1900.

Lamoreaux, Naomi R. "The Structure of Early Banks in Southeastern New England: Some Social and Economic Implications." *Business and Economic History*, 2nd ser. 13 (1984): 171-84.

_____. "Banks, Kinship, and Economic Development: The New England Case." *Journal of Economic History* 46 (September 1986), 647-667.

Lanier, Henry W. *A Century of Banking in New York, 1822-1922*. New York: Gilliss, 1922.

Lewis, Lawrence, Jr. *A History of the Bank of North America*. Philadelphia: Lippincott, 1888.

Licht, Walter. *Working for the Railroad: The Organization of Work in the Nineteenth Century*. Princeton: Princeton University Press, 1982.

Main, Jackson Turner. *The Antifederalists: Critics of the Constitution, 1781-1788*. Chapel Hill: University of North Carolina Press, 1961.

_____. *Political Parties Before the Constitution*. Chapel Hill: University of North Carolina Press, 1973.

Mana-Hatin: The Story of New York. New York: Bank of the Manhattan Company, 1929.

McBain, Howard L. *DeWitt Clinton and the Origin of the Spoils System in New York*. Studies in History, Economics and Public Law 28, No. 1. New York: Columbia University Press; reprint, New York: AMS Press, 1967.

McClurkin, A.J. "Summary of the Bank of North America Records." *Pennsylvania Magazine of History and Biography* 64 (1940): 88-96.

McDonald, Forrest. *We the People: The Economic Origins of the Constitution*. Chicago: University of Chicago Press, 1968.

Miller, Harry E. *Banking Theories in the United States Before 1860*. Cambridge: Harvard University Press, 1927.

Miller, John C. *Alexander Hamilton: Portrait in Paradox*. New York: Harper and Row, 1959.

Miller, Nathan. *The Enterprise of a Free People: Aspects of Economic Development in New York State During the Canal Period, 1792-1838*. Ithaca: Cornell University Press, 1962.

Mints, Lloyd W. *A History of Banking Theory in Great Britain and the United States*. Chicago: University of Chicago Press, 1945.

Mitchell, Broadus. "Inflation: Revolution and Its Aftermath." *Current History* 24 (May 1953): 257-63.

_____. *Alexander Hamilton: Youth to Maturity, 1755-1788*. New York: Macmillan, 1957.

Nash, Gerald D. *Perspectives on Administration: The Vistas of History*. Berkeley: Institute of Governmental Studies, University of California, 1969.

Nelson, John R., Jr. *Liberty and Property: Political Economy and Policy-Making in the New Nation, 1789-1812*. Baltimore: Johns Hopkins University Press, 1987.

Nevins, Allan. *History of the Bank of New York and Trust Company, 1784-1934.* New York: Bank of New York, 1934.

_____. "Alexander Hamilton." *Dictionary of American Biography* 4: 171-9.

Nuxoll, Elizabeth M. "The Bank of North America and Robert Morris's Management of the Nation's First Fiscal Crisis." *Business and Economic History*, 2nd ser. 13 (1984): 159-70.

Papenfuse, Edward C. *In Pursuit of Profit: The Annapolis Merchants in the Era of the American Revolution, 1763-1805.* Baltimore: Johns Hopkins University Press, 1975.

Platt, John D.R. "Jeremiah Wadsworth: Federalist Entrepreneur." Ph.D. diss., Columbia University, 1955.

Pollard, Sidney. *The Genesis of Modern Management: A Study of the Industrial Revolution in Great Britain.* Cambridge: Harvard University Press, 1965.

Pomeranz, Sidney I. *New York: An American City, 1783-1803: A Study of Urban Life.* New York: Columbia University Press, 1938.

Pursell, Carroll W., Jr. "Christopher Colle's Steam Engine for the New York Water Works, 1775." *Technology and Culture* 10 (1969): 567-9.

Pusateri, C. Joseph. *A History of American Business*, 2nd ed. Albuquerque: University of New Mexico Press, 1988.

Rappaport, George David. "The Sources and Early Development of the Hostility to Banks in Early American Thought." Ph.D. diss., New York University, 1970.

Redlich, Fritz. *Essays in American Economic History.* New York: G.E. Stechert, 1944.

_____. *The Molding of American Banking: Men and Ideas.* 2 vols. New York: Hafner Publishing, 1947, 1951; reprint, New York: Johnson Reprint Company, 1968.

_____. "Bank Administration, 1780-1814." *Journal of Economic History* 12 (Fall 1952): 438-53.

_____. "American Banking and Growth in the Nineteenth Century: Epistemological Reflections." *Explorations in Economic History* 10 (Spring 1973), 305-14.

Reubens, Beatrice G. "Burr, Hamilton and the Manhattan Company. Part I: Gaining the Charter." *Political Science Quarterly* 72 (December 1957): 578-607.

_____. "Burr, Hamilton and the Manhattan Company. Part II: Launching a Bank." *Political Science Quarterly* 73 (March 1958): 100-25.

_____. "State Financing of Private Enterprises in Early New York." Ph.D. diss., Columbia University, 1960.

Riesman, Janet A. "Republican Revisions: Political Economy After the Panic of 1819." Unpublished paper delivered at the Conference on New York and the Rise of American Capitalism, May 18-19, 1984, New-York Historical Society.

Robertson, James Oliver. *America's Business.* New York: Hill and Wang, 1985.

Rockoff, Hugh T. "Varieties of Banking and Regional Economic Development in the United States, 1840-1869." *Journal of Economic History* 35 (March 1975), 160-77.

____. *The Free Banking Era.* New York: Arno Press, 1975.

Rose, Peter S. *The Changing Structure of American Banking.* New York: Columbia University Press, 1986.

Schwartz, Anna Jacobson. "The Beginning of Competitive Banking in Philadelphia, 1782-1809." *Journal of Political Economy* 55 (October 1947): 417-31.

_____. "An Attempt at Synthesis in American Banking History." *Journal of Economic History* 8 (1947): 208-17.

Schweikart, Larry. "Banking in the American South, 1836-1865." Ph.D. diss., University of California, Santa Barbara, 1983.

_____. "Antebellum Southern Bankers: Origins and Mobility." *Business and Economic History*, 2nd ser. 14 (1985): 79-103.

_____. "Private Bankers in the Antebellum South." *Southern Studies* 25 (Summer 1986): 125-34.

_____. *Banking in the American South From the Age of Jackson to Reconstruction.* Baton Rouge: Louisiana State University Press, 1987.

Seavoy, Ronald E. "The Origins of the American Business Corporation, 1784-1855: New York, the National Model." Ph.D. diss., University of Michigan, 1969.

_____. *The Origins of the American Business Corporation, 1784-1855: Broadening the Concept of Public Service During Industrialization*. Westport: Greenwood Press, 1982.

Spaulding, E. Wilder. *New York in the Critical Period, 1783-1789*. New York: Columbia University Press, 1932.

Stokes, Howard Kemble. *Chartered Banking in Rhode Island, 1791-1900*. Providence: Preston and Rounds, 1902.

Streeter, Edward. *Window on America: The Growth of a Nation as Seen by New York's First Bank, 1784-1959*. New York: Bank of New York, 1959.

Studenski, Paul, and Herman Kroos. *Financial History of the United States*. New York: McGraw-Hill, 1962.

Sylla, Richard. "Early American Banking: The Significance of the Corporate Form." *Business and Economic History*, 2nd ser. 14 (1985): 105-23.

Sylla, Richard, John B. Legler, and John J. Wallis. "Banks and State Public Finance in the New Republic: The United States, 1790-1860." *Journal of Economic History* 47 (June 1987): 391-403.

Tarr, Joel A., and Gabriel Dupuy, eds. *Technology and the Rise of the Networked City in Europe and America*. Philadelphia: Temple University Press, 1988.

Thayer, Theodore. "The Land Bank System in the American Colonies." *Journal of Economic History* 13 (Spring 1953): 145-59.

Trescott, Paul B. *Financing American Enterprise: The Story of Commercial Banking*. New York: Harper and Row, 1963.

Vickers, Douglas. *Studies in the Theory of Money, 1690-1776*. Philadelphia: Clinton Company, 1959.

Walsh, John J. *Vignettes of Old Utica*. Utica: Utica Public Library, 1982.

Water for Old New York. New York: Chase Manhattan Bank, no date.

Weidner, Charles. *Water for the City*. New Brunswick: Rutgers University Press, 1974.

White, Lawrence H. *Free Banking in Britain: Theory, Experience and Debate, 1800-1845*. New York: Cambridge University Press, 1984.

Wilentz, Sean. *Chants Democratic: New York City and the Rise of the American Working Class, 1788-1850*. New York: Oxford University Press, 1984.

Williams, Ben Ames, Jr. *Bank of Boston 200: A History of New England's Leading Bank, 1784-1984*. Boston: Houghton Mifflin, 1984.

Williams, William Appleman. "The Age of Mercantilism: An Interpretation of American Political Economy, 1763-1828." *William and Mary Quarterly* (1958): 419-37.

Wilson, Janet. "The Bank of North America and Pennsylvania Politics: 1781-1787." *Pennsylvania Magazine of History and Biography* 66 (1942): 3-28.

Wilson, John Donald. *The Chase: The Chase Manhattan Bank, N.A., 1945-1985*. Boston: Harvard Business School Press, 1986.

Wood, Gordon. *The Creation of the American Republic, 1776-1787*. Chapel Hill: University of North Carolina Press, 1969.

For Product Safety Concerns and Information please contact our EU representative GPSR@taylorandfrancis.com Taylor & Francis Verlag GmbH, Kaufingerstraße 24, 80331 München, Germany

Printed and bound by CPI Group (UK) Ltd, Croydon, CR0 4YY

08/05/2025

01864377-0004